LIBRARY IN A BOOK

INTERNET PREDATORS

Harry Henderson

Facts On File, Inc.

INTERNET PREDATORS

Facts On File, Inc.
132 West 31st Street
New York NY 10001

Library of Congress Cataloging-in-Publication Data

Henderson, Harry, 1951
   Internet predators / Harry Henderson.
      p. cm.—(Library in a book)
   Includes bibliographical references and index.
   ISBN 0-8160-5739-7
   1. Computer crimes. 2. Computer crimes—United States—Prevention. I. Title.
II. Series
HV6773.H45 2005
364.16′8—dc22   2004027537

Facts On File books are available at special discounts when purchased in bulk quantities for businesses, associations, institutions, or sales promotions. Please call our Special Sales Department in New York at (212) 967-8800 or (800) 322-8755.

You can find Facts On File on the World Wide Web at http://www.factsonfile.com

Text design by Ron Monteleone
Graphs by Jeremy Eagle

Printed in the United States of America

MP Hermitage 10 9 8 7 6 5 4 3 2 1

This book is printed on acid-free paper.

To the citizens of cyberspace and
everyone who is trying to make it a better place.

CONTENTS

PART III
APPENDICES

PART I

OVERVIEW OF THE TOPIC

CHAPTER 1

INTRODUCTION TO COPING WITH INTERNET PREDATORS

It has been only about a decade since the Internet became a pervasive and essential part of modern society. Today there are few aspects of daily life that it does not touch in some way. In particular, the World Wide Web has become both the world's shopping mall and the focus of a great variety of social interactions.

Consider some online encounters that could be typical for anyone in the United States and other industrialized countries who has access to the Internet at home, work, or school.

- Going to an auction site, bidding for and winning a new 21″ LCD computer monitor, one of several being offered at attractive starting prices because they were "bought by a failed dot-com and never used."

- Receiving e-mail that touts an investment in a little known but "hot" technology stock. The linked web site seems to offer abundant testimonials and figures to back the claim that the stock is poised to increase in value a hundred times in a matter of months.

- Receiving a startling e-mail that warns, "Your Citibank account has been suspended because of possible fraud. Please click here to verify your account information."

- Typing messages in her favorite chat room, a teenage girl becomes intrigued with "Kyle," because he is witty, entertaining, and seems to share her taste in music and movies.

For millions of Internet users these interactions might represent useful opportunities—to get bargains, deal quickly with a bank problem, or pursue an exciting relationship. But by now many people have already learned that things in the cyberworld are often not what they seem:

3

- The auction required that payment be made by cashier's check or money order "because of the nature of this liquidation sale." After payment, the buyer waits for weeks. At first, he is offered various excuses. But nothing ever comes, and the money is gone.
- The "hot tech stock" does go up, because people who got the e-mails are buying it. However, thousands of shares are quickly sold by the "pump and dump" promoters, who make a good killing as the stock plunges back to worthlessness. The company actually had no realistic growth prospects.
- After clicking on that Citibank link, the user sees a very authentic-looking web site complete with the bank's usual logo and typeface. But the site actually belongs to a hacker, and the account number and password being "verified" are sold to a group of identity thieves. In a few weeks the customer will learn that her bank account has been drained.
- "Kyle" offers to meet the young woman in "RL" (real life). When the meeting takes place in a nearby café, she discovers that she had been chatting online not with another teenager but with a man in his 30s. If she is lucky, she will have learned a useful lesson. If not, she may be molested or exploited for the production of child pornography.

In each case our typical Internet user has had an encounter with an Internet predator. Whether primarily economic or personal in its motives, computer-related crime has grown in rough proportion to Internet usage. But what exactly is meant by computer crime or, as it is often called, cybercrime?

WHAT IS CYBERCRIME?

One of the first problems in dealing with computer crime is to clarify the actual role of computers and the Internet in the offenses. What crimes are really cybercrimes? There are basically four possible roles for the computer in criminal activity:

The computer might be only an incidental tool for the criminal. For example, a bank robber might use a computer to print out a holdup note, or even use a service like MapQuest to get a map showing the possible getaway route. Most researchers would not really consider the ensuing robbery to be a computer crime, because the computer does not play a distinctive role that should be addressed by regulators, law enforcers, or the public. The robbery is no more a computer crime than using a car to get away would make it a car crime.

An intermediate case is when computers and networks make it easier in important ways for criminals to commit traditional crimes. For many years fraudsters have taken out magazine ads offering bogus work-at-home schemes or even sent letters offering a hefty cut for helping an alleged Nigerian official move money out of his country.

With the Internet, however, unsolicited bulk e-mail, or spam, can be used to send fraudulent solicitations to thousands or millions of recipients at virtually no cost to the sender. Here the computer greatly multiplies the chances for profitable fraud by vastly increasing the pool of potential suckers.

Stalking, harassment, and child molestation are also in this intermediate category. All of these offenses have long been committed by way of direct contact or using available technology (such as mail, telephone, camera, and so on). However, as we will see, the Internet's anonymous nature and the ready accessibility of private information have made these crimes easier to commit and harder to pursue.

In some computer-related crime the computer is itself the target of the criminal. For example, hackers may seek to get into a computer system to obtain valuable information (such as credit card numbers) or perhaps just for bragging rights.

Finally, there is a criminal technique that is in effect made possible only by the existence of the Internet. The gathering of personal information for use in identity theft is an example. For a long time criminals have stolen mail from mailboxes or Dumpster dived to obtain credit card receipts and other identifying information. Now, however, criminals can use deceptive e-mails to frighten or persuade recipients to reveal sensitive personal information by following links to cleverly disguised web sites (this practice, called phishing, will be discussed in detail later.) Clearly, here criminals have taken advantage of a combination of new technologies (e-mail and web sites) to operate on a scale not practicable before.

The criminal activity that is the focus of this book involves individual predators who prey on other individuals where computers and the Internet are either extremely useful or are actually essential to carrying out the crime.[1] Specifically, the focus is on four categories of cybercrime:

- Frauds and scams carried out by e-mail or online
- Identity theft and other crimes related to personal information
- Stalking and harassment primarily using the Internet
- Sexual exploitation of children using online contacts and distribution of child pornography online

PREVALENCE AND IMPACT

The growth of cybercrime has roughly paralleled the growth of the Internet economy. In 2003 the estimated value of online retail sales in the United

States reached $114 billion. Although this still represents only 5.4 percent of all retail sales, it is one of the fastest-growing sectors of the economy. Meanwhile, the cost of cybercrime in the United States alone is estimated at about $5 billion annually. This does not include the noneconomic costs of stress to victims of identity theft or the even more severe impacts on victims of violent stalking, harassment, or child sexual abuse by Internet-based predators. As former vice president Al Gore noted in 1999: "Unlawful activity is not unique to the Internet—but the Internet has a way of magnifying both the good and the bad in our society . . . . What we need to do is to find new answers to old crimes."[2]

Thus far the impact of cybercrime has not led to a corresponding commitment of resources and effort by law enforcement. Indeed, recent surveys suggest that

> *only about 10% of all cybercrimes committed are actually reported and fewer than 2% result in a conviction. This is primarily due to two reasons. First, businesses and financial institutions feel that they have more to lose by reporting computer security breaches. They argue that customers will lose confidence in the company if business and financial transactions are known to be insecure. Second, a majority of cybercrime victims do not report crimes against them, assuming that law enforcement will provide little or no assistance . . .*[3]

Because of differing definitions of what crimes are cybercrimes, the standard sources of crime statistics are not always as helpful as they could be. The National Incident-Based Reporting System (NIBRS) and the older Uniform Crime Reports (UCR) are the main source for U.S. national crime data. Neither source has a category for cybercrimes as such, although some NIBRS Category A offenses will certainly include an unknown (but probably growing) proportion of cybercrimes. These offenses include counterfeiting/forgery, destruction/damage/vandalism of property, embezzlement, extortion/blackmail, fraud offenses, gambling offenses, larceny/theft, pornography/obscenity, prostitution-related, sex offenses (nonforcible), and stolen property offenses. Many cybercrime experts believe there is an urgent need to develop an appropriate national reporting system to specifically track computer-related crimes.

PERPETRATORS AND VICTIMS

Cybercriminals generally share the same motives as conventional criminals—principally, the desire to get money or other things of value with a minimum of effort and risk. Criminals whose crimes require a considerable amount of technical knowledge, such as hackers or even the designers of deceptive e-mail messages and web sites, are likely to be better educated, more intelligent and flexible, and less predictable than the common run of robbers or burglars. Personally, they may more or less fit the stereotype of the computer nerd, although some hackers combine technical expertise with the manipulative social skills of the traditional con artist.

However the growing access of ordinary people to facilities such as e-mail and the Internet has meant that many cybercrimes do not require exceptional skills or intelligence. Anyone who can master an e-mail program or use a chat room can use these communications tools to try to deceive or harass a victim, much as an earlier generation might have used the telephone. A growing number of criminals may opportunistically use computer services but will not necessarily stop short of physical theft or violence in order to get what they want.

As for the victims of cybercrime, it is fair to say that while anyone can be targeted, the most vulnerable are people who have little experience with the Internet and other modern communications technologies. This means that college-educated young and middle-aged adults are more likely to be net-savvy, while a greater proportion of older people and minorities who have had less opportunity to develop computer skills are more vulnerable—for example, they may not be able to easily identify the source of an e-mail or know how to evaluate the credibility of a web site.

Younger children are inexperienced both in computer skills and in dealing with possibly deceptive or dangerous behavior by adults. Older teenagers may actually be more computer-savvy than their parents, but they are still learning to use good judgment and how to manage risks in social situations.

Whatever one's age and level of computer experience, it is wise to not be complacent. Fraudsters, scammers, and other Internet predators are constantly developing more deceptive, plausible e-mails and web sites. Meanwhile, developers of dangerous software such as viruses, Trojan horse programs, and spyware that can be used to steal personal information engage in a constant technological battle with people who are trying to build better defenses for personal computers.

ONLINE FRAUDS AND SCAMS

The number of deceptive offerings that arrive by e-mail or can be found on the Web seems limited only by the criminal imagination. And it is clear that criminals are indeed taking to Internet crime in increasing numbers. According to the Federal Trade Commission's Consumer Sentinel database of fraud and identity theft complaints, in 2004:

- The FTC received over 635,000 complaints of fraud or identity theft.
- Sixty-one percent of complaints were for fraud, and 39 percent were related to identity theft.
- Total fraud complaints increased by about 20 percent from 2003 to 2004.
- Fifty-three percent of reported fraud complaints involved the Internet, with reported losses of $265 million.
- The median loss for Internet fraud was $214.00 per incident.
- Thirty-five percent of frauds began with e-mail contact, while 22 percent began with someone clicking on a web site.
- Internet auctions were the leading source of fraud complaints (16 percent), followed by shop-at-home and catalog sales (8 percent).

Overall, the picture that is emerging is quite clear. Internet-based fraud is already having a serious impact on millions of Americans, and the problem is growing worse every year.

WHY THE INTERNET ATTRACTS SCAMMERS

What is it about the Internet that seems to make it such an attractive place for running frauds or scams? There are a number of plausible reasons why Internet fraud is growing rapidly:

- Criminals go where the victims are and the money is to be had. As noted, e-commerce is one of the fastest-growing business sectors.
- It is possible to send thousands or even millions of spam e-mails for virtually no cost. Such e-mails are the main vehicle for Internet fraud, either directly or by enticing readers to link to deceptive web sites.
- Because it is so easy to disguise one's true identity on the Internet (such as by sending e-mail through a remailer that strips away the real return address), it is hard for investigators to track down the source of Internet frauds and scams. Thus the risk of getting caught, let alone sent to jail, is low. And if one bogus address or web site is shut down, it is a simple matter to set up another.
- Many frauds originate outside the United States, making it impractical in most cases for U.S. officials to prosecute the perpetrators. Even within the United States there are often perplexing legal questions about which state's court has jurisdiction.
- Many victims do not report Internet frauds. This might be because they do not know who to report them to, they do not think the report will do

any good, or (as with conventional frauds) they are embarrassed about having been taken.

AUCTION FRAUD: GOING, GOING . . . GONE

The leading position of auctions in the Internet fraud hit parade is no doubt related to their incredible popularity. For example, on eBay, by far the leading online auction service, about $24 billion in merchandise was sold in 2003. The vast majority of buyers and sellers are somewhere between satisfied and greatly pleased with their transactions, which is a testimony both to most people's fairness and honesty and to the innovative feedback mechanism by which eBay users can rate their satisfaction with each transaction.

When fraud occurs, the most common type involves auctions in which the winning bidder makes payment and receives nothing in return. In more subtle types of fraud, the winner gets the item, but it is defective or, in the case of collectibles, is not authentic or not as described. Often fraudulent sellers will try to string out their victims as long as possible by claiming payment or shipping problems or unavoidable delays. The object is to make as much money as possible before negative feedback and complaints to eBay leads to closure of the seller's account. (Unfortunately, when an account is closed it is not hard for the fraudster to open another, possibly using bogus identifying information.)

Although most auction fraud involves sellers victimizing buyers, there are also buyers who defraud sellers, such as by using stolen credit cards or counterfeit cashier's checks or money orders.

The bidding process itself is also susceptible to fraud. In shill bidding the seller arranges to have bogus bids made to drive up the price—the bids can come from duplicate accounts set up for the purpose or from other users who are in on the fraud. Shill bidding is less destructive than other forms of auction fraud because, while it may raise the price paid by the legitimate winning bidder, at least that bidder presumably paid no more than he or she was willing to spend. Also, eBay attempts to identify shill bidding situations and warn or close the offending accounts.

The defense against auction fraud involves several levels: the seller, the item description, and the use of payment services. Sellers who have no feedback (because they are new to eBay) or more than a few negative feedback comments may be risky. However, a 100 percent positive feedback rating is not a guarantee that the seller is not fraudulent. Some fraudulent sellers may run legitimate auctions for a while in order to get a good feedback rating. Sellers may also create multiple accounts and buy and sell among them to create bogus feedback ratings.

The description of the item is also important. Some specialized areas, such as coins or stamps, can involve subtle distinctions as to variety or grade that can make the difference between a $50 item and a $50,000 one. Recently eBay has developed relationships with hobby organizations such as the American Philatelic Society (the nation's leading stamp collecting organization) where experts help screen listings for fraud or inadvertent errors of description. Anyone buying art or collectibles online should seriously consider requiring third-party authentication or grading for the more expensive items.

Finally, how one pays for an auction greatly affects whether there is any recourse in case of fraud. Obviously cash is not recoverable, but some buyers may not realize that instruments such as cashier's checks and debit cards are essentially the same as cash. Using a credit card allows the cardholder to dispute the charge if the item is not received (or is not as described). Most individual sellers cannot accept credit cards, but, fortunately credit cards can be used to pay for many auctions via PayPal and other payment services, which allow legitimate sellers to offer a "Buyer Protection" option and also gives the buyer an opportunity to purchase a money-back guarantee for certain types of transactions.

Another alternative for some auctions is the use of an escrow service. The escrow service is a third party who can help ensure that a transaction is completed properly. The typical sequence of events is:

1. The buyer sends the payment for the auction to the escrow service.
2. The escrow service notifies the seller that the funds are good.
3. The seller ships the goods to the buyer.
4. The buyer notifies the escrow service that the goods have been received.
5. The escrow service sends the funds to the seller.

Using an escrow service is a bit cumbersome and, of course, a fee is involved. Generally, escrows are used for relatively expensive items. Buyers should make sure that the escrow service itself is legitimate—fraudsters have been known to recommend a fake escrow service to their trading partners. Once the funds are sent to that service, the buyer is out of luck.

Auction fraud raises some important issues about the role of online auction services. On the one hand eBay, like all services, wants its users to be satisfied and has provided or encouraged mechanisms such as feedback, escrow services, and PayPal to increase user confidence. On the other hand, eBay has disclaimed legal responsibility for the accuracy of descriptions and the authenticity or fitness of goods. Its position is that eBay is merely a facilitator that brings sellers and buyers together. The actual auctioneer is the seller.

If online auction fraud increases, users may pressure regulators to make the auction services assume responsibilities more like those of traditional auction venues. Traditional art and collectibles auction houses perform expensive cataloging and are supervised by a staff of experts. If online auction sites were forced to do likewise, auction fees would have to be increased substantially, items might have to be sent to the service for inspection before the auction, and the advantages of online auctions for selling a great variety of inexpensive as well as premium items would likely be lost.

BUYER TAKE CARE: ONLINE SHOPPING

Fraud involving Internet-based stores shares many common features with auction fraud. In both cases buyers must make an attempt to determine the seller's legitimacy before paying their money. A store that is an offshoot of a reputable physical (brick-and-mortar) business is probably equally safe. Businesses that are affiliated with a major online service such as eBay or Yahoo! shops are subject to policies designed to promote customer satisfaction, and dissatisfied customers have certain specified recourse.

What about other independent businesses? There are a number of ways to check them out:

- Check with traditional sources such as *Consumer Reports* and the Better Business Bureau.
- Be aware of other Internet-based services such as Trust-E and WebAssured. A company that is affiliated with such a service must agree to abide by its guidelines for privacy and/or resolving consumer complaints.
- Do a Web search on the company name to see if there are complaints or other discussion available. Not all complaints may be valid, but one can at least get a sense of whether a company is problematic.

Even if a business seems legitimate, customers must check a few more things to avoid vulnerability to fraud or identity theft:

- Does the store have a prominently posted privacy policy? Does that policy either guarantee that the customer's personal information will not be sold or shared with anyone else, or at least provide a way to opt out of having that information shared?
- Where is the store located? Web addresses in the United States typically do not include as country code. If a code appears in the address just before the .com part (such as www.mystore.ru.com), it indicates that the site is based outside the United States. Many such companies may be legitimate, but

U.S. consumers who run into problems will have little practical recourse if the company is located outside the United States.

- The Whois service (available at http://www.internic.net/whois.htm) can provide the registered address and contact information for any Web domain. This is often useful for finding the location and parent company for a business.
- Is the payment processing done through a secure web page? This can be determined by a URL beginning with "https" (not "http") and the presence of a padlock symbol in the bottom of the browser window.
- Finally, as with auctions, payments should be made with a credit card or a service such as PayPal. This allows charges to be disputed if the product is not received or is unsatisfactory. If allowed by the merchant, PayPal and other payment services offer the additional advantage that the buyer's credit card number does not have to be transmitted.

HIDDEN CHARGES AND AUTOMATIC PAYMENTS

Another growing source of consumer fraud is the misuse of prearranged automatic payments. These allow consumers to arrange for recurring payments, such as for mortgages, insurance, or memberships in a gym or club. This can be a convenience, but fake charges can also be created by fraudsters who obtain the necessary credit card details.

Even charges that were originally legitimate can sometimes continue even after the consumer has ended the service—and even after the credit card account has been closed. (Card issuers claim that some legitimate charges must still be applied to closed accounts.) According to the National Automated Clearing House Association, unauthorized automatic charges have increased by more than 68 percent since 2001.

Consumers should review their monthly credit card statements carefully for bogus charges, and they should make sure that when a service is discontinued, the charges also stop. Unauthorized charges can be disputed with the credit card issuer, and they will generally be removed unless the company making the charge can substantiate it.

SECURITIES FRAUD: PUMP AND DUMP

At an age where many teenagers are still preoccupied with video games, 15-year-old Jonathan G. Lebed was playing for keeps. He bought some inexpensive stock shares and touted them by using spam e-mail and postings on Yahoo! Finance message boards that claimed to be from stock experts who predicted that the price of the shares would rise. When investors became intrigued and began to buy the shares, Lebed sold his shares for a profit of $285,000. When he was charged with stock manipulation the Securities and Exchange Commission (SEC) settled the case. Perhaps because of his age, he was offered a settlement that spared him a prison sentence. He had only to return the ill-gotten gains and promise not to do it again.

This fraud is called "pump and dump," and it represents a dangerous trap for unwary online investors. It works as follows. First, the scammer acquires a block of some inexpensive, little-known stock. Because so little money is invested in such companies, they are often called microcaps (microcapitalized) or penny stocks. The attraction of such stocks for the fraudulent promoter is that little money is needed to buy a large number of shares. Because there is so little capitalization, any change in demand for the stock is likely to produce a big upswing in the price.

As for the type of business involved, the only requirement is that the stock be vaguely related to some popular investment area such as biotechnology, energy, or whatever else is currently being hyped among investors.

In the "pump" part of the scam, e-mails and chat room messages are used to tout the stock's prospects. Typically the promoter shares what is claimed to be inside information about a forthcoming invention, patent, or drug. Alternatively, it might be claimed that the company is about to receive a lucrative government contract (homeland security is a currently popular area) or perhaps that it will be bought by a major company. Whatever the supposed event, it is something that, if true, would mean that the stock would be expected to soar in value, perhaps from pennies to tens of dollars or more.

The promoters watch as the price of the stock increases because of the demand generated by the false information. When it seems to have reached a plateau, they quickly sell, or dump, their shares. They get a profit, while the investors who bought the stock during the pumping phase lose virtually all of their investment.

Occasionally the scheme can be run in reverse. In 2000 Mark S. Jakob sold shares in Emulex Corporation "short," meaning that he was counting on the stock's value to go down. He then tried to ensure that outcome by issuing a phony press release to online news services. The release claimed that Emulex was under SEC investigation and that the company's chief executive officer (CEO) would soon resign. The stock promptly went down, yielding Jakob a profit on the short sale and an opportunity to buy more stock at a temporarily depressed price. Other investors who had held the stock lost a reported $110 million. Jakob was eventually arrested, pleaded guilty, and received a sentence of 44 months in prison. He was also required to pay about $500,000 in fines and restitution.

"Pump and dump" and other stock touting schemes are not new: In the old days they were done by boiler room operations, where likely prospects were phoned and talked into investing in supposedly hot stocks. But just as the Internet allows investors to respond quickly to market changes in attempting to capture gains, it also makes it easy to attempt to manipulate the market by quickly spreading false information.

The SEC responded to the growing fraud in 1998 by forming the Office of Internet Enforcement with an initial "Cyberforce" of 135 members. Besides monitoring chat rooms and other areas for signs of stock manipulation, the agency has distributed special investor alerts and education materials through its web site. The SEC even created its own web site for a fake company, McWhortle Enterprises. The site tries to persuade visitors to invest in the stock: if the visitor clicks on the Invest link he or she is given an explanation of deceptive online investment frauds.

Although many stock manipulation schemes do result in the perpetrators being tracked down and prosecuted, this is often of little consolation to investors who cannot recover their losses. Education is ultimately the key to avoiding being victimized by this type of Internet predator. Investors should be suspicious of information from unknown sources and be wary of unsubstantiated claims. An investor who is interested in a particular company should obtain and carefully examine its official filings with the SEC.

OTHER INVESTMENT SCAMS

There are many types of fraudulent investment that do not involve buying stock. In the classic pyramid or Ponzi scheme (named for Charles Ponzi, a notorious 1920s con artist), the first investors actually do receive the promised returns, with the money coming from subsequent investors. But the hype can carry the scheme for only a brief time: Soon the lack of new investors putting money into the scheme means that incoming investors can no longer be paid. The promoter pockets the money skimmed from the original investments and then disappears, likely to surface again with a new scheme. Pyramid schemes are illegal because they are inherently fraudulent in that they cannot be sustained and the underlying investment is misrepresented as being valuable.

Multilevel marketing (MLM) also has a pyramid-type structure in which participants receive returns only if new participants come in. Essentially a person signs up for the program, gets access to the product, and gets some sort of commission each time he or she sells it to someone. The product might be software, a "make money at home kit," or some other item that is often of little real value. In some schemes, once the product is sold to someone, the seller in turns gets a percentage of *that* person's future sales. Some types of MLM are legal if they involve legitimate products and a realistic chance at a sustained return through sales and recruiting. However, potential participants need to be very careful and should try to seek unbiased opinions.

Other investment schemes are more complex—indeed, their very complexity tends to disguise fundamental problems. For example, so-called prime bank investments use terminology that suggests they are connected with some of the world's leading financial institutions. They also suggest (using official-looking documents) that they are providing access to special investment opportunities used by millionaires. (There seems to be the assumption here that people get to be millionaires because they have secret knowledge, not because they are lucky or skilled at business.) The "financial instruments" described offer unrealistic rates of return (up to 200 percent) and claim to be issued by the World Bank, International Monetary Fund (IMF), Federal Reserve, or another prominent international or central bank.

In fact, the instruments are wholly fictitious, and any money invested will be lost beyond recovery. Asking a few common-sense questions would quickly expose the dubious nature of this and similar banking "investments":

- Why would a major international financial institution have to offer such high interest rates for money when they have access to the world's institutional investors?

- Would such an institution even be looking for ordinary individual investors?

- If so, would it use random Internet mailings or work through established brokerages or other channels?

- Assuming one wants to invest in such a program, how would one go about verifying its legitimacy?

That last question is perhaps the key. If something claims to be a program of the World Bank, a logical next step would be to go to that institution's web site—in this case, http://web.worldbank.org. There one can find a press release titled "World Bank Group Warns of Fraudulent Investment Schemes Misrepresenting Its Name."

Another type of e-mail or web site solicitation features day trading. Day trading is a legitimate, though risky, investment technique. Its basic idea is to identify stocks that are rising and quickly buy and sell them (often within minutes) to lock in small profits. (Alternatively, a falling stock can be sold short for a profit.) There are several problems, with this type of trading, however:

- The investor needs to risk a large amount of money to make a worthwhile profit on relatively small moves in price.

- Timing the market is difficult even for seasoned professionals—beginners typically lose a lot of money as part of the "learning curve," and some never turn a profit.

- The frequent buying and selling means a high overhead in trading commissions.

- Day traders must spend hours each day carefully watching the market. It is not really a part-time job.

Courses or seminars in day trading sold through e-mail spam or other means vary greatly in their completeness and accuracy. A particular warning flag should be raised if students are offered special "hot tips" (or access to them) for a fee.

The theme of offering insider knowledge is also expressed in trading schemes involving initial public offerings (IPO)—the first stock offered by a company that is opening itself to public investment. Sometimes investors are offered the opportunity to buy a stake in a company that is "pre-IPO"—that is, has not yet made an official public stock offering. The lure here is the chance to get in on the ground floor of a company that the e-mail claims might be the next Microsoft or Google. However, even if the pre-IPO stock actually exists, it is probably an unregistered security, which means investors have no recourse if, for example, the company never goes public and the shares become essentially worthless. At any rate, investment in legitimate IPOs is usually handled through select brokers or offered to employees. Even then, investors should carefully research the company's assets, track record, future business plans, and management before participating in an IPO.

OLD SCAMS IN NEW CLOTHING: THE MONEY LETTER

Over the years most people have probably received mail (or e-mail) purporting to be from a government official (often in Nigeria). This person has a problem: He has a large amount of money (usually there is a hint of corruption). He wants to get the money out of the country, and he offers the recipient a hefty cut in exchange for the use of his or her bank account for receiving the transfer.

The outcome is depressingly predictable. Typically, if the recipient accepts the offer it is explained that certain amounts will be needed up front to pay for bank fees, bribes, and other expenses. Although there always seem to be delays, reassuring, official-looking documents seem to suggest that the big day is almost here.

What happens next varies. If the victim is lucky, he or she eventually backs out after losing a few thousand dollars in fees. If not, the victim may be lured into going to Nigeria or some other country. Virtually out of reach of the protection of the United States, the victim might then be held for ransom, subjected to extortion, or, in a few cases, even killed.

In a quicker variation, sometimes the bank information provided by the letter recipient is simply used to execute a funds transfer in the other direction, cleaning out the account.

There has been some cooperation between other nations and Nigeria in shutting down these 419 scams (named for the relevant section of Nigeria's penal code). However, many other countries have been used for similar scams—as of 2004, Iraq is becoming a popular choice. The advice given about such opportunities is simple: Avoid them.

ONLINE GAMBLING

Online casinos offer virtual Vegas style games such as blackjack. The user establishes an account and is paid through credit card transfers. If the casino is totally illegitimate, the account setup may simply be a ruse to get credit information for identity theft or fraud purposes.

If the casino actually operates the advertised games, the games may not operate fairly. The virtual cards dealt, the position of the virtual roulette wheel, and other matters can easily be rigged by suitable programming to give the house much better odds (and the player correspondingly worse odds). Generally the only way to tell this is going on would be for someone to play enough games to demonstrate that the results are not in accordance with chance. Another likelihood is that players are not paid their winnings.

Because they are only a click or two away, online casinos can accelerate the fall of compulsive gamblers into bankruptcy. Lisa Harding, a 39-year-old retail-store manager, ruefully recalled how she spent hours every night playing blackjack, roulette, slots, and other casino games online: "Soon I started gambling more than we were earning. You don't realize what you're spending. Betting is so easy." Lisa's husband Andy added, "You can bet in your own home, in your pajamas, 24 hours a day."[4]

Because of its invisibility, it is hard to tell how many compulsive gamblers now bet online, and how much they are losing. However, the problem has attracted the attention of regulators and lawmakers. Since the casinos themselves are often outside U.S. jurisdiction, regulators are focusing on the major credit card companies. For example, Senator Jon Kyl (Rep.–Arizona) proposed a bill in 2003 that would make it unlawful to process credit card payments relating to online gambling.

Of course, as with traditional casinos, many players gamble moderately and do not get into trouble. Libertarians would argue that authorities should focus on educating the gamblers and closing down illegitimate online casinos and lotteries rather than enacting a new prohibition that, like those against drugs, may have little effect.

GRAY MARKETS AND FAKE MERCHANDISE

An Internet user (perhaps a college student on a limited budget) receives an e-mail offering a $500 Microsoft Office software suite for only $75 or perhaps Windows XP, normally about $200, for only $50. (The software might also be offered via a web site or online auction.) The software CD received will almost certainly be a "pirated" counterfeit copy.

After installation the program may appear to run correctly. However, if there is a problem, contacting the manufacturer for technical support will be out of the question because the program's serial number is not valid. Worse, the CD may contain viruses, spyware, or other forms of "malware" in addition to the featured program. And although individual home users are unlikely to face legal consequences, businesses where pirated software is in use have faced costly lawsuits from manufacturers or the Software Publishers' Association (SPA).

Microsoft has tried to reduce piracy by requiring that the program be activated after installation. This requires a unique, valid serial number, so pirated copies will not be usable. Ever since the early days of personal computers (when copy-protected discs were often used), there has been a tradeoff between making programs harder to copy and making them easier to install and use.

Most people have heard the saga of Napster and similar file-sharing services. The original idea was basically to have everyone convert their favorite music tracks to the MP3 file format and store them in a publicly accessible area of their hard drive. Users could then browse to find who had a desired track, and download it for free instead of having to pay $15–$20 for the commercial CD. Naturally, this threatened the revenue of the record labels, which successfully sued to shut down the service. (Belatedly the music industry also learned how effective the online channel might be for selling their product, and the result was Apple's iTunes and similar services.)

File-sharing has not gone away, however. Unlike the old Napster, many later file-sharing programs did not use a central database, so it was hard to target them with legal action. The result is a vast gray market which, along with illegally copied music, movies, or software features a wide assortment of pornographic images and other dubious files. Naturally this underground exchange also gives wide scope for distributing viruses, spyware, and other predatory programs.

Besides software and music, other fake products have recently been featured in spam e-mail. In late 2004, for example, people received endless offers of "genuine fake Rolex watches." These, at least, are not advertised as genuine.

Internet sales of strictly illegal products such as narcotics, certain weapons, and banned substances (such as ivory) are likely to come to the attention of the relevant authorities. Persons venturing into such markets are clearly beyond the purview of consumer advice.

In general, gray markets illustrate the ambiguity of Internet predation. Although not everything available in such venues is necessarily illegal, in many cases the victims have gone outside of the law and thus cannot seek the protection of the law. Because people naturally do not want to reveal their illegal activity, it also becomes hard to determine the extent of gray markets and thus of victimization.

A PRESCRIPTION FOR TROUBLE

A growing Internet market that is subject to considerable fraud and abuse is the sale of prescription drugs. One of the most popular spam categories is e-mails offering low-cost drugs. Many sites are offering common prescription drugs such as Viagra or Cialis (for erectile dysfunction) or cholesterol-lowering statin drugs such as Lipitor.

Legitimate online pharmacies require a prescription from a physician (and verify it, as would a local drugstore.) In a gray area are online pharmacies that have their own doctors who review brief questionnaires filled out by the would-be customer who, of course, they have not examined. Finally, the type of sites advertised via spam generally do not require prescriptions at all. However, the drugs (if any are actually shipped) are likely to be fake, adulterated, or expired.

Some users may visit such sites because they want to obtain addictive drugs and do not have a prescription. Many others are simply struggling with the high prices of prescription drugs in the United States and are looking for better prices, such as from Canadian pharmacies.

Many of the cautions described earlier in connection with online shopping also apply to online pharmacies. In addition, online pharmacies based in the United States can be checked with the National Association of Boards of Pharmacy to determine whether they are properly licensed. This organization also offers a certification for pharmacies that meet a vigorous review of their practices.

The Food and Drug Administration (FDA) generally prohibits individuals from importing prescription drugs into the United States. Nevertheless, high drug prices have led to many Americans in border areas driving to Canada, where the same drugs are often available at much lower than domestic prices. Similarly, a small but growing number of Internet users are buying drugs from foreign online pharmacies. As with Internet gambling, the problem is that what is not legal cannot be regulated. However, some states are setting up foreign drug purchase programs even against the opposition of the FDA. Public pressure on Congress may also lead to the legalization of foreign drugs (with some type of accompanying regulation) and perhaps treaties with countries such as Canada to regulate cross-border commerce in prescription drugs.

Recent data from the Pew Internet and American Life survey reflects the misgivings that many Internet users have about buying prescription drugs online, despite the possible financial benefits. As of 2004 only about 4 percent of Internet users have ever bought medicines online. A majority, 62 percent, said that they were concerned about the safety of drugs purchased from online pharmacies compared to those from their local drugstore.

Consumers who wish to buy drugs online that they are not currently taking should check with a medical professional to make sure that the drug is safe and appropriate for them. It should also be noted that many materials sold as "dietary supplements," as well as "natural" or herbal products, are just as much drugs as something sold in a bottle with a prescription label. They can have serious side effects, either alone or in combination with prescription drugs.

Information can be as important as drugs as a factor in the quality of health care. According to recent surveys from the Pew Internet and American Life Project, more than 93 million Americans now seek health information online. At a time when many doctors can allow only a few minutes for a patient visit, reliable health information sites (such as those of the National Institutes of Health, the Mayo Clinic, or other reputable institutions) can provide much helpful information. For example, diabetics can get help with managing their diet and blood sugar, asthma sufferers can learn how environmental factors might be aggravating their condition, and the baby boom generation can find tips on coping with the problems of aging.

On the other hand, unreliable information can have serious consequences if it leads patients to seek unproven or even dangerous treatments for diseases such as breast or prostate cancer, to avoid vaccinations, or to misuse antibiotics. Internet predators who sell 21st-century "snake oil" (dubious patent "medicines") electronically may damage their victim even more than the perpetrators of financial frauds or identity theft.

Further, a November 2004 study by researchers at University College, London, suggests that even good online information can cause problems if taken in too large a "dose." Their study looked at 4,042 patients suffering from chronic illnesses such as diabetes, asthma, and cancer. According to the researchers, patients who found health information, programs, and support groups on the Web learned more about their condition and options, and they received an emotional boost from the support groups. However, surprisingly, most of these patients did not change their behavior (such as diet) to reduce health risks. The researchers have suggested that this disappointing outcome may be due in part to patients not understanding the statistics they were reading online and not realizing the actual degree of risk involved in behaviors such as smoking or poor diet.

In the long run both health care providers and patients must become better educated about how to use and find online health resources. The result of better cooperation between providers, patients, and institutions may be better (and more appropriately targeted) information, and timely, effective warnings about health-related scams. Meanwhile the FDA and other government and private sources offer guidelines for those seeking health information online.

Fads and panic situations can also spawn drug-related online scams. For example, following the anthrax attacks in late 2001, many scammers offered antibiotics and other drugs. Cipro, for example, is a legitimate treatment for anthrax, but it is recommended only for people who may have been exposed to the disease. Widespread inappropriate use of antibiotics can have serious consequences: Not only do the drugs have potential side effects, overuse can lead to the emergence of resistant strains, making it harder to treat legitimate cases.

FAKE CHARITIES

Given the large number of people online (and their higher proportion of discretionary income), it is not surprising that charities and other nonprofit groups have taken to e-mail and web sites as a way to reach prospective donors. Unfortunately, Internet predators are also ready to take advantage of people's desire to help one another, particularly in times of crisis such as the aftermath of the Asian tsunami in December 2004. Only a few hours after the terrorist attacks of September 11, 2001, for example, e-mail appeals claiming to be from various charitable organizations began to appear. Because many legitimate charities also use the Web for fund-raising, it takes some effort to determine whether one is giving money to a bona fide group. Fortunately, as with fraudulent businesses, the Internet can also serve as a mechanism for alerting and educating consumers. For example, the

GuideStar web site provides a database that includes descriptions of nonprofit organizations as well as the Form 990s that they are required to file with the IRS. The Better Business Bureau also tracks charities. If an organization is not listed with either source, it is probably either very new or is not legitimate.

IN A FAMILY WAY: ADOPTION FRAUDS AND INTERNET BRIDES

Some of the cruelest online frauds involve intimate decisions about finding a mate or creating a family. It is the very emotional investment that people have in such matters that provides the hook for fraudulent services.

Fraudsters often troll for victims in chat rooms for prospective adoptive parents. As the CBS News program *48 Hours* reported, one couple, Steven and Kelly Motl, turned in spring 1998 to Tender Hearts Family Services, a Philadelphia-based online adoption service and one of its agents, Sonya Furlow. Kelly Motl was impressed with what she found, recalling later that "her Web site really made you believe like caring and responsibility went all together."[5] The Motls arranged to adopt a child through the service.

Several months and about $7,000 later, the Motls were told that Laurel, the birth mother, had decided to keep the child. Unknown to them and to another couple who had been promised the same child, there actually was no child and no birth mother. Eventually the Federal Bureau of Investigation (FBI) learned that Furlow had defrauded 43 couples out of more than $200,000. Furlow pleaded guilty to mail fraud and was sentenced to almost four years in prison. The Motls and the other couple were both financially and emotionally devastated.

This and other adoption frauds take advantage of several factors. Thousands of couples desperately want to adopt children but cannot deal with the complex procedures and long waiting times involved with the legitimate adoption process. Furlow and other adoption fraudsters take advantage of the tools that allow people to quickly and inexpensively build attractive, professional-looking web sites. In general, people tend to associate a professional appearance with legitimacy. Anxious and hopeful that their long wait for a child will soon be over, they often fail to do the checking that is necessary before undertaking any major transaction or life step.

To avoid such nightmares, would-be adoptive parents should demand references from adoption web sites and check them thoroughly. This should include verifying that the organization is registered with the state in which it does business. If the agency claims to be nonprofit, it can also be checked through the services mentioned earlier in connection with nonprofit charities. A red flag should be raised if an agency claims that it can complete in a few months an adoption process that typically takes at least a year.

Once in contact with a birth mother, the adoptive parents should be very cautious when presented with requests for money for expenses. In some states it is illegal to give money to the birth mother; doing so may void the adoption. Obtaining the advice of an attorney is recommended.

Online marriage scams are also prevalent and represent a real risk to lonely Internet users. Some "marriage" sites are simply disguised prostitution rings. For those that do offer marriage, the user is shown photographs of attractive women (usually purportedly in Russia), together with biographical and other information. If the user expresses interest in an individual, contact usually begins with encouraging messages that give the sense that a real relationship is starting to form.

The expenses then begin to mount. Sometimes the site charges fees for translating messages between the prospective bride and groom. Money may also be asked for language lessons, health checkups, and other preliminary expenses. The big "hook" usually occurs when the user is asked to provide money for visa and travel expenses to bring the bride to the United States—or sometimes, to bring the groom to Russia or to some third country.

As with the Nigerian money letter scam, sometimes the user reaches a point when he finally realizes that his money is gone and he is going to get nothing for it. However, sometimes the would-be groom and bride actually meet. At this point there may be more demands for money, or even an actual marriage. Unfortunately, the marriage may turn out to be just a sham to allow the "bride" to enter the United States legally. By then, in some cases, the unfortunate groom may be implicated in criminal immigration fraud.

Some online marriage services are legitimate (although expensive) and users actually do find themselves with happy marriages. Unfortunately, the "industry" lacks a reliable way to police itself, and by the time immigration authorities become involved, the damage to the duped user of an illegitimate agency has been already done. And for many women who have been persuaded to be "offered" by such services, disappointment and possibly abuse may wait.

EDUCATION SCAMS

Certainly most people would agree that education can help one get ahead. The problem is that it is hard to go to school while keeping an existing job. Is there an alternative? One common type of spam e-mail reads like this:

Earn more money with a college degree! MBA and other degrees available from prestigious institution. No course requirements or examinations, low fees, financing available.

Of course a "prestigious institution"—a legitimate accredited one—is not going to award a degree without the completion of work and other requirements on the student's part. These online solicitations represent later-day versions of "diploma mills." Any degrees they award are essentially worthless.

Persons seeking educational opportunities and new career possibilities should not despair, however. Thousands of legitimate colleges and universities now offer distance learning programs that allow students to complete all or most of the work for a degree from home, without interrupting their current employment. Before enrolling, however, students should verify that any claimed accreditation is legitimate.

Many students also seek money for educational expenses. They may encounter web sites that claim to offer the inside scoop on millions of dollars in scholarships and grants, both government and private. If the site requires substantial up-front fees before one can receive the scholarship or loan, chances are that it is a scam and the student will receive nothing. Legitimate institutions do not charge applicants for "processing." Sites such as www.finaid.org as well as government and college sites can offer reliable information.

EMPLOYMENT SCAMS

Not surprisingly, a variety of scams can be disguised as employment opportunities. For example, some scams offer lucrative overseas jobs. Generally they offer some plausible reason for the jobs being available (such as oil development in former Soviet republics). They generally mislead clients by claiming that they have many prospective employers lined up or that they have extensive databases for matching clients to employers.

However, as the Federal Trade Commission has reported, in numerous cases the job seeker receives nothing after paying advance fees of hundreds of dollars. Generally, job seekers would be better advised to research the economic activity in a country of interest and then contact major employers directly.

Domestic job seekers have a variety of well-known online job sites that can be quite helpful. Again, a sign of a reputable site is that it does not make extravagant promises or demand up-front fees. Indeed, most reputable sites make their money primarily from fees charged to employers with whom they have successfully placed applicants.

Alternative forms of employment such as telecommuting and "work at home" opportunities are attractive to many people. Such employment offers flexibility and may be especially attractive to stay-at-home parents. However, most such offers are scams. Some examples include:

- Address and stuff envelopes (an old favorite)
- Type or scan documents on a home computer
- Prepare medical billing forms for health care providers
- Assemble products or create craft work according to specifications

One thing nearly all of these offers have in common is the requirement to pay a fee up front, usually for some sort of kit that is supposed to provide the necessary information for setting up the home business. The potential for these types of home businesses is limited at best. For example, mass mailings are conducted using machines, not persons stuffing envelopes, and outsourcing of medical billing is much more likely to go to India or other countries than into American homes. Persons who pay to enroll in home assembly or craft work usually find that the company will make various excuses as to why their work is unacceptable and will not be paid for.

There are, of course, legitimate ways to make a living working at home, including performing clerical duties. However, agencies should have verifiable references and not charge fees until work is actually obtained.

"REPAIR YOUR BAD CREDIT"

In today's consumer-driven society, many people find they have fallen way behind on their credit card payments, mortgages, loans, or other financial obligations. The result is a bad credit record, which can persist even if the consumer succeeds in catching up with the debts. Bad credit can mean the inability to obtain further credit.

People who are desperate to restore their credit (and perhaps obtain new credit cards) are the prey for credit repair scams. Typically, these scams offer to remove negative information from one's credit records, such as information about defaults or overdue payments. Some agencies even offer to create a new record so the consumer can start over with a clean slate. However, as the FTC explains:

> *First, accurate and timely negative information cannot be removed from a credit report in an effort to repair it. Second, it's not only a bad idea to try to create a new credit identity using a false Social Security Number, it's also illegal. And third, when it comes to credit repair, only time and a personal debt repayment plan will improve your credit report.*[6]

Legitimate credit counselors can help consumers develop a plan to consolidate and pay off debts but, as with most things in life, there is no quick, painless solution to the problem of bad credit.

TAX SCAMS

A final area in this survey of online scams involves taxes—certainly a major concern for most people. Because the tax rules are incredibly complicated, it is easy to confuse legally permitted loopholes with bogus schemes that are likely to result in heavy penalties from the Internal Revenue Service (IRS) and possible criminal charges of tax fraud.

Some of these schemes involve convoluted transactions, often involving overseas institutions (which may not even exist) or the setting up of fake businesses (such as at home) in order to claim deductions. Other scams involve claims for special refunds that do not exist, such as claiming that African Americans are entitled to a special payment in compensation for their ancestors' enslavement. Some right-wing antitax groups even offer kits with legal arguments that claim that ordinary individuals are not liable for income tax at all. No courts have ever accepted these arguments, and people who use them are liable for civil and criminal penalties, as well as the unpaid taxes.

OTHER INTERNET SCAMS

There are some general considerations for evaluating online scams and schemes. First is that old saw, "If it's too good to be true, it probably is." If the offer looks somewhat plausible, it is time to ask the following:

- Who is making this offer? Are they what they claim to be? Is there any way to check?
- Does it make sense that a legitimate agency would be contacting me about this? (For example, one usually cannot win a lottery one has not entered.)
- Is what is offered something that can be found on the Web (or obtained from the government, etc.) for free?
- What could go wrong if I bought into this?

FIGHTING ONLINE FRAUD: GOVERNMENT AND PRIVATE EFFORTS

The battle against online fraud involves the efforts of many types of agencies. The federal government regulates securities (Securities and Exchange Commission), general advertising and promotion (Federal Trade Commission), and drugs and health claims (Food and Drug Administration). All of these agencies provide alerts about scams and guidelines for investors or consumers; many also provide facilities for reporting scams online. In addition, these agencies have sometimes conducted special sweeps looking for online fraud, such as the series of "Surf Days" run by the Federal Trade Commission.

Certain kinds of fraud can also involve the Secret Service (which traditionally investigates counterfeiting and analogous activities) and the U.S. Postal Inspection Service, which deals with fraud carried out through the mails.

Every state has an office of consumer protection or consumer affairs (the names vary slightly). District attorneys' offices can investigate Internet scams operated from within their jurisdiction or that affect their residents.

Besides general groups like the Better Business Bureau, most industries have private groups that certify products or practices. Before relying on such groups, however, it is necessary to verify that they are legitimate and independent, since scammers can create their own plausible-sounding groups and web sites.

Besides reporting scams they encounter to the appropriate agencies, individuals can also discuss scams in newsgroups, chat rooms, weblogs, and the many other kinds of expression available on the Internet. Just as the opportunities for consumers have vastly expanded with the coming of the Internet, so has the necessity (and the means) to become well informed.

INFORMATION AND IDENTITY THEFT

As destructive as Internet frauds and scams can be, they usually involve a one-time loss. If an Internet predator can obtain the information needed to assume a victim's identity, however, the results can be even more devastating. While a single fraud is perhaps the virtual equivalent of having one's pocket picked for a few dollars, identity theft is like losing one's wallet and house keys.

COSTS AND IMPACTS

According to a 2003 survey prepared by the research firm Synovate for the Federal Trade Commission, about 10 million Americans were the victims of some sort of identity theft during the year. The Federal Trade Commission logged 516,740 actual identity theft complaints in 2003, up from 404,000 the previous year.

The average loss was $4,800 per victim, and the total cost was approximately $50 billion, of which about two-thirds was borne by financial institutions and businesses and the rest by the victims.

Some experts believe that the statistics regarding identity theft have been exaggerated. Ness Feddis, senior federal counsel for the American Banking Association, suggests that "people call identity theft what they would before have called a stolen check."[7] It has also been pointed out that many states classify a stolen credit card as an identity theft even if no attempt is made to assume the owner's identity.

The banking and financial services industries, on the other hand, have an incentive to downplay the incidence of identity theft. Until fairly recently, many institutions preferred to treat identity theft as part of the cost of doing business, just as stores might do with shoplifting.

The problem is that the impact of identity theft on its victims is more than financial. On average, identity theft victims reported spending 30 hours trying to obtain police reports, stop collection of bills, and remove negative information from their credit files. Beyond that there is a psychological impact: The sense of violation and loss of control can cause considerable stress and depression. Media coverage of the incidence and impact of identity theft is now leading many banks and credit card companies to offer education about identity theft and to provide monitoring services to spot potential problems with accounts.

As President George W. Bush noted while signing federal legislation enhancing prison sentences for identity thieves:

> *The crime of identity theft undermines the basic trust on which our economy depends. Identity theft harms not only its direct victims, but also many businesses and customers whose confidence is shaken.*[8]

Occasionally identity theft can have a more sinister aspect. In about 15 percent of cases reported in the survey, the perpetrators of the identity theft were not primarily interested in money. In 4 percent of cases, criminals used the stolen identity when stopped by law enforcement officers. This means that the real owner of the identity might find that a routine traffic stop turns into arrest, booking, and a difficult attempt to prove that one is not a wanted criminal.

STEALING INFORMATION: TRADITIONAL METHODS

Identity theft did not begin with the development of e-commerce. The idea of falsely claiming the identity of another person in order to use that person's resources is as old as the development of money substitutes, such as checks or money orders. However, check forgery is difficult to do on a large scale. It involves the forging of signatures and of accompanying identification and usually exposes the criminal through personal contact with a bank or store.

Starting in the 1950s, the development of credit cards increased the scope for identity fraud, but the credit cards still had to be used in person with accompanying identification. What really boosted the possibilities for identity theft was the growth in telephone and online ordering of merchandise, electronic funds transfers, and debit cards, online banking, and similar systems. What all these systems have in common is that they allow a person to obtain merchandise or money simply by presenting certain information such as an account number or credit card number. No personal contact with the store or financial institution is necessary, and the risk to the criminal is lessened.

How do criminals get the numbers and account information needed to tap into their victims' financial resources? The traditional sources, still prevalent today, involve the following:

- Credit card receipts, checks, and so on diverted by unscrupulous employees (such as waiters)
- Similar materials stolen from home mailboxes or trash
- Preapproved credit offers sent through the mail

Once the criminals obtain the account numbers and other identifying information, such as full name and Social Security number, there are several ways they can cash in on the information. A common scenario involves filling in a stolen preapproved credit offer but changing the address to one used by the criminals. As a result, the criminal receives a shiny new credit card in the victim's name. The number can then be used to order merchandise that can be sold, or "fenced," for cash, or even to get cash advances.

THE THIEVES GO ONLINE

Identity theft experts have urged individuals to make life harder for identity thieves by securing their mailboxes, not putting outgoing bills in the door slot for the mail carrier, and shredding any credit card offers or other documents that contain personal information. This remains good advice. But just as students can now search the world's libraries online, modern identity thieves have access to a huge array of databases that can contain personal identifying information. Sometimes that access requires that hackers figure out a password or find some technical vulnerability. Some hackers sell or swap stolen credit cards in chat rooms, while others, such as the infamous Kevin Mitnick, seemed to value them more for bragging rights.

Often, however, no hacking is necessary. For example, convicted fraud-ster Thomas Seitz explained to a reporter that his actions were a "crime of opportunity." Taking advantage of the free Internet access at a local public library, he found a database belonging to the Securities and Exchange Commission. The database included various legal forms filed by individuals, and the forms included that Holy Grail of identity theft, Social Security numbers. Seitz began to apply for car loans using the names and numbers and eventually succeeded in getting a $44,000 sports car. "It became something like 'Let's see if I can do it,' he noted later."[9]

All he needed then was some fake identification to take to the car dealer, and he had no problem finding someone who could provide a false birth certificate and a W-2 form that matched the name under which he had received the loan.

Seitz eventually got caught when he tried to register his newly purchased car. What is significant about the story is not that he was a particularly smart criminal, but that all the information and tools for identity theft were readily available online.

Belatedly, governments have responded to try to make Social Security numbers less available to thieves. Many states now prohibit their use as customer numbers. Many universities no longer use them as student identification numbers, and while banks must still obtain them, they can use separate identification numbers.

The majority of identity thefts—an estimated 70 percent—are the work not of sticky-fingered Web surfers but of insiders. In the largest case to date, the U.S. Department of Justice charged a help desk worker at Teledata Communications, Inc., with obtaining thousands of credit reports and selling them to a coconspirator for use in identity fraud. In another high-profile case, a University of Texas student stole 55,000 Social Security numbers from the school's database. Congress responded in 2004 by including in the Identity Theft Penalty Enhancement Act a special sentencing enhancement for offenders who were in trusted positions and abused their access to data.

PHISHING: PART CON, PART THEFT

The latest threat to personal identity and information is based on a rather diabolic idea. Why work hard to uncover credit card and account numbers when you can actually get people to give them to you voluntarily? As Mitnick recounts in his book *The Art of Deception*, hackers have long used social engineering tricks to deceive or intimidate people into giving them the means to access systems.

Phishing combines two elements: a spam e-mail with the hook that persuades the victim to provide information, and a back end, consisting of an authentic-looking web site that the victim thinks belongs to the bank or other institution in question. Criminals have taken to phishing with a vengeance: Between September 2003 and May 2004 the number of different deceptive e-mails used climbed from 279 to 247,027. By mid-2004, it estimated 60 million Internet users received at least one such message. According to a survey by Gartner Research, about 11 million users bit on the hook, clicking on the included link to go to the phony web site containing the form requesting information. About 2 million went on to provide personal information. In one particular case, studied by the research firm Mail-Frontier, 40 percent of the people who read a fraudulent e-mail claiming to be from Citibank thought that it was really from that institution.

Major Internet companies have become concerned that if phishing cannot be brought under control it may become a drag on an e-commerce sector that has been gradually recovering from the dot-com bust of 2000–02. According to Dan Maier, a spokesperson for the Anti-Phishing Working Group:

> *It's a problem for Internet-related companies because their customers are starting to lose their trust in e-mails and communications. So these organizations are challenged about what to do next.[10]*

Why does phishing seem to be so effective? It begins with the hook, as can be seen in the following examples.[11]

The most common type of hook tries to get the victim to fix some sort of problem in order to prevent loss of a valuable service such as PayPal.

> *It has come to our attention that your PayPal® account information needs to be updated as part of our continuing commitment to protect your account and to reduce the instance [sic] of fraud on our web site. If you could please take 5–10 minutes out of your online experience and update your personal records you will not run into any future problems with the online service.*
>
> *However failure to update your records will result in account suspension. Please update your records on or before July 15, 2004.*

Similar hooks have been used citing Citibank and other banks and citing eBay.

Another variant claims that fraud has already occurred, as in the following example:

> *We recently reviewed your account, and suspect that your U.S Bank account may have been accessed by an unauthorized third party. . . . Therefore, as a preventative measure, we have temporarily limited access to sensitive U.S*

Bank account features. Click the link below in order to regain access to your account . . .

The following example tries to make the victim think that money is about to be lost:

Your request for Express Transfer from your Citi account to your bank account ending in 6297, has been received and is in process. See, Change or Cancel this Transfer at: . . .

Variants of this hook look like invoices for orders from Amazon or other companies. It is hoped that the victim, seeing an expensive order that he or she did not make, will panic and provide information to cancel the order.

One wave of phish e-mails brought out the big guns. It claimed that the recipients had been selected for "E-audits" by the IRS, and were urged to confirm their personal information. The IRS has tried to publicize this scam and let the public know that it does not conduct this type of audit.

A smaller number of hooks concentrate on the carrot instead of the stick. For example:

Ebay offer [sic] this month a great prize for members. All you need to do is to login in your account and enter this number . . .

Once the victim has clicked on the link included in the e-mail, the continuing success of the deception depends on the fake web site. Unfortunately, with modern Web authoring software it is easy to make a convincing duplicate of almost any web site. The logos can be copied and any characteristic typefaces or layout matched.

With early phishing schemes there was often a giveaway in that the URL (Web address) that appeared in the user's browser did not match the normal one used by the institution being simulated, or spoofed. Unfortunately, flaws in the browser and other techniques can be used to replace the actual address of the fake web site with the address used by the real institution.

As with other forms of Internet fraud, fighting phishing requires a multipronged approach. At least for the near future, user awareness and education is the most important line of defense. In an effort by the Information Technology Association of America backed by major online companies such as eBay, the industry is becoming increasingly committed, according to Greg Garcia, vice president of information security for the association, to

public awareness and education, to get people to understand more about their responsibilities, how to protect their identity online, and what to look out for in terms of phishing and spoofing scams.[12]

Here are some questions recipients of possible phishing e-mail should ask:

- Do I have an account with this bank or institution? (Phishers generally choose popular banks or services in the hope that many recipients will have accounts.)
- If I have an account, why would this service be contacting me in this way? (Many banks and stores have said that they will never ask people to confirm information by e-mail)
- If there's a link, does it really go to the service? (As noted, however, links can be spoofed. When in doubt, users should use the browser to go directly to the site in question, not through the link in the e-mail.)
- Does the e-mail have grammatical or spelling errors? This is often characteristic of phishing messages.

Beyond these particulars, the key is for the user not to be intimidated by the threatened consequences or enticed by any promised reward. As with all cons, phishing depends on a kind of short-circuiting in the victim's thought processes.

The growth in phishing has been accompanied by increasing efforts in investigation and education by the FTC and state consumer protection agencies. In the first FTC phishing case, a 17-year-old California teenager was sued for using phishing letters and a phony web site to get credit card numbers from America Online users. A settlement was reached involving restitution and a promise to spam no more.

On the technical front, phishers have combined their deceptive art with that of virus writers. Many viruses are spread when users click on an e-mail. This activates the virus, which then finds e-mail addresses in the user's mailbox and proceeds to mail itself to those contacts. Since the deceptive e-mails used to spread viruses are similar to those used in phishing, it becomes a simple matter to combine a phishing message with a virus.

However innovative technology can also be used to fight the spread of phishing. Services such as EarthLink have developed and offered e-mail filters (similar to spam filters) that also look for and block e-mails that have language typical of phishing hooks. PayPal and eBay have also offered software that works with the user's browser to give warnings about web sites being visited. Green indicates a legitimate web site, red means a fraudulent or spoofed site, and gray indicates the status is unknown. The software uses a constantly updated database of known fraudulent sites.

The largest private effort is that of the Anti-Phishing Working Group. This organization consists of more than 200 companies, including major banks such as Wells Fargo and large Internet service providers such as EarthLink.

SPYWARE AND OTHER VULNERABILITIES

A final way for identity thieves to obtain personal information is to get it directly from the user's computer. *Spyware* is a generic name for software that surreptitiously transmits information from the user's hard drive to some site on the Internet. Most people whose computers are infected with spyware are unaware that it is there—they just wonder why their computer has slowed down or started behaving erratically.

Typically, spyware is included in a popular file-sharing program, shopping aid, or other application that users want to have. As part of getting the free software the user also receives the spyware component—this fact is often buried somewhere in a user agreement.

Some of these programs represent mainly a threat to privacy. Adware, for example, tracks the web sites being visited by the user and downloads and displays advertising with a related topic. Like cookies, the little marker files that identify previous web site visitors and their activities, adware does not transmit personal information.

Spyware, on the other hand, actively seeks out and sends information that can compromise privacy or open up the user to identity theft. Spyware can include keyloggers that can record the information typed by the user—including user names, passwords, and account numbers used to access services. Whatever it does, spyware represents a breach in the basic security and privacy of Internet users.

A survey conducted by EarthLink and Webroot, a maker of privacy software, found that about one in three of the computers surveyed contained some form of spyware. Fortunately, a number of companies have developed free or low-cost programs such as Spy Sweeper and SpyBot Search and Destroy that can scan computers for spyware and remove it. (In 2005 Microsoft joined the battle, offering a free antispyware program to Windows users.) As with viruses, the developers of antispyware programs are in constant competition with spyware creators, and users need to keep their defenses up to date.

On the legislative and legal front, Congress in 2004 considered (but did not pass) several bills that would ban some of the most problematic components of spyware (such as keyloggers) and require that users definitively opt in before spyware could be installed on their machines or allowed to transmit information. The legislative effort is expected to resume in the following session of Congress.

Identity theft remains the most troubling cybercrime likely to be faced by most people. However, some Internet users will face a more personal and possibly even deadly kind of Internet predator.

ONLINE STALKING AND HARASSMENT

In 1997 20-year-old Amy Boyer became the object of the obsessive affections of 21-year-old Liam Youens, whose other hobby appeared to be collecting weapons. Youens, who had been a classmate of Boyer's in 10th grade, created two web sites on which he chronicled his feelings about Boyer as he stalked her in real life and took pictures. His musings then took a sinister turn involving his killing himself—and possibly killing her first. Youens then went to a web site that offered information on anyone for a price. For less than $100, he soon knew where Boyer worked. Youens noted in his online journal, "It's actually obscene what you can find out about a person on the Internet."[13]

On October 15, 1999, Youens's online obsession had irrevocable real-life consequences. He showed up outside the dentist's office where Boyer worked, and he waited until she emerged, got in her car, and drove away. Youens then drove alongside Boyer's car and shot her several times with a 9-millimeter Glock pistol, which he then used to kill himself.

Fortunately, most cyberstalking incidents do not end in injury or death, but fear, stress, and disruption of victims' lives accompany this crime, which is one of the most frequently reported cybercrimes. As Vice President Al Gore prefaced a 1999 report from the U.S. Attorney General's office: "Make no mistake; this kind of harassment is as frightening and as real as being followed and watched in your neighborhood or in your home."[14]

DEFINING THE CRIME

The root behavior of cyberstalking is, of course, stalking. One common legal definition of *stalking* is:

> *the act or an instance of following another by stealth or the offense of following or loitering near another, often surreptitiously, with the purpose of annoying or harassing that person or committing a further crime such as assault or battery.*[15]

The same dictionary goes on to define the new term *cyberstalking* as:

> *the act of threatening, harassing or annoying someone through multiple e-mail messages, as through the Internet, esp. with the intent of placing the recipient in fear that an illegal act or an injury will be inflicted on the recipient or a member of the recipient's family or household.*[16]

Stalking first became a crime in the early 1990s in the aftermath of the stalking and murder of actress Rebecca Schaeffer. Toward the end of the decade, stalking and harassment began to be carried on through online newsgroups and chat rooms. From January 1996 to August 2000, more than 180 cases of cyberstalking were investigated by the New York City police department. As a pair of FBI experts note:

> *By enabling human interaction without the constraints of physical barriers and with the perception of anonymity, the Internet has become the ideal instrument for individuals who wish to intimidate, threaten, and harass others. A stalker can use the Internet to send alarming messages anywhere, within a matter of moments, under the guise of a fictitious screen name or pseudonym.*[17]

An early example of online harassment with a nonsexual motive occurred when author Jayne Hitchcock posted online newsgroup articles criticizing the spamming advertising practices and fees charged by Woodside Literary Agency. In return she received harassing e-mail, phone calls, death threats, and unwanted club memberships and magazine subscriptions. Hitchcock fought back with a civil suit against Woodside and two of its corporate officers. She also publicized the case and helped Maryland pass the nation's first law against e-mail harassment. The New York state attorney general also filed charges against Woodside, and the agency shut down in 1999. Meanwhile, Hitchcock went on to write about cybercrimes and founded the group Working to Halt Online Abuse (WHOA).

STALKERS AND THEIR MOTIVES

According to a survey conducted in the mid-1990s by the National Violence Against Women Prevention Research Center, about 87 percent of stalkers are male and about 78 percent of the victims are female. Sexual obsession is one of the most common motives for cyberstalking. Other motives can include the desire to avenge some perceived wrong. Studies suggest that most stalkers have a mental disorder in some degree, such as schizophrenia or paranoia, a personality disorder, and/or a history of substance abuse.

The profile for cyberstalkers does differ in some ways from that of traditional stalkers. Cyberstalkers tend to be better educated, at least moderately experienced with computers, and often able to hold a fairly good job.

Some of the typical actions found in cyberstalking cases include:

- sending repeated obscene or threatening e-mail
- attaching pornographic images or viruses to messages

- obtaining the victim's e-mail or physical address and subscribing the victim to various magazines, clubs, and so on
- posting descriptive profiles or pictures of the victim on sexually oriented or pornographic web sites or services
- obsessively pursuing further information or details about the victim

E-mail is by far the most common way for stalkers to contact and harass their victims. Instant messages (IM) are being used increasingly. Less frequent venues include chat rooms and message boards.

WHO ARE THE VICTIMS?

As noted earlier, the majority of victims are female. Additionally, children or teenagers, minorities, inexperienced Internet users, and the disabled tend to be at higher risk. According to a survey by WHOA, 59 percent of the victims had some prior relationship or acquaintance with the stalker.

Many victims do not report being cyberstalked. This may be due to a variety of feelings: embarrassment, fear that reporting the stalking will make it worse, and belief that law enforcement agencies will not take online stalking seriously. Because of the potential danger, particularly when stalking includes extreme obsession, violent threats, and physical approaches, the victim should report it and insist on prompt investigation and appropriate action.

PROSECUTING CYBERSTALKERS

There are a number of difficulties involved in prosecuting this type of Internet predator. Some cyberstalkers are adept at disguising their identity. As investigators have noted,

> *If someone writes a threatening letter, the victim often can recognize the writing. If someone makes a threatening phone call, the victim often can recognize the stalker's voice. With electronic devices, the person on the other end is an unknown. It's the coward's way to stalk.*[18]

Technically adept stalkers can further disguise their identity by sending e-mails through anonymous remailing services that strip away their original return addresses. If the suspect's Internet service provider (ISP) can be identified, there is still the matter of obtaining a subpoena or a search warrant (depending upon law and circumstances). If the ISP has retained records of the relevant online transactions, then they must be expertly analyzed to serve as evidence in court that the suspect sent the harassing messages.

If a suspect is identified, there is still the matter of jurisdiction. If both suspect and alleged victim reside in the same state, this is pretty straightforward. However, if the harassment is being conducted across state lines, prosecutors in the alleged victim's state must decide whether to invest the resources involved in extraditing the suspect. Many may be reluctant to do so if the case appears to be weak. If the state from which extradition is being requested does not have a law specifically addressing cyberstalking, it may not honor the extradition request.

Further difficulties can be encountered in determining how to charge the defendant. It can be difficult to prove that a specific series of actions amounts to illegal stalking, A report from the U.S. Department of Justice notes:

> *Stalking is a distinctive form of criminal activity composed of a series of actions (rather than a single act) that taken individually might constitute legal behavior. For example, sending flowers, writing love notes, and waiting for someone outside her place of work are actions that, on their own, are not criminal. When these actions are coupled with an intent to instill fear or injury, however, they may constitute a pattern of behavior that is illegal.[19]*

Fortunately, legislators have been addressing many of these issues. All states have basic stalking laws, and most now have language dealing with cyberstalking. More uniform laws and extradition procedures are making it easier to bring cyberstalking suspects to trial. And although there is still no federal cyberstalking law, the Interstate Stalking Law of 1996 does make it illegal to travel across state lines with the intent to injure or harass another person. There are also federal laws against making threats of violence or death using interstate communications.

Victims of cyberstalking can still face great stress and uncertainty as they attempt to deal with the legal system. However, several groups offer support and resources for victims. Besides WHOA, mentioned earlier, there is also CyberAngels, an offshoot of the Guardian Angels crime victims' advocacy group.

CHILDREN: THE ULTIMATE VICTIMS

Children and teenagers are receiving many benefits from the Internet access that is common in schools, libraries, and many homes. According to a study by the Pew Internet and American Life project, as of 2001 about 17 million youths ages 12 to 17 used the Internet. This represents about 73 percent of people in this age bracket; no doubt these numbers have increased. The same survey found that 55 percent of parents believed the Internet to be "a good thing" for their children. In addition, 55 percent believed that learning about the Internet was "essential" for children; and 40 percent agreed that it was at least "important."

Young people turn to the Internet for learning and entertainment, but perhaps most importantly, to communicate and pursue social relationships. The survey found that 48 percent of online teens believed that their use of the Internet improved their relationship with friends and 32 percent said the Internet helped them make new friends. Seventy-four percent of online teens used instant messaging, the most fluid form of online communication, as compared to only 44 percent of online adults. As seems to be usually the case, young people adopt (and adapt to) technology more quickly than adults.[20]

These statistics should establish a context for considering the risks and dangers of the online world for children and teens. Internet predators who target children are indeed online, and their numbers have also grown with Internet use. The challenge is how to protect children from these predators without depriving them of the benefits of the Internet, a sense of privacy, and the ability to pursue their interests effectively.

PEDOPHILES AND THE INTERNET

Most people can recall warnings from parents or from visiting police officers in schools. Their purpose was to explain that some people wanted to harm children and to give rules about encountering adult strangers in places such as parks or malls. In the pre-online days the stereotypical pedophile trolled playgrounds for kids, using candy, toys, or various pretexts for luring them to where they could be abducted and molested.

Most sexual offenders against children are male. Child abuse expert Dr. Leigh Baker identifies 10 general characteristics of offenders:

- *Refusal to take responsibility for his or her actions and blames others or circumstances for failures*
- *A sense of entitlement*
- *Low self-esteem*
- *A need for power and control*
- *A lack of empathy*
- *An inability to form intimate relationships with adults*
- *A history of abuse*
- *A troubled childhood*

- *Deviant sexual behaviors and attitudes*
- *Drug and/or alcohol abuse*[21]

While the motivation of pedophiles (adults with sexual interest in children) has not changed, online interactions are rather different than those in real life. For example, the ability to easily assume identities in online chat rooms and message boards makes it easy for an adult predator to appear to be another young person or teen. Just as old-style pedophiles made sure they could talk about things that interested kids (such as sports or games), online predators can easily blend into teen culture—and without physical appearances that warn this is really an adult.

To what extent are children exposed to pedophiles and other exploitive predators online? According to a June 2000 survey by the Crimes Against Children Research Center, which sampled youths age 10 to 17 who used the Internet regularly:

- About one in five received a "sexual solicitation or approach" online during the past year.

- About one in 33 received an "aggressive" sexual solicitation, such as one where the teen was given money or gifts or asked to meet the person somewhere.

- About one in 17 was threatened or harassed.

- About a quarter of teens who received a sexual solicitation told a parent. Less than 10 percent of solicitations were reported to some authority such as the police, an Internet service provider, or a hotline.

- Only about 17 percent of online teens (and only 10 percent of parents) knew about any of the agencies or groups to which reports could be submitted and help sought.[22]

These statistics suggest that just as pedophiles in the past took advantage of the relative anonymity of public spaces like parks, many have become attracted to using the Internet, which provides both large numbers of potential targets and the ability to disguise identity.

THE ROLE OF CHILD PORNOGRAPHY

Pedophiles have often acquired large accumulations of child pornography—photos, and in more recent years, videos. Here, too, the Internet has provided something of a bounty to the predators. Pornographic images and videos can be easily transmitted via e-mail attachments or downloads from web sites and exchanged over peer-to-peer file-sharing networks. Besides using the images to gratify themselves sexually and collecting them as trophies, pedophiles sometimes also provide them to children in order to suggest that sexual relations between adults and children are normal or to desensitize them.

Manufacture, possession, or distribution of child pornography is illegal in all jurisdictions. Supreme Court decisions (such as *Miller v. California*) have distinguished between obscene materials (including child pornography) that are not protected by the First Amendment and other material that might be indecent but is legal for adults.

Child pornography is also prohibited because it can be assumed that children were abused as part of its manufacture. However the growth in computer image manipulation techniques has added a complication. In the case *Ashcroft v. Free Speech Coalition* (2002), a federal appeals court overturned the part of the Child Pornography Prevention Act of 1996 that banned virtual child pornography created either by digitally manipulating pictures of adults or wholly from scratch. The court reasoned that the law as written was too broad in that it could be construed to ban images protected by the First Amendment. Thus an element in future prosecutions of child pornography will be the attempt to prove that the images did or did not derive from actual children.

STINGS AND OTHER PROSECUTION TOOLS

Despite legal complications, targeting online distribution of child pornography remains an effective way to prosecute pedophiles without having to catch them in the act of molesting children. In 2000, for example, FBI agents learned that a Yahoo! discussion group called Candyman was engaged in posting and exchanging pornographic photos of children. As the agents investigated, the scale of the operation became apparent: The group involved more than 7,000 unique e-mail addresses, of which 4,600 were in the United States. Agents were able to obtain information about more than 1,400 members living in every part of the United States.

On March 18, 2002, the agents launched a coordinated sweep, searching 231 homes and businesses and arresting 86 suspects in 26 states. Twenty-seven suspects eventually confessed to molesting children. Meanwhile, law enforcement agencies in other countries were provided with information on members residing abroad.

As an illustration of the limited value of stereotypes in identifying pedophiles, the Candyman suspects included members of the clergy, law enforcement officers, a nurse, a teacher's aide, and a school bus driver—all persons likely to be trusted with and by children.

Federal agencies in particular have also mounted large-scale sting operations against child pornographers. Typically, they send out e-mail offers or create a web site that purports to offer child pornography. As people respond and order material, the transactions are documented and the purchasers identified. Arrests are then made, typically in a batch to minimize the chance that suspects will be able to destroy the evidence on their computers.

Since 1995 the FBI's Innocent Images National Initiative has especially targeted interstate pedophile rings and groups distributing child pornography on the Internet. The number of cases investigated by this unit rose from 113 in 1996 to 2,370 in 2002.

Child molesters are also directly targeted by stings. Law enforcement agents pose online as young people in chat rooms or other areas known to be frequented by pedophiles. They attempt to get suspects to be explicit about their interest in a sexual relationship and to get them to agree to a physical meeting, at which the arrest is made. If done with careful regard to avoiding legal entrapment, these stings can be quite effective in removing pedophiles from circulation.

PROTECTION OR CENSORSHIP?

Many parents and citizens in general are concerned about the exposure of children to all pornography, not just child pornography. Besides the fact that adult pornography can also attract children or be used by predators to entice them into sexual activity, most people would agree that there are types of images, such as extreme sadomasochism, rape, torture, or bestiality, that are likely to be harmful to young viewers.

Here the issue becomes how to protect children while allowing adults their First Amendment rights. Attempts to ban any online pornography that might be harmful to children began with the Computer Decency Act of 1996. All such laws have been overturned by the courts as violating the First Amendment. For example, in *Reno v. ACLU* (1997) the Supreme Court ruled that requiring Web users to provide proof of age (such as a credit card) before accessing web sites deemed harmful to children was unconstitutional. The Court noted that noncommercial web sites would not have practical access to credit card verification.

The most popular approach to protecting children from harmful online content is the use of Web filtering or blocking software. These programs can use lists of known good and bad web sites, scan for keywords associated with harmful material, or combine these and other techniques. However, Web filtering in public libraries has been controversial because the programs can also block large numbers of valuable web sites (such as sites devoted to information on breast cancer or prevention of sexually transmitted disease). Further, many library computers are shared by children and adults.

When this issue reached the Supreme Court in *United States v. American Library Association* (2003), the Court upheld a law requiring that federally funded libraries install Web filtering software on any computers that were accessible to children. The Court seemed to suggest that adults should be given access to unblocked computers on demand, but the practical consequences are uncertain.

Children are subject to other online risks besides sexual molestation. Like adults, they can be stalked and harassed online—it is no longer uncommon for children to create web sites that target classmates or groups. On the other hand, with concern about school violence exacerbated after the Columbine High School shootings in Colorado in 1999, authorities have sometimes overreacted and suspended students who posted poems or other material that had violent themes but did not involve specific threats to individuals. Here, too, the desire to prevent an atmosphere (or even an actuality) of violence runs up against the right of self-expression.

KEEPING CHILDREN SAFE

There are a number of ways to minimize the chance that children will encounter online predators and, if there is contact, to help them avoid becoming entangled in their snares. Among the many suggestions put forth by government agencies and child protection groups, the following seem reasonable and appropriate:

- Parents should have some familiarity with what their children are doing online, including web sites and chat rooms visited and any frequent online correspondents.

- Parents should talk to children about their use of the Internet, perhaps setting some basic ground rules—such as no giving out of personal information online and no real world meetings with online correspondents without the parent's permission.

- Parents should assure children that if they encounter someone or something online that disturbs or confuses them, the parent will help them sort it out without heavy-handed, punitive responses.

- Parents should be familiar with their child's school's policy toward Internet use and with what resources and guidance is available there.

Some parents may want to go further and use software to monitor and control their children's Internet use. Besides Web blocking and filtering programs, there is also software that monitors and records online activity (including web sites visited and even transcripts of chat sessions). It is tempting to use such software in order to be sure nothing dangerous is happening online. However, such close monitoring and control is likely to make children feel resentful at the invasion of privacy and perceive the parents as lacking trust in them. More computer-savvy children may be able to disable or override the software or shift their activities to computers outside the home.

Beyond particular recommendations, it is important to consider the overall process by which children learn to appropriately navigate in a technological and social world that is being transformed by universal access to information and global communications, as well as by new forms of media and of self-expression.

Consider the use of multiple or disguised identities. On one level online teens are used to the idea of multiple identities. Most have more than one screen name or use certain e-mail accounts for communicating with particular groups of friends. Popular role-playing and fantasy videogames also encourage the idea of having multiple identities. Experts such as psychologist Sherry Turkle see this exploration of multiple identities as a potentially rich creative process. Part of helping children stay safe online is helping them learn to manage their identities while learning to recognize how identities can also be used to disguise people who have harmful intentions. In other words, the best protection from Internet predators in the long run is a deeper understanding of what it means to communicate online.

POLICING THE NET

The final section of this introduction looks at issues and challenges that are common to all the various types of Internet predation. Whether a cyber-crime is primarily economic or personal in nature, the nature of the online world provides certain advantages to criminals, challenges to investigators, and possibilities for making online experience safer while preserving its richness and diversity.

CAN WE AFFORD ANONYMITY?

A common thread in confronting Internet predators is that their activities often take advantage of the anonymity of the Internet. Spammers, e-mail fraudsters, and phishers can all effectively hide or disguise their true identity, as can pedophiles trawling for children in chat rooms. Makers of defamatory or hate speech also often hide behind the Internet's anonymity.

On the other hand, the ability to use made-up screen names and conceal one's true identity can be very helpful for people engaged in positive pursuits. For example, rape victims or recovering drug addicts can share their stories and offer support without using real names that might make them more vulnerable. A whistleblower could expose the sleazy practices of his or her employer without facing dismissal, perhaps by sending e-mail through an anonymous remailing service.

There is a distinction between anonymity and pseudonymity, however. True anonymity removes any possibility of identifying the sender or poster. The screen names provided by services such as America Online should be thought of more as pseudonyms: the service actually knows the identity and account information that goes with each screen name. If compelled by a subpoena, the service must divulge this information.

Some online communities such as the Well do not allow anonymity or pseudonymity. Users can assign themselves something like a screen name, but the user's actual identity is present in every posting. This reflects a belief that if people are identified with their words they will have to take responsibility for them, and discussions will be more civilized and productive and less prone to flaming. As computer pundit Esther Dyson has remarked, "Anonymity is the opposite of community."[23] Thus another writer suggests that

> *The ultimate implication, I believe, is that to achieve a civilized form of cyberspace, we have to limit the use of anonymous communications. Many early citizens of cyberspace will bitterly oppose any such development, arguing that anonymous and pseudonymous electronic communications are vital to preserve electronic freedoms and allow free expression of human personality. But the problem with that view is that [. . .] we must collaborate in groups to build a rich social fabric, and we know that the ability to act anonymously, sporadically, in large groups brings out the worst in human character.[24]*

Although the structure of the Internet makes it easy to exercise relative anonymity in online interactions, the concept of anonymity seems to be under increasing pressure in the larger society, particularly in the wake of terrorist attacks. For example, the use of cash (anonymous) in financial transactions can bring increased suspicion by authorities. Travelers (particularly in airports and at borders) must prove their identity. Some observers believe that a national ID card and the universal use of biometric features (such as fingerprint scanning) is just around the corner.

In fighting Internet predators, much legislative and policy effort focuses on trying to remove the anonymity behind which offenders hide. Examples include measures requiring spammers to identify themselves. It has even been suggested that the e-mail system be fundamentally changed so that mail can be sent only by people who have been identified or registered in some way. While some form of verification of e-mails and Web content—

perhaps using certificates and encryption—might end the scourge of spam, e-mail fraud, and phishing, it would inevitably give the government the ability to control who uses the Internet and the ability to identify the source of any online communication. While fighters against online crime or terrorism may say that society can no longer afford anonymity, civil libertarians would reply that we cannot afford to give possibly repressive governments that much power and control.

JURISDICTION IN A BORDERLESS WORLD

At the time the United States was founded, jurisdiction was a rather simple affair. Nearly all offenses involved a perpetrator and victim residing in the same state. The powers and prerogatives of the federal government deriving from the Constitution gave it jurisdiction over matters that could not be confined to any one state, such as disputes involving navigation, interstate commerce, the seas (admiralty law), and international relations.

Advances in communications and transportation added complications to this scheme. The federal government gained increasing regulatory jurisdiction over railroads. Crimes such as extortion or conspiracy that used mail or the telephone to communicate between states required new federal laws such as for wire fraud.

The Internet adds a new dimension in that it is inherently global—any user, any site can connect to any other. As some writers in the emerging field of cyberspace law have noted:

Cyberspace radically undermines the relationship between legally significant (on-line) phenomena and physical location. The rise of the global computer network is destroying the link between geographical location and: (1) the power of local governments to assert control over on-line behavior; (2) the effects of on-line behavior on individuals or things; (3) the legitimacy of a local sovereign's efforts to regulate global phenomena; and (4) the ability of physical location to give notice of which sets of rules apply.[25]

As seen in many of the cases discussed in the next chapter, these are quite real considerations. It is often not clear whether a state law will be effective in dealing with an Internet-wide problem (such as spam or identity fraud) or how Internet-based businesses or other organizations can cope with a maze of conflicting state regulations. However, there is a more practical way to look at many cybercrimes:

The skeptics [of Internet regulation] completely ignore the spillover effects of cyberspace activity itself. They do not consider these effects because they take it as an article of faith that cyberspace participants form a self-contained group that can internalize the costs of its activity . . . . [But] they are real people in real space transacting in a fashion that produces real-world effects . . . . Cyberspace users solicit and deliver kiddie porn, launder money, sexually harass, defraud, and so on.[26]

In other words, one can focus on specific crimes: who commits them and who they affect. However, there is still the question of who will have jurisdiction over the case. Although there are elaborations, basically a state has jurisdiction over an offense if:

- The illegal conduct takes place in the state or produces its effect in the state.
- Conduct outside the state constitutes an attempt to commit an offense in the state.
- Conduct outside the state constitutes a conspiracy and an act in furtherance of the conspiracy that occurs within the state.
- Conduct in the state constitutes an attempt, solicitation, or conspiracy to commit an offense in another jurisdiction that is also an offense in this state.

On the Internet, of course, any user can be in any U.S. state or in any country in the world. There is thus a tendency to throw up one's hands and say that Internet crimes do not really fit within state or local jurisdictions and therefore only federal or even international law can be applied. However, many of the types of Internet predation featured in this book can be prosecuted at the state level even if federal laws may be needed for others.

For example, if someone creates fraudulent e-mail and sends it to victims within the same state, the state can certainly apply appropriate computer fraud laws to the case. If the person sends such e-mail to other states that also have laws against doing so, either the originating or receiving state can prosecute.

Problems occur when states have differing laws (or no laws) concerning a particular action. The principle that obscenity can be defined according to local standards becomes problematic when Tennessee, for example, prosecutes a pornographic bulletin board in California, a state with more liberal obscenity laws. In general, there is also a problem if a state tries to regulate the Internet in such a way that it imposes undue burdens on or diminishes rights of users in other states. Such cases usually have to be decided in federal court in relation to constitutional rights such as those protected by the First Amendment.

Thus the borderless nature of the Internet can make it difficult to prosecute some types of Internet predators. As a practical matter, law enforcement agencies are often reluctant to spend scarce resources prosecuting crimes that seem to have little connection with their own jurisdiction. Federal agencies, however, can prosecute most offenses under federal laws that regulate interstate commerce and telecommunications. The greatest need seems to be for more coordination between federal, state, and local agencies in prosecuting crimes such as Internet fraud and identity theft.

WANTED: BETTER CYBERCOPS

Once the decision is made to investigate and pursue Internet predators, the law enforcement officer or agent must face a variety of challenges that are unique to cybercrime, including characteristics of the offender, the mechanisms by which the offense is committed, and the nature of electronic evidence.

Like any good cop, an effective cybercop must become familiar with his or her beat. However, when that beat consists of message boards, chat rooms, and web logs, this means broad familiarity with Internet culture, including its customs, special slang, and subcultures (such as hackers). This is particularly true of agents who go undercover in the cyberworld to catch pedophiles or traders in stolen credit card numbers.

All investigators need a reasonable familiarity with the Internet and related software, although expert help can usually be obtained for matters such as tracing e-mails or interpreting the IP (Internet address) routing of communications or transactions.

The cybercop also needs to be familiar with legal matters such as how to obtain search warrants for evidence for Internet crimes and know what conduct is acceptable in approaching a target undercover and what crosses the line into entrapment.

Assuming the investigator gets the goods on an Internet predator, the job is really only half done. Regular police detectives are trained in how to collect, properly bag and log evidence, such as a gun at a crime scene. But in computer crimes, while some aspects of the evidence are physical (such as a hard drive or a printout), the actual data, such as e-mail messages or image files, are rather fragile. Many large police departments and all federal agencies now have special units that secure electronic evidence. For example, when the evidence is on a hard drive:

- The computer must be seized in such a way that neither the user nor some automatic program can erase the data.
- The data must be copied to a backup medium in such a way that it can be proven in court that it was not tampered with.

- Some evidence may be encrypted. Depending on available resources, it may be possible to decrypt it.
- Some evidence may already have been deleted by the suspect. But in many cases deleted data can be recovered using appropriate technical tools.

This brief look at the complexity of computer investigation and forensics shows the need for more extensive training for the cybercops of the future. A number of organizations, such as the International Association of Chiefs of Police and the High Technology Crime Investigators Association, as well as the FBI Cyber Crimes Unit, provide training and resources.

Historically, computer-related crime has not had a high status in law enforcement circles or in the police culture, as noted by one observer:

Globally, cybercrime is not a priority for most police departments. Reasons for this international lack of concern include scarce resources, insufficient training and fear of technology, lack of public outcry, and the police culture itself. For example, training officers to investigate cybercrime requires an extensive and ongoing educational program. In addition, the equipment necessary to investigate cybercrime is expensive and must be updated constantly. Third, public crime polls indicate that people are more concerned with and would rather have police investigate rapes, murders, thefts and drugs. Finally, because heroism, physical bravery, and catching violent offenders are rewarded, police departments intentionally or unintentionally place a lower value on apprehending nonviolent offenders.[27]

The good news is that high-tech investigation and law enforcement is an exciting field that appeals to many young people who have grown up with technology and are looking for a challenging and secure career. Private cybersleuth Michael Allison believes that

It's exciting getting into the hunt. You never know what you're going to find. And when you identify and finally catch someone, it's a real rush. The bad guys will always be out there. But we're getting better and better. And we're catching up quickly.[28]

BUILDING A SAFER INTERNET

One principle of modern criminology is that the environment in which a crime takes place has a considerable effect on the incidence and type of crime that occurs. For example, parks and housing projects can be designed in ways that minimize the kind of concealed areas or access routes favored by individual criminals or gangs.

Similarly, the Internet infrastructure—the way data is organized, transported, and accessed—can also be designed to make it less attractive to predators. Some possible examples might include:

- Use of biometrics such as fingerprint scanners connected to the computer to verify identity in e-commerce or electronic banking transactions
- More secure operating systems for personal computers. Microsoft Windows has long emphasized power and programmability over security, but public concern and perhaps government pressure are leading to an overhaul of the Windows XP system to provide built-in security features, such as an Internet firewall
- Redesigning the e-mail system (SMTP) so that senders are verified before mail is forwarded to its destination
- Having the browser use third-party certificates and encryption to verify the identity of web sites, as is currently done for verifying the source of software before installation
- Artificial intelligence software that works with Web browsers and e-mail programs to provide real-time warnings of possibly fraudulent messages or web sites
- Better analytical systems—perhaps applying data mining and other techniques to identify phishing and other deceptive e-mails and web sites
- More educational programs for school and home Internet users, particularly children and new adult users—perhaps featuring interactive, simulated encounters with various types of Internet predators
- Greater cooperation between private businesses (such as service providers and e-commerce firms) and government agencies

THE FUTURE OF A FRONTIER

That last bullet point is particularly important. The Internet has been a remarkably libertarian enclave within an increasingly regulated world. There seems to be widespread recognition that the tremendous economic and social benefits of the Internet would be jeopardized by trying to apply traditional regulatory schemes to such a rapidly changing, complex environment.

At the same time, the very success of the Internet means that it now carries a significant portion of the commerce and social life of every developed nation (and a growing number of developing ones). When people perceive significant risks or problems, they tend to demand that they be addressed by government. The question is whether the regulations enacted in coming years will be informed by an understanding of how the Internet works so that the online world can be made safer without making it poorer.

Whatever can be achieved by carefully considered regulations, a safer Internet infrastructure, and more effective law enforcement, the individual Internet user will always have a major responsibility to educate him- or herself about Internet safety issues and to become a more responsible and savvy citizen of cyberspace.

---

[1] There are related types of activity involving the Internet that are beyond the scope of this book. These include industrial espionage and other crimes committed against organizations and computer attacks on behalf of terrorist groups (cyberterrorism). The latter is covered in the Library in a Book volumes titled *Global Terrorism* and *The Terrorist Challenge to America*. Hacking activities and attacks against computer systems are covered here only to the extent they are used to help Internet predators gain access to their victims. Additionally, privacy issues are closely involved both in cybercrimes and in legislation and law enforcement practices. For coverage of these issues, see the Library in a Book volume *Privacy in the Information Age*.

[2] Quoted in "The Electronic Frontier: The Challenge of Unlawful Conduct Involving the Use of the Internet: A Report of the President's Working Group on Unlawful Conduct on the Internet." March 2000. Available online. URL: http://www.usdoj.gov/criminal/cybercrime/unlawful.htm.

[3] Chris Hale. "Cybercrime: Facts and Figures Concerning the Global Dilemma." *Crime & Justice International*, vol. 18, September 2002, pp. 5–6, 24–26.

[4] Quoted in Alex Tresniowski [and others]. "Gambling Online." *People*, vol. 60, October 13, 2003, pp. 119ff.

[5] Quoted in "Preying on Hope." CBSNews.com *48 Hours*. Available online. URL: http://www.cbsnews.com/stories/2001/01/23/48hours/main266460.shtml. Posted on January 25, 2001.

[6] Federal Trade Commission. "Surf's Up for Crackdown on 'Credit Repair' Scams." Available online. URL: http://www.ftc.gov/opa/2000/08/credit.htm. Posted on August 21, 2000.

[7] Quoted in Orla O'Sullivan. "ID Theft Overstated? Some Think So." *ABA Banking Journal*, vol. 96, February 2004, pp. 8ff.

[8] Quoted in Tim Lemke. "Penalties Stiffened for Identity Theft; New Law Gives Harshest Sentences to Terrorists, Corporate Insiders." *The Washington Times*, July 16, 2004, p. C11.

[9] Quoted in Margaret Mannix [and others]. "The Internet's Dark Side: Internet Crime." *U.S. News & World Report*, vol. 129, August 28, 2000, pp. 36ff.

[10] Quoted in Pete Barlas. "Anti-Phishing Group Intends to Reel In Online Identity Thieves; Crooks Use Phony Sites; Yahoo, eBay, Even FBI Have Been Impersonated by Internet Scam Artists." *Investor's Business Daily*, March 12, 2004, p. A04.

[11] The phish e-mails cited are archived by the Anti-Phishing Working Group at http://www.antiphishing.org/phishing_archive.htm.

[12] Quoted in Donna Howell. "Internet Auctions Still Lead FTC's Fraud Complaints." *Investor's Business Daily*, January 26, 2004, p. A06.

[13] Quoted in J. A. Hitchcock, *Net Crimes and Misdemeanors*. Medford, N.J.: Information Today, 2002, p. 113.

[14] Quoted in "Cyberstalking: A New Challenge for Law Enforcement and Industry: A Report from the Attorney General to the Vice President, August 1999." Available online. URL: http://www.usdoj.gov/criminal/cybercrime/cyberstalking.htm.

[15] Garner, Bryan A., editor. *Black's Law Dictionary*, 2d Pocket Edition. Eagan, Minn.: West Publishing Co., 2001, p. 660.

[16] Garner, Bryan A., editor. *Black's Law Dictionary*, p. 169.

[17] Robert D'Ovidio and James Doyle. "A Study on Cyberstalking: Understanding Investigative Hurdles." *The FBI Law Enforcement Bulletin*, vol. 72, March 2003, pp. 10ff.

[18] G. Miller and D. Maharaj. "Chilling Cyber-Stalking Case Illustrates New Breed of Crime; Internet: Mother's Account of Daughter's Ordeal Points Up the Unique Problems Such Web Crimes Present for Law Enforcement." *Los Angeles Times*, January 23, 1999, Part C, Page 1, (quoting Los Angeles Deputy District Attorney Rhonda Saunders).

[19] Quoted in J. Travis. *Domestic Violence Stalking, and Antistalking Legislation: An Annual Report to Congress under the Violence Against Women Act*. Washington, D.C.: U.S. Department of Justice, 1996.

[20] For more statistics and survey results about children and teens on the Internet, see Amanda Lenhart [and others]. "Teen Life Online: The Rise of the Instant Message Generation and Its Effects on Friendships and Family Relationships." Pew Research Center Internet & American Life Project. Available online. URL: http://www.pewinternet.org/pdfs/PIP_Teens_Report.pdf. Downloaded December 17, 2004.

[21] Leigh Baker, *Protecting Your Children from Sexual Predators*. New York: St. Martin's Press, 2002, p. 16.

[22] For more data from this survey see David Finkelhor, Kimberly J. Mitchell, and Janis Wolak. *Online Victimization: A Report on the Nation's Youth by the Crimes Against Children Research Center*. National Center for Missing and Exploited Children, 2000. Also available online. URL: http://www.unh.edu/ccrc/pdf/Victimization_Online_Survey.pdf.

[23] From a speech quoted in Sara Baase, *A Gift of Fire*. Upper Saddle River, N.J.: Pearson Education, 2003, p. 217.

[24] David R Johnson. "The Unscrupulous Diner's Dilemma and Anonymity in Cyberspace." Electronic Frontier Foundation. Available online. URL: http://www.eff.org/legal/anonymity_online_johnson.article. Posted on March 4, 1994.

[25] David R. Johnson and David Post. "Law and Borders: The Rise of Law in Cyberspace." *Stanford Law Review*, vol. 48, 1996, p. 1367ff.

[26] Jack L. Goldsmith,. "Against Cyberanarchy." *University of Chicago Law Review*, vol. 65, 1998, p. 1199ff.

[27] Chris Hale. "Cybercrime: Facts and Figures Concerning the Global Dilemma." *Crime & Justice International,* vol. 18, September 2002, pp. 5–6, 24–26.

[28] Quoted in Christopher S. Stewart. "Online Crime Engenders New Hero: Cyber-sleuth." *International Herald Tribune,* June 11, 2004, p. 17.

CHAPTER 2

THE LAW AND
INTERNET PREDATORS

The four types of Internet predation that are the focus of this book have been the object of a variety of federal and state laws. Some of these underlying offenses, such as fraud, child pornography, and child molestation, became the subject of extensive legal attention long before the Internet era began. Others, such as identity theft and stalking, have been recognized as distinct crimes for only a decade or so—the result of changing technology and social interactions.

The legal system depends on laws being precise as to the actions for which people will be held accountable. If a law is not precise, neither defense nor prosecution will know what elements constitute the alleged crime. They will not be able to advocate effectively. Further, citizens will not be able to know whether any particular action is permissible under the law.

One might think it would be a simple matter to treat, for example, the illegal obtaining of credit card numbers from a computer as analogous to stealing them from slips in a store's cash register. A person doing this could simply be charged with larceny. But computer data is intangible and fluid. It can be stolen without the victim being deprived of it. It is thus a different kind of property from, say, a bicycle. Entering a computer need not involve picking a lock or breaking down a door. Sometimes, indeed, the door is carelessly left open. Is this a trespass? Burglary? Or something else? Thus legislators have had to devise laws that specifically forbid various uses of computers and networks for criminal purposes.

Fraud

In simple terms, fraud is the use of misrepresentation or deception to induce someone to hand over money or something else of value. A related concept is embezzlement, or the surreptitious, unauthorized taking of money or valuables, often through the use of forged or faked documents or their electronic equivalent.

Computers can be used both to defraud consumers and to embezzle funds, such as from an employer. Most computer fraud statutes have been aimed more at the use of technical skills to steal funds or valuable information from businesses than at protecting consumers. However, information stolen from business computers can also be used to victimize consumers, such as through identity theft. Thus, strong computer fraud laws help protect consumers as well.

LEGISLATION

LANHAM ACT (1946)

This law's purpose is primarily to protect corporate trademarks against misuse, copying, or counterfeiting. However, it could be used against fraudsters or phishers who use corporate trademarks as part of creating deceptive e-mails or web sites. There is also a possible action for "false designation of origin"—by definition, phishers are falsely claiming that their mail is coming from the business being spoofed.

COMPUTER FRAUD AND ABUSE ACT (CFAA) (1984)

This federal law applies to all computers used in interstate commerce (as a practical matter, this will apply to virtually all businesses and many networks). It prohibits the theft (unlawful acquisition) of computer data. The law allows for civil as well as criminal proceedings, allowing victims the potential of recovering their losses.

The CFAA could also be applied by businesses in response to unlawful access to (for example) an online banking system using stolen account or credit card information or information obtained through phishing. Phishers could also be sued for misuse of corporate logos, trademarks, or other elements in creating their deceptive web sites. Another cause of action would be the cost in system resources and support or customer service time involved in responding to customers who have been phished. Of course, not many phishers would have the resources to make a civil suit worthwhile, and injunctions are of little use, given the constantly changing identities of the offenders.

ACCESS DEVICE FRAUD ACT (1984)

This law can be viewed as a complement to the CFAA. It has a wide-ranging definition of devices or methods used to gain illegal access to funds, including counterfeit credit cards. Courts have even extended the law to cover stolen passwords (see *United States v. Fernandez*, SDNY 1993). This law can also be applied to phishing, which involves an "intent to defraud" both the holder of the "access device" (that is, the credit card or bank account) and the issuing institution.

ANTICYBERSQUATTING CONSUMER PROTECTION ACT (1999)

Cybersquatting is the intentional obtaining of an Internet domain name that closely resembles that of an existing business or other organization. Cybersquatting has been used as a money-making scheme (registering the domain and then selling it to the affected company) and as a way to create sites that criticize a company or provide a forum for disgruntled customers. However, phishers often use web site addresses designed to very closely resemble that of the company being spoofed—for example, paypal.com instead of paypal.com (the former using a numeral *1* instead of a letter *l*).

CAN-SPAM ACT (2003)

Officially the "Controlling the Assault of Non-Solicited Pornography and Marketing Act," this law requires that unsolicited commercial e-mail messages (commonly known as spam) be labeled and include opt-out instructions for recipients as well as an actual (physical) address for the sender. The law also authorized the Federal Trade Commission to establish a "do not e-mail" registry. However, this idea was rejected when critics pointed out that spammers would simply use the list to obtain confirmed e-mail addresses.

Spam is frequently a vehicle for fraud and deceptive phishing e-mail, so restraining it is a reasonable legal objective. Unfortunately, most spam cannot be effectively tracked down and prosecuted. This law might be useful in fraud cases where the sender has been identified.

PENDING ANTISPYWARE LEGISLATION

In October 2004 the Securely Protect Yourself Against Cyber Trespass Act (SPY Act) was passed by the House of Representatives. While it was not passed by the Senate before the end of the congressional session, this law or something similar is likely to pass in the near future.

The law provides civil penalties for various deceptive practices involving the installation and use of intrusive software (spyware). Programs that take over control of the browser or Internet connection without user consent would be prohibited. The software would be required to notify the user and receive permission before transmitting any data from the user's computer.

The House also passed the Internet Spyware Prevention Act (I-SPY Act), which would add criminal sanctions for many of the same practices prohibited by the SPY Act. It, too, awaits further action in 2005.

OTHER BASIC FRAUD LAWS AND REGULATIONS

Fraudulent schemes can involve multiple communications methods. Thus messages sent through the U.S. mail are subject to 18 U.S.C. § 1341 (mail fraud) and those carried over phone or fax lines fall under 18 U.S.C. § 1343 (wire fraud).

There are also laws and regulations covering specific types of fraud. Fraudulent advertising of consumer goods is regulated by the Federal Trade Commission (FTC), which can bring civil actions. In 1983 the agency issued a letter summarizing the basic principles as follows:

Certain elements undergird all deception cases. First, there must be a representation, omission or practice that is likely to mislead the consumer. Practices that have been found misleading or deceptive in specific cases include false oral or written representations, misleading price claims, sales of hazardous or systematically defective products or services without adequate disclosures, failure to disclose information regarding pyramid sales, use of bait and switch techniques, failure to perform promised services, and failure to meet warranty obligations.

Second, we examine the practice from the perspective of a consumer acting reasonably in the circumstances. If the representation or practice affects or is directed primarily to a particular group, the Commission examines reasonableness from the perspective of that group.

Third, the representation, omission, or practice must be a "material" one. The basic question is whether the act or practice is likely to affect the consumer's conduct or decision with regard to a product or service. If so, the practice is material, and consumer injury is likely, because consumers are likely to have chosen differently but for the deception. In many instances, materiality, and hence injury, can be presumed from the nature of the practice. In other instances, evidence of materiality may be necessary.

Thus, the Commission will find deception if there is a representation, omission or practice that is likely to mislead the consumer acting reasonably in the circumstances, to the consumer's detriment.

These standards remain in force today. In addition, the FTC requires that advertisers have a "reasonable basis for advertising claims before they are disseminated." If an ad claims to have certain types of substantiation, such as studies, tests, or doctors' recommendations, the advertiser may be required to produce them.

For investment-related fraud, the Securities and Exchange Commission (SEC), created by the Security Exchange Act of 1934, comes into play. SEC regulations are complex but are generally directed to requiring that certain information be provided and, on the other hand, that information provided not be deceptive, fraudulent, or misleading. Since the late 1990s the SEC has been active in uncovering and prosecuting Internet-based investment scams.

STATE COMPUTER FRAUD LAWS

All states have consumer protection statutes that have language about deceptive trade practices and fraud similar to that used by the FTC. As e-commerce continues to grow into an integral part of the economy, the public increasingly demands that state agencies become proactive in prosecuting Internet-based frauds. However, since many transactions involve businesses in one state and customers in another, the question of which state has jurisdiction can become complicated.

Identity Theft

The use of instruments such as forged checks, implying impersonation of the legitimate owner, has been part of the criminal world for centuries. However, the development of credit cards and highly automated banking in the latter part of the 20th century made feasible the systematic creation and exploitation of false identities. This was recognized in the 1990s by the development of federal and state laws specifically targeting identity theft.

LEGISLATION

IDENTITY THEFT AND ASSUMPTION DETERRENCE ACT (1998)

This law makes it a federal crime when anyone:

knowingly transfers or uses, without lawful authority, a means of identification of another person with the intent to commit, or to aid or abet, any unlawful ac-

tivity that constitutes a violation of Federal law, or that constitutes a felony under any applicable State or local law.

IDENTITY THEFT PENALTY ENHANCEMENT ACT (2002)

This act essentially adds a penalty for crimes in which identity theft plays a part. Concern about identity theft as a tool for terrorists prompted the special higher penalty for such cases.

Sec. 1028A. Aggravated identity theft
a) Offenses —
1) In general—Whoever, during and in relation to any felony violation enumerated in subsection (c), knowingly transfers, possesses, or uses, without lawful authority, a means of identification of another person shall, in addition to the punishment provided for such felony, be sentenced to a term of imprisonment of 2 years.
(2) Terrorism offense—Whoever, during and in relation to any felony violation enumerated in section 2332b(g)(5)(B), knowingly transfers, possesses, or uses, without lawful authority, a means of identification of another person or a false identification document shall, in addition to the punishment provided for such felony, be sentenced to a term of imprisonment of 5 years.

Consumer Protections and Identity Theft Victims

FEDERAL LEGISLATION

Several other laws can help consumers prevent identity theft or help them to repair their credit following an incident.

FAIR CREDIT REPORTING ACT (1971)

The Fair Credit Reporting Act (with recent amendments) gives consumers the right to obtain their credit reports. Both the major national credit agencies and the merchants or others reporting information to the agencies have responsibilities for investigating, correcting, and verifying erroneous information. A recent amendment to the FCRA allows credit card holders to request one free credit report per year from each of the three major credit reporting agencies.

FAIR CREDIT BILLING ACT (1975)

The Fair Credit Billing Act provides protections to consumers who believe that their credit cards have been charged erroneously or fraudulently. The financial responsibility of the cardholder for unauthorized charges is capped at $50. Charges must be disputed by writing to the credit card provider.

FAIR DEBT COLLECTION PRACTICES ACT (1978)

Victims of identity theft have often found themselves pursued by merchants or collection agencies, even after they have attempted to explain that they are not responsible for the charges. The Fair Debt Collection Act limits the times and places where the alleged debtor can be contacted; the alleged debtor can also demand that no further contacts be made until the debt is resolved or some specific action is taken. If the supposed debtor sends the collector notice that no money is actually owed (which should be done in cases of identity theft), collection activity must stop unless the collector can provide proof that the debt is valid. (However, such proof might just be a copy of the bill generated by the fraudulent purchase.)

ELECTRONIC FUNDS TRANSFER ACT (1978)

This law covers many kinds of electronic funds transfers, including debit cards, ATMs, direct deposits, and online banking. One relevant requirement is that when an account is opened the holder must be told the amount for which he or she would be liable in case of an unauthorized transaction.

The act provides that the holder of a debit or ATM card will not be liable if its loss is reported before it has been misused. If the loss is reported within two business days of the owner realizing the card is missing, the maximum liability is $50. If it is reported between two and 60 days, the cap rises to $500. Beyond that, the loss is limited only by the amount of money in the account or line of credit.

GRAMM-LEACH-BLILEY ACT (1999)

This law, also called GLBA or the Financial Modernization Act of 1999, added new requirements for financial institutions (such as banks, investment services, mortgage brokers, and insurance companies) to safeguard customers' personal information. The institution must provide a clear privacy notice and give customers the right to opt out of some sharing of information with third-party companies. The GLBA also bans pretexting, or the obtaining of information by third parties pretending to be customers.

STATE LAWS

All states now have laws against identity theft or identity fraud. For example, the following North Carolina statute clearly specifies the intent of fraudulent misrepresentation, the types of information applicable, and the legitimate uses of such information:

Article 19C.

　Financial Identity Fraud.

§14–113.20. Financial identity fraud.

(a) *A person who knowingly obtains, possesses, or uses identifying information of another person, living or dead, with the intent to fraudulently represent that the person is the other person for the purposes of making financial or credit transactions in the other person's name, to obtain anything of value, benefit, or advantage, or for the purpose of avoiding legal consequences is guilty of a felony punishable as provided in G.S. 14–113.22(a).*

(b) *The term "identifying information" as used in this*
Article includes the following:

　(1) *Social Security numbers.*

　(2) *Driver's license numbers.*

　(3) *Checking account numbers.*

　(4) *Savings account numbers.*

　(5) *Credit card numbers.*

　(6) *Debit card numbers.*

　(7) *Personal Identification (PIN) Code as defined in G.S. 14–113.8(6).*

　(8) *Electronic identification numbers.*

　(9) *Digital signatures.*

　(10) *Any other numbers or information that can be used to access a person's financial resources.*

　(11) *Biometric data.*

　(12) *Fingerprints.*

　(13) *Passwords.*

　(14) *Parent's legal surname prior to marriage.*

(c) *It shall not be a violation under this Article for a person to do any of the following:*

    (1) *Lawfully obtain credit information in the course of a bona fide consumer or commercial transaction.*

    (2) *Lawfully exercise, in good faith, a security interest or a right of offset by a creditor or financial institution.*

    (3) *Lawfully comply, in good faith, with any warrant, court order, levy, garnishment, attachment, or other judicial or administrative order, decree, or directive, when any party is required to do so. (1999–449, s. 1; 2000–140, s. 37; 2002–175, s. 4.)*

Many states also include civil provisions allowing victims to sue the perpetrator.

Stalking and Harassment

LEGISLATION

Stalking was first defined as a specific crime in the early 1990s in response to the case of Rebecca Schaeffer, an actress who was stalked and then murdered by Robert Bardo. Although statutory definitions of stalking vary, the crime generally involves repeated following or other intrusions on a person's privacy such that a reasonable person would feel threatened. The development of online communications led to the need to apply the law to stalking-type behavior that does not involve direct physical contact. This behavior is often called cyberstalking.

INTERSTATE STALKING AND PREVENTION ACT (1996)

This law made it a crime to travel across state lines with intent to injure or harass another person. It did not deal with harassment carried on via phone or the Internet.

U.S. CODE 18: 41, § 875(C)

This language is more useful because it does cover communications technology:

Whoever transmits in interstate or foreign commerce any communication containing any threat to kidnap any person or any threat to injure the per-

son of another, shall be fined under this title or imprisoned for not more than five years, or both.

COMMUNICATIONS DECENCY ACT (CDA) (1996)

The original Communications Act language dealt only with the telephone. The CDA broadened this language to include the Internet and other communications devices. It makes illegal any use of a telecommunications device that:

makes, creates, or solicits, and initiates the transmission of, any comment, request, suggestion, proposal, image, or other communication which is obscene, lewd, lascivious, filthy, or indecent, with intent to annoy, abuse, threaten, or harass another person
-or-
makes a telephone call or utilizes a telecommunications device, whether or not conversation or communication ensues, without disclosing his identity and with intent to annoy, abuse, threaten, or harass any person at the called number or who receives the communications;
-or-
makes repeated telephone calls or repeatedly initiates communication with a telecommunications device, during which conversation or communication ensues, solely to harass any person at the called number or who receives the communication.

Although other parts of the CDA relating to Internet pornography were overturned by the Supreme Court, the antiharassment language was not challenged. It potentially covers a much broader range of actions than did the earlier language that referred only to threats of kidnapping or violence.

VIOLENCE AGAINST WOMEN ACT (2000)

This act extends the federal stalking statute to include stalking that is carried out by telephone, mail, or the Internet.

STALKING PREVENTION AND VICTIM PROTECTION ACT OF 2000

This law expanded the definition of stalking in the U.S. Code to include the use of "the mail or any facility of interstate or foreign commerce" to place a person "in reasonable fear of . . . death, or serious bodily injury." Threatening a person's spouse, intimate partner, or family member is also covered.

Thus the Internet, online communications services, and any similar technologies developed in the future are covered.

FEDERAL LAWS

As of 2004 there are no federal laws that deal explicitly with cyberstalking. However, many stalking cases involve personal contacts or other offline offenses. The following laws may be useful to cyberstalking victims in some cases.

18 U.S.C. 875(c) makes it a federal crime, punishable by up to five years in prison and a fine of up to $250,000, to transmit any communication in interstate or foreign commerce containing a threat to injure the person of another. Note the two limitations implicit in the law. The "interstate or foreign commerce" qualification would be satisfied by most online services. However, the law applies only when a communication contains an explicit threat of injury.

Under 47 U.S.C. 223 it is a federal crime, punishable by up to two years in prison, to use a telephone or telecommunications device to annoy, abuse, harass, or threaten any person at the called number. This law covers a wider range of abusive behavior, but it applies only to direct person-to-person communication, not postings on web sites, chat rooms, or newsgroups.

The Interstate Stalking Act (1996) makes it a crime for any person to travel across state lines with the intent to injure or harass another person and, in the course thereof, places that person or a member of that person's family in a reasonable fear of death or serious bodily injury. If online stalking by someone in another state turns into in-person stalking, this law might become a useful tool for prosecution.

STATE LAWS

As of 2004 all states have antistalking laws; most of the laws include provisions that deal specifically with communications (including threats) conveyed electronically. One important element of criminal stalking is the making of a credible threat of harm; another is harassment. For example, the California Penal Code specifies as follows:

Cal. Penal Code § 646.9
646.9. (a) Any person who willfully, maliciously, and repeatedly follows or harasses another person and who makes a credible threat with the intent to place that person in reasonable fear for his or her safety, or the safety of his or her immediate family, is guilty of the crime of stalking, punishable by imprisonment in a county jail for not more than one year or by a fine of not more

than one thousand dollars ($1,000), or by both that fine and imprisonment, or by imprisonment in the state prison.

(b) Any person who violates subdivision (a) when there is a temporary restraining order, injunction, or any other court order in effect prohibiting the behavior described in subdivision (a) against the same party, shall be punished by imprisonment in the state prison for two, three, or four years.

(c) Every person who, having been convicted of a felony under this section, commits a second or subsequent violation of this section shall be punished by imprisonment in the state prison for two, three, or four years.

(d) In addition to the penalties provided in this section, the sentencing court may order a person convicted of a felony under this section to register as a sex offender pursuant to subparagraph (E) of paragraph (2) of subdivision (a) of Section 290.

(e) For the purposes of this section, "harasses" means a knowing and willful course of conduct directed at a specific person that seriously alarms, annoys, torments, or terrorizes the person, and that serves no legitimate purpose. This course of conduct must be such as would cause a reasonable person to suffer substantial emotional distress, and must actually cause substantial emotional distress to the person.

Stalking can also be treated as a tort, allowing the alleged perpetrator to be sued in civil court. For example, California defines civil stalking as follows:

Cal. Civil Code § 1708.7

1708.7. (a) A person is liable for the tort of stalking when the plaintiff proves all of the following elements of the tort:

(1) The defendant engaged in a pattern of conduct the intent of which was to follow, alarm, or harass the plaintiff. In order to establish this element, the plaintiff shall be required to support his or her allegations with independent corroborating evidence.

(2) As a result of that pattern of conduct, the plaintiff reasonably feared for his or her safety, or the safety of an immediate family member. For purposes of this paragraph, "immediate family" means a spouse, parent, child, any person related by consanguinity or affinity within the second degree, or any person who regularly resides, or, within the six months preceding any portion of the pattern of conduct, regularly resided, in the plaintiff's household.

(3) One of the following:

(A) The defendant, as a part of the pattern of conduct specified in paragraph (1), made a credible threat with the intent to place the plaintiff

> *in reasonable fear for his or her safety, or the safety of an immediate family member and, on at least one occasion, the plaintiff clearly and definitively demanded that the defendant cease and abate his or her pattern of conduct and the defendant persisted in his or her pattern of conduct.*
>
> (B) *The defendant violated a restraining order, including, but not limited to, any order issued pursuant to Section 527.6 of the Code of Civil Procedure, prohibiting any act described in subdivision (a).*

Harassment is typically defined as repeated nonconsensual contact that would cause a reasonable person to suffer "substantial emotional distress."

Sexual Exploitation of Children

Because of their inherent vulnerability, children have always received a special degree of legal protection. Since minors are not legally capable of consenting to sex, any sexual activity involving them is potentially subject to prosecution. Generally, the greater the age difference, the more heinous the offense, with child molestation by adults being the most heavily sanctioned category.

The development of online communications services and the Internet led to a need to apply laws against sexual exploitation of children to this new medium. Generally, the most controversial area has been the attempt to prevent children from having access to pornography in general, as well as to prevent the online distribution of child pornography

LEGISLATION

COMMUNICATIONS DECENCY ACT (1996)

Signed into law as part of the Telecommunications Act of 1996, the CDA was controversial from the very beginning. The law attempted to ban pornography and other indecent or "patently offensive" material from computers that could be accessed by children. Offenders faced up to two years in jail and a $250,000 fine per offense.

In 1997, however, the Supreme Court overturned these provisions, ruling that there was no means to ensure that children did not access web sites or online services that did not also prevent adults from viewing material to which they were entitled under the First Amendment—material that might be indecent, but is not legally obscene.

CHILD PORNOGRAPHY PREVENTION ACT (1996)

This law was the first attempt to deal with the production of "virtual" or "morphed" child pornography. In such productions adults could be posed in various sexual acts and then digitally transformed to look like children. However, in 2002 the Supreme Court ruled that because children were not actually used, such productions were protected by the First Amendment.

CHILDREN'S ONLINE PRIVACY PROTECTION ACT (1998)

This law prohibits the collection of personal information from children under 13 without parental consent. It was passed in response to concern that children could be exploited by marketers or that their information could in turn become available to predators.

Additionally, in 1998 a statute, 18 U.S.C. 2425, was enacted that makes it a federal crime to use any means of interstate or foreign commerce (such as a telephone line or the Internet) to knowingly communicate with any person with intent to solicit or entice a child into unlawful sexual activity.

CHILD ONLINE PROTECTION ACT (COPA) (1998)

The COPA was enacted in an attempt to prevent children from being exposed to pornography while answering the Supreme Court's objections to the CDA. The law provided that persons who make "harmful" material available to children could be fined up to $50,000 a day; they could also be sued in federal court for up to $50,000 per violation.

In 2004 the Supreme Court ruled in *Ashcroft v. ACLU* that these provisions appeared to be in violation of the First Amendment. The Court allowed the government to reargue its case in the lower court, but the law is likely to remain inactive.

CHILD PROTECTION AND SEXUAL PREDATOR PUNISHMENT ACT (1998)

This law addressed the growing use of computers and the Internet by sexual predators to exploit children. Because the Internet's anonymity and the presence of a large number of unsupervised children make it so attractive to predators, Congress responded by adding to the federal sentencing guidelines sentence enhancements to "ensure that persons who misrepresent themselves to a minor, or use computers or Internet-access devices to locate and gain access to a minor, are severely punished."

CHILDREN'S INTERNET PROTECTION ACT (CIPA) (2000)

The CIPA represents a third attempt to deal with exposure of pornography to children. Instead of making it illegal to distribute such material, it focused on the other end of the computer link. Specifically, it required that schools that received so-called E-rate technology funding must install Web blocking or filtering software on their computers. Although library and civil liberties groups objected on grounds that such software often blocks legitimate educational material, the Supreme Court upheld the law in June 2003. (*U.S. v. American Library Association.*)

CHILD OBSCENITY AND PORNOGRAPHY PREVENTION ACT (2003)

This law tries to sidestep the constitutionally treacherous question of virtual child pornography by focusing on the intent of the participants. It outlaws any solicitation to buy or sell child pornography (or anything represented as child pornography).

PROSECUTORIAL REMEDIES AND TOOLS AGAINST THE EXPLOITATION OF CHILDREN TODAY ACT (PROTECT ACT) (2003)

A provision of the PROTECT Act represents another attempt to deal with virtual child pornography. It would make it illegal to use pornographic images that appear to be indistinguishable from actual children. However, pornographers would be able to defend themselves in court by proving that no actual children were used in making the images but the burden of proof is essentially shifted from the prosecution to the defense. Another provision would make it illegal to use Internet domain names that mislead children into visiting pornographic sites.

OTHER APPLICABLE LAWS

Depending on the circumstances, a variety of other federal charges can be brought in connection with Internet sexual exploitation of children. Some relevant chapters of Section 18 of the U.S. Code include:

§ 1462. Importation or Transportation of Obscene Matters
§ 1465. Transportation of Obscene Matters for Sale or Distribution

§ 1466. Engaging in the Business of Selling or Transferring Obscene Matter

§ 2241(a)(b)(c). Aggravated Sexual Abuse

§ 2251(a)(b)(c). Sexual Exploitation of Children

§ 2251A(a)(b). Selling or Buying of Children

§ 2252. Certain Activities Relating to Material Involving the Sexual Exploitation of Minors

§ 2252A. Certain Activities Relating to Material Constituting or Containing Child Pornography

§ 2260(a)(b). Production of Sexually Explicit Depictions of a Minor for Importation into the US

§ 2421. Transportation Generally

§ 2422. Coercion and Enticement

§ 2423(a). Transportation of Minors with Intent to Engage in Criminal Sexual Activity

§ 2423(b). Interstate or Foreign Travel with Intent to Engage in a Sexual Act with a Juvenile

§ 2425. Use of Interstate Facilities to Transmit Information About a Minor

§ 13032. Reporting of Child Pornography by Electronic Communication Service Providers

Other Computer-Related Offenses

Most states have laws prohibiting computer-related offenses such as unauthorized access, disruption of services, damaging equipment or data, or attacking a computer in order to further a scheme involving theft or fraud. (Since all Internet activity depends on underlying computer systems, general laws against abuse or misuse of computer equipment are often relevant to prosecution of Internet predators.) For example, the Florida penal code includes the following provisions, which include civil remedies as well as criminal sanctions.

815.06 Offenses against computer users. —
(1) Whoever willfully, knowingly, and without authorization:
(a) Accesses or causes to be accessed any computer, computer system, or computer network;
(b) Disrupts or denies or causes the denial of computer system services to an authorized user of such computer system services, which, in whole or part, is owned by, under contract to, or operated for, on behalf of, or in conjunction with another;

(c) Destroys, takes, injures, or damages equipment or supplies used or intended to be used in a computer, computer system, or computer network;

(d) Destroys, injures, or damages any computer, computer system, or computer network; or

(e) Introduces any computer contaminant into any computer, computer system, or computer network, commits an offense against computer users.

(2)(a) Except as provided in paragraphs (b) and (c), whoever violates subsection (1) commits a felony of the third degree, punishable as provided in s. 775.082, s. 775.083, or s. 775.084.

(b) Whoever violates subsection (1) and:

1. Damages a computer, computer equipment, computer supplies, a computer system, or a computer network, and the monetary damage or loss incurred as a result of the violation is $5,000 or greater;

2. Commits the offense for the purpose of devising or executing any scheme or artifice to defraud or obtain property; or

3. Interrupts or impairs a governmental operation or public communication, transportation, or supply of water, gas, or other public service, commits a felony of the second degree, punishable as provided in s. 775.082, s. 775.083, or s. 775.084.

(c) Whoever violates subsection (1) and the violation endangers human life commits a felony of the first degree, punishable as provided in s. 775.082, s. 775.083, or s. 775.084.

(3) Whoever willfully, knowingly, and without authorization modifies equipment or supplies used or intended to be used in a computer, computer system, or computer network commits a misdemeanor of the first degree, punishable as provided in s. 775.082 or s. 775.083.

(4)(a) In addition to any other civil remedy available, the owner or lessee of the computer, computer system, computer network, computer program, computer equipment, computer supplies, or computer data may bring a civil action against any person convicted under this section for compensatory damages.

(b) In any action brought under this subsection, the court may award reasonable attorney's fees to the prevailing party.

(5) Any computer, computer system, computer network, computer software, or computer data owned by a defendant which is used during the commission of any violation of this section or any computer owned by the defendant which is used as a repository for the storage of software or data obtained in violation of this section is subject to forfeiture as provided under ss. 932.701-932.704.

(6) This section does not apply to any person who accesses his or her employer's computer system, computer network, computer program, or computer data when acting within the scope of his or her lawful employment.

(7) For purposes of bringing a civil or criminal action under this section, a person who causes, by any means, the access to a computer, computer system,

or computer network in one jurisdiction from another jurisdiction is deemed to have personally accessed the computer, computer system, or computer network in both jurisdictions.

LAWS AFFECTING INVESTIGATION OF COMPUTER CRIMES

The investigation of computer crimes and subsequent gathering of evidence is affected by a number of constitutional and statutory requirements. The Fourth Amendment to the U.S. Constitution states that "no warrants shall issue, but upon probable cause, supported by oath of affirmation, and particularly describing the place to be searched, and the persons or things to be seized." Under the Fourth Amendment, government agents such as police (but not private parties) are required to obtain a warrant before seizing computer data when the owner has an "expectation of privacy."

Determining whether an expectation of privacy exists has been the source of much high-powered litigation. In general, a person would have an expectation that data stored on the hard drive of her home computer is private. However, that data might not be considered private if it is stored on a computer at work, or if it is stored at home in a directory made accessible to a peer-to-peer file-sharing program. It would certainly not be private if posted on a publicly accessible web site or chat room.

The specific content and procedural requirements for a search warrant are given in the appropriate federal or state code of criminal procedures. These, too, have had to be interpreted in the light of the complex and fluid nature of computer technology. For example, would a warrant that mentions "computer equipment" cover a cell phone that includes computerlike functions such as text messaging and an address directory?

Generally, when a warrant is executed it must either be served (handed to) the person in control of the premises being searched or, if that person is not present, must be left where it will be readily seen. There are two exceptions. In some cases where it is believed that evidence could be quickly destroyed (such as a computer rigged to erase data), a "no knock" warrant might be authorized, allowing police to break into the premises without any kind of announcement. The other exception, embodied in the USA PATRIOT Act passed following the terrorist attacks of September 11, 2001, can allow for "sneak and peak" warrants. In such cases the search is done surreptitiously without informing the persons involved.

While this controversial provision was designed for use in terrorism cases, it and some other USA PATRIOT Act provisions may also be applied in some conspiracy or organized crime cases.

There are some cases in which no warrant is necessary:

- The party involved consents to the search.
- The property is considered abandoned (such as in the garbage).
- The item is in plain view when a police officer has legitimately entered the area.
- The search is part of an arrest where it involves the contents of a wallet or purse or is necessary to assure the officer's safety.
- There is an "exigent circumstance" allowing officers to enter the area, such as their hearing a person's cry for help. This can also apply to cases where evidence is about to be destroyed, such as through equipment failure.

There are also privacy considerations that affect the issuing of warrants. Under the federal Privacy Protection Act, material held by journalists or publishers is generally not subject to a warrant because of the need to protect activities under the First Amendment. (The case *Steve Jackson Games, Inc. v. United States Secret Service* extended this principle to many nontraditional online publications, such as computer games.)

The Electronic Communications Privacy Act was designed to correct the fact that warrants were not required for police to tap into emerging forms of communication such as pagers, cell phones, e-mail, and other data being transmitted over the Internet. However, the requirements of this act and other wiretap acts were modified by provisions of the USA PATRIOT Act. For example:

- Some additional types of information can now be subpoenaed from Internet service providers (ISPs), such as customers' credit card information and the Internet addresses that had been assigned for their use at various times.
- ISPs can divulge customer information in emergency situations, including threat of terrorist attack, and can use these circumstances as a defense in civil suits.
- The traditional phone methods of pen register and trap and trace (hardware devices for tracing calls) can be used analogously to intercept routing information for e-mails, but not the content of the messages themselves.
- Search and pen register warrants can now be issued to apply nationwide.
- Under a 1999 intelligence act, authorities can use roving wiretaps that can apply to whatever communications devices a person of interest is

using, rather than being limited to a particular phone. Also phones that are "proximate" to the person of interest can be tapped even if they do not actually belong to that person.

ILLUSTRATIVE CASES

The following cases raise important issues involved with the prosecution of Internet predators and the application of criminal and civil law. It should be noted that some cases do not deal directly with the types of predators discussed in this book, but bear on questions such as jurisdiction and liability that may well apply to crimes such as Internet fraud or identity theft. More cases bearing directly on these crimes are likely to emerge as recent legislation is tested.

The following table indexes the cases by the major legal issues covered:

Child Molestation
 United States of America v. Anthony F. Murrell
Children, Online Protection of
 Ashcroft v. ACLU
 Ashcroft v. Free Speech Coalition
 Reno v. ACLU et al.
 United States v. American Library Association
 United States of America v. Chance Rearden
Cyberstalking
 Helen Remsburg v. DocuSearch
 United States of America v. Abraham Jacob Alkhabaz
Defamation
 Bochan v. La Fontaine
 Carafano v. Metrosplash.com, Inc.
 Cubby, Inc. v. CompuServe, Inc.
 Stratton Oakmont, Inc. v. Prodigy Services Company
First Amendment Protections
 Ashcroft v. ACLU
 Ashcroft v. Free Speech Coalition
 American Library Association v. Pataki
 Miller v. California
 Reno v. ACLU et al.
 Steve Jackson Games, Inc. v. United States Secret Service
 United States v. American Library Association
Information Brokers
 Helen Remsburg v. DocuSearch

Jurisdiction Issues

Obscenity and Pornography

Search and Seizure

Service Providers, Liability of

Spam

Spyware and Adware

Web Filtering

MILLER V. CALIFORNIA 413 U.S. 15 (1973)

Background

The appellant sent sexually explicit advertisements in a mass mailing, hoping to sell various books that, while purporting to be studies of the history of pornography and of various sexual behaviors, consisted mainly of sexually explicit photographs. He was arrested after some recipients complained about the unsolicited mailing. He was convicted of violating a California obscenity statute. His conviction was affirmed by the California appeals court; his appeal then reached the U.S. Supreme Court.

Legal Issues

The fundamental question was where the boundary lay between unlawful obscene materials and materials protected by the First Amendment guarantee of freedom of the press.

Decision

The Court essentially revised earlier standards for defining obscenity (such as the material being "utterly without redeeming social value") as being unworkable. They came up with the following three-part definition:

> *The basic guidelines for the trier of fact must be: (a) whether "the average person, applying contemporary community standards" would find that the work, taken as a whole, appeals to the prurient interest . . . (b) whether the work depicts or describes, in a patently offensive way, sexual conduct specifically defined by the applicable state law, and (c) whether the work, taken as a whole, lacks serious literary, artistic, political, or scientific value.*

The lower court decision was thus vacated so that the new obscenity test could be applied.

Impact

What became known as the *"Miller* test" sets a rather stringent standard for what materials will be judged obscene and thus not protected under the First Amendment. Child pornography has been held to be obscene under this standard, but the general trend has been to not attempt to prosecute cases of adult pornography. In the mid-1990s aspects of the Miller test would become problematic when applied to the Internet, a global network for which it is not easy to define "community standards" (see *Reno v. ACLU*).

CUBBY, INC. V. COMPUSERVE, INC., 776 F. SUPP. 135 (S.D.N.Y. 1991)

Background

The online service CompuServe runs hundreds of separate forums where users can discuss various topics. The journalism forum, which was edited and managed by a contractor (not by CompuServe itself), made available to users a daily online journal called Rumorville. Cubby, Inc., developer of Skuttlebut, a rival news service, brought suit in a New York federal district court against CompuServe, claiming that Rumorville had published false and defamatory statements about their firm.

Legal Issues

The core issue is when an online service is legally responsible for defamatory or other actionable material carried on its servers. In traditional libel law, a publisher who edits, selects, and is otherwise involved in the shaping of the content is liable for it. However, a distributor who merely makes the content available is not liable unless it actually knows (or has reason to know) that the material it is distributing is defamatory (per the 1959 U.S. Supreme Court ruling in *Smith v. California*). For example, a bookstore is not ordinarily responsible for libelous contents of the books it carries.

Decision

The court decided that CompuServe was not a publisher, since it did not exercise any editorial control over the contents of Rumorville. It simply provided space in its file library. CompuServe was thus only a distributor, did not have any way to know about the content being defamatory, and could not be sued.

Impact

It may be natural for victims of defamation or online harassment to seek the service provider as a "deep pockets" defendant. However, both courts and the Congress have shown a desire to protect online service providers from such legal action because if the services had to carefully check all material for legal problems, the free flow of information and the expression protected by the First Amendment would likely be choked off.

STEVE JACKSON GAMES, INC. V. UNITED STATES SECRET SERVICE, 816 F. SUPP. 432 (W.D. TEX. 1993)

Background

In 1990 the Secret Service launched a wide-ranging investigation of computer hackers, particularly a group that called itself the Legion of Doom. They believed the group had stolen a confidential document relating to BellSouth telephone company's emergency 911 phone system, which the company valued at almost $80,000. (In reality the value of the document was vastly overinflated, and it was actually available to the public for only a few dollars.)

Tracing postings on computer bulletin boards, Secret Service agents concluded that Lloyd Blankenship, operator of the Illuminati bulletin board, was involved in hacking activity. The agents seized the computer equipment used for the bulletin board. However, the Illuminati bulletin board was actually operated on behalf of Steve Jackson Games. The materials and discussion on the board were not about real-world hacking, but hacking as the theme of a role-playing game. Jackson tried to explain this and requested that the equipment, which contained vital business records, be returned. The Secret Service ignored his pleas. As a result, the Steve Jackson Games company faced considerable delays in developing new games as well as loss of business. Jackson then sued the Secret Service for damages caused by their equipment seizure.

Legal Issues

Steve Jackson argued that the Secret Service had violated the Privacy Protection Act of 1980, which states that it is "unlawful for a government officer employee to search for or seize any work product materials possessed by a person reasonably believed to have a purpose to disseminate to the public a newspaper, broadcast, or other similar form of public communication." Jackson argued that the game materials were a publication and thus immune from seizure. He also argued that the Secret Service had unlawfully intercepted, read, and destroyed private e-mail rather than allowing it to reach its intended recipients.

The Secret Service responded that the game materials were not a publication in the sense intended by Congress in the Privacy Act. The agents had acted in good faith and had reasonable cause to suspect that the Illuminati bulletin board had a copy of the stolen BellSouth document.

Decision

The Court found in favor of Jackson, noting that

> *The Court does fault Agent Foley and the Secret Service on the failure to make any investigation of Steve Jackson Games prior to March 1, 1990, and to contact Steve Jackson in an attempt to enlist his cooperation and obtain information from him as there was never any basis to suspect Steve Jackson or Steve Jackson Games, Inc. of any criminal activity.*

If they had investigated, the court said, they would have found they had no reason to seize any of the computer equipment, and Jackson's business would not have been seriously affected. (The court declined, however, to find that electronic mail had been intercepted and destroyed. An appeals court upheld that part of the decision.) Jackson was awarded $50,000 in damages plus $1,000 in statutory damages plus attorney's fees.

Impact

For privacy advocates and civil libertarians, the main impact of the case was to mobilize them to found such groups as the Electronic Frontier Foundation and to actively advocate on issues surrounding Internet-related legislation. For investigators of computer crimes, the lesson was that they needed to take a broad approach to possible First Amendment protections for computer systems used to create new forms of content such as Web pages and weblogs, or blogs. When seizing evidence, they should opt where possible for less disruptive procedures, such as promptly and carefully making a copy of the data on a system and then returning it to its owner.

STRATTON OAKMONT, INC. V. PRODIGY SERVICES COMPANY, 1995 WL 323710 (N.Y. SUPP. MAY 24, 1995)

Background

A user of the Prodigy online service made a forum posting stating that Daniel Porush, the president of the investment firm, was "soon to be proven criminal" and that the firm "was a cult of brokers who either lie for a living or get fired." Porush filed suit against Prodigy, claiming that the service was liable for spreading these defamatory statements.

Legal Issues

Prodigy claimed that it was only a distributor of its online forums, not a publisher. (As in *Cubby, Inc. v. CompuServe,* courts have ruled that distributors are not liable for defamatory material unless they know or have reason to know of its existence.) The plaintiff Stratton Oakmont, however, argued that Prodigy exercised editorial control over material on the service. That would make it a publisher, and publishers are liable for defamatory materials.

Decision

In this case the court sided with the plaintiff. The Prodigy service posted guidelines for users warning them not to post messages that are harassing or insulting or are "grossly repugnant to community standards." The company used Board Leaders who enforced these guidelines and also used software to screen for offending postings. All of this amounted to Prodigy being a publisher, and thus liable for the contents of the postings it carried.

Impact

This case illustrates a general Catch-22 in the legal system. If a service refrains from screening or editing, it will probably not be liable for the material it carries. But if a service actively tries to screen for and avoid defamatory material, it becomes a publisher and thus liable.

Recognizing this problem, Congress acted in 1996 by passing the Communications Decency Act (CDA), which states that "no provider or user of an interactive computer service shall be treated as the publisher or speaker of any information provided by another information content provider." Further, providers will not be liable if they make good faith efforts to screen out offensive material, either through human or technical means.

In *Zeran v. America Online* (1997) this provision of the CDA was cited to prevent the online service from being held liable for an online hoax in which a user's address and phone number were posted in connection with advertisements for souvenirs glorifying the 1995 Oklahoma City bombing.

In *Doe v. America Online, Inc.* (1997) this interpretation of the CDA was carried still further: The court ruled that the service provider could not be held liable under either civil or state law for postings using child pornography featuring the plaintiff's 11-year-old son. (The pornographer himself, of course, can be held responsible.)

MINNESOTA V. GRANITE STATE RESORTS, 568 N.W. 2D 715 (DEC. 11, 1996)

Background

The defendants advertised Wagernet, an early Internet gambling service based in Belize. Upon establishing an account, a customer could place sports bets online. The service agreement specified that if any dispute arose, the service could file suit at their option, either in the customer's home state or in Belize. On learning that several Minnesota residents had responded to the advertising by seeking further information, the state attorney general filed suit against the service, charging fraud, false advertising, and other violations of the state's consumer protection laws.

Legal Issues

The defendants argued that the state had no jurisdiction in this case because the service was not operated from Minnesota. The only contact Minnesota had with the service was that the Internet ads were accessible there. They also made the interesting argument that the web site did not transmit any gambling-related information to the Minnesota residents who contacted it. Rather, by clicking on links, customers were transmitting information to themselves!

Decision

The court did not buy this novel but technically unsound argument. It noted that the Minnesota Web surfers would not have seen anything on their screen if the defendant's Web server did not open an electronic link and send the text and pictures to them. The web site was the equivalent of an advertisement in a national magazine, which implicitly offers its products to Minnesota residents.

Impact

This is another pragmatic attempt to bring Internet transactions into the same legal framework as traditional business practices. It is well settled that if a business advertises in a state it is subject to that state's consumer protection laws.

UNITED STATES V. THOMAS, F. 3D 701 (6TH CIRC., 1996)

Background

The defendant operated a commercial pornography computer bulletin board called Amateur Action BBS. A computer user in Tennessee complained to U.S. postal inspectors about the bulletin board, and a postal inspector signed up with the board and was able to download images of bestiality, oral sex, incest, and sadomasochism. A Tennessee federal grand jury then indicted the defendant under federal laws prohibiting the use of communications devices and computer systems for transmitting obscene materials across state lines.

Legal Issues

In district court the defense argued first that the material transmitted or downloaded was "intangible," consisting only of a stream of bits. They also argued that the community standards of Tennessee regarding obscenity could not be applied to the defendant's California-based operation. To do so would impose the most conservative, restrictive standards on all users of the global Internet.

Decision

The district court rejected both arguments. The transmissions may be only "ones and zeroes," but they begin and end with an image that is as subject to obscenity laws as anything in print or on film. The court also ruled that the appropriate community standards to apply in obscenity are those in which the offense takes place—in this case, Tennessee, to which the images were transmitted.

While the court acknowledged concerns about local standards being imposed on the Internet as a whole, it also noted that subscribers to this commercial service had to give their location of residence. Thus the bulletin board operators could easily restrict or deny access to residents of states such as Tennessee where the images were illegal.

Impact

While the distinction between cases where technological localization is possible and those where it not may be workable, the question remains whether forcing Internet services to deal with 50 different state laws is too burdensome. In the case *American Library Association v. Pataki* the court ruled on the side of not overburdening communication and commerce on the net.

AMERICAN LIBRARY ASSOCIATION V. PATAKI, 969 F. SUPP. 160 (S.D.N.Y. 1997)

Background

As an expression of the growing concern in the mid-1990s about exposure of children to harmful material on the Internet, the state of New York enacted a law that made it illegal for residents to distribute material "harmful to minors" over the Internet. The American Library Association (ALA) and affiliated groups sued in federal district court to block enforcement of the law.

Legal Issues

The ALA raised two issues. First, it argued that the law denied New York residents the exercise of their First Amendment rights. After all, material that is indecent (and presumably harmful to minors) but not obscene has been ruled by the Supreme Court to be within the First Amendment rights of adults. Second, the ALA argued that New York's state law violated the Commerce Clause of the Constitution. By interfering with communication (and thus commerce) between the states, the law attempts to exercise a power that the Constitution gives only to Congress.

Decision

The court began by noting the conflicting attempts of various states to regulate speech, advertising, and commercial activity on the Internet. Examining the nature of the Internet, in which most communications pass through computers in multiple states, the court suggested that any user might thus be subjected to "haphazard, uncoordinated, and even outright inconsistent regulations by states that the actor never intended to reach and possibly was unaware were being accessed." Applying a standard judicial test, the court went on to say that the New York law overreached by having the effect of regulating commerce outside the state, in effect imposing the state's policies on outsiders. Even granting the legitimate objective of protecting children, the burdens the act imposes on interstate commerce exceed any benefit to the residents of New York. Finally, the regulations that the act would impose would subject outside Internet users to inconsistent and conflicting regulations.

The injunction to block the law was thus granted. Because the law was deemed to violate the interstate commerce clause, there was no need to consider the First Amendment issues.

Impact

This legislation is perhaps characteristic of early attempts to regulate a new medium. It is simply not practicable for states to issue such sweeping regulations on Internet content. And at the federal level, the attempt to ban indecent or harmful speech has also been overturned on First Amendment grounds. However, regulation of Internet business practices by (and affecting) residents of a state is generally not barred if not preempted by federal law (see *State of Washington v. Heckel*).

COMPUSERVE, INC. V. CYBER PROMOTIONS, INC., 962 F. SUPP. 1015 (S.D. OHIO 1997)

Background

CompuServe is a major online service that provides Internet and e-mail access to its members. Cyber Promotions specializes in sending bulk unsolicited advertising e-mail, commonly known as spam. CompuServe notified Cyber Promotions that the sending of such mail using its facilities was prohibited. When Cyber Promotions not only persisted but increased the volume of such mail, CompuServe sued in an Ohio federal district court for damages and an order to cease the mailings.

Legal Issues

CompuServe argued that the high volume of spam messages was driving customers away from its service as well as slowing down and threatening to overload the mail servers. CompuServe tried to use software to automatically block the mailings, but Cyber Promotions was able to evade the filtering mechanism by disguising the origin of its mailings. CompuServe said that these activities amounted to a "trespass against property"—that is, they interfered with use of CompuServe's computer systems.

The defendant, Cyber Promotions, responded that it had the right to send as much mail as it wanted over the Internet. It was not their fault that when the mail arrived at CompuServe it caused problems for the servers. That CompuServe offered full Internet connectivity implied that it was open to receive all e-mail. Finally, Cyber Promotions made a First Amendment argument that CompuServe's major presence on the Internet might obligate it to allow free expression, including the spam messages.

Decision

The court ruled that CompuServe had shown that CyberPromotions had interfered with its equipment and caused real damage to its operations and customer goodwill. The First Amendment argument was rejected because there were other ways that Cyber Promotions could have reached CompuServe subscribers. Cyber Promotions was ordered to pay attorney's fees and not to send e-mail to any CompuServe subscriber unless the subscriber had given them explicit permission.

Impact

The attempt to restrain the use of spam is important in fighting Internet fraud because e-mail is the most common way to reach and entice Internet users with scams and deceptive phishing messages. (The federal CAN-SPAM Act was passed in 2003.) However, most spam is not sent by high-profile companies that can be effectively pursued in court.

NEW YORK V. LIPSITZ, 663 N.Y.S. 2D 468 (NEW YORK SUPP. CT. JUNE 23, 1997)

Background

The respondent, Kenneth Lipsitz, resided in New York and operated a magazine subscription service that used spam e-mails to promote magazines. These advertisements typically included glowing but fake testimonials. The

New York attorney general received numerous complaints that paid-for subscriptions never arrived or were fulfilled late or only in part. Customers who complained were stalled or ignored. The state therefore sued Lipsitz for consumer fraud and false advertising, seeking that the defendant be ordered to cease his activities.

Legal Issues

Lipsitz argued that the court had no jurisdiction over him because his business was carried out over the Internet and involved numerous states, not just New York. It would be unfair to be able to sue an Internet business in any state where a complaint arose. The state countered that Lipsitz and his business were in New York, as were his alleged victims.

Decision

The court concluded that the case fulfilled all the tests for jurisdiction. The respondent was physically present in New York and his business was conducted through a New York–based Internet service provider. The magazine subscriptions were sold to the New York residents on whose behalf the attorney general was acting. It was also proper for the attorney general to consider complaints from other states in seeking to show that the respondent should be restrained. On the facts of the case, the court found for the state and ordered that the respondent pay restitution and other penalties and post a bond before being allowed to conduct business again.

Impact

This decision represents a pragmatic approach. It is easy to get caught up in "the rarified [sic] air of cyberspace" (to quote the judge), but when the perpetrator of a fraud and his or her victim are in the same state, the fact that the transaction was solicited via the Internet is of little importance.

RENO V. ACLU ET AL., 521 U.S. 844 (1997)

Background

Lurid stories about a flood of pornography on the Internet prompted demands for regulation. In 1996 Congress passed the Communications Decency Act (CDA), amending the Telecommunications Act. One of the CDA's provisions criminalized the use of computer services to make "indecent" or "patently offensive" materials available to minors. However, the law did not define these terms. The American Civil Liberties Union (ACLU) filed a lawsuit against U.S. Attorney General Janet Reno and won a temporary restraining act against enforcement of the CDA. As the case went to a hearing on the merits, the American Library Association joined the plaintiffs.

Legal Issues

During the lower court hearing, both sides agreed that the court needed to be educated about the way the Internet worked, its impact as an emerging global medium, and how First Amendment concerns were to be interpreted in this new medium. The ACLU contended that the terms *indecent* and *patently offensive* were unconstitutionally vague, and that enforcing the CDA would deprive adults of access to materials to which they were entitled under the First Amendment. This is because service providers would be unable to determine what material was potentially illegal under the CDA and would tend to err on the side of banning material that was even slightly risqué. In *Miller v. California*, the Supreme Court had ruled that obscene material was not protected by the First Amendment. But material that is merely "indecent" does not meet the stricter definition of obscenity.

The government argued that it had a compelling interest in "shielding minors from access to indecent materials." In general, children are often given more limited constitutional rights than are adults.

Decision

The lower court sided with the plaintiffs, ruling that the CDA was unconstitutionally vague. It cited a number of examples, such as an AIDS education web site, that used sexually explicit slang terms in order to reach people who were thought to be at high risk for the infection. Under the CDA, however, the site might be prosecuted for being indecent or patently offensive.

Further, the court noted that because the Internet is a global medium with worldwide connections, there was no technically feasible way to limit access to a given site to communities that found it acceptable (this is the "community standards" test for obscenity under *Miller v. California*).

In addition, while proponents of the CDA had argued that online services or sites could verify that visitors were adult through requiring a credit card for access, the court concluded that this would be impracticable for personal or noncommercial sites that are not equipped to process credit cards.

The lower court concluded, "Just as the strength of the Internet is chaos, so the strength of our liberty depends upon the chaos and cacophony of unfettered speech the First Amendment protects." The court declared the CDA to be "unconstitutional on its face."

On appeal, the U.S. Supreme Court concurred. While acknowledging the "governmental interest in protecting children from harmful materials," the Court said this did not justify "an unnecessarily broad suppression of speech addressed to adults."

Impact

Civil libertarians rejoiced in this ruling as protecting the robust freedom of speech that had been characteristic of the Internet. However, Congress, still under pressure to protect children from pornography, would continue its attempts at regulation.

UNITED STATES OF AMERICA V. ABRAHAM JACOB ALKHABAZ, NO. 95-1797 (6TH CIRCUIT, 1997)

Background

The defendant, known online and generally as Jake Baker, posted fictional stories to the newsgroup alt.sex.stories that featured the abduction, rape, torture, and murder of women and young girls. They culminated in a story that featured the torture, rape, and murder of a female classmate at the University of Michigan. Baker also shared similar fantasies via e-mail with a male classmate, Arthur Gonda.

Baker and Gonda were arrested and charged on a criminal complaint alleging violations of 18 U.S.C. § 875(c), which prohibits interstate communications containing threats to kidnap or injure another person. (Note that Baker was not charged based upon his public postings in the newsgroup.)

Legal Issues

Baker filed to quash the indictment in district court. The district court did dismiss the indictment against Baker, ruling that the e-mails exchanged between the two men did not constitute true threats and were thus protected by the guarantee of free speech in the First Amendment. The government appealed, arguing that the e-mails did amount to true threats.

Decision

Because the lower court did not consider whether the e-mails met the basic requirements of the cited federal law, the appeals court began with that question. The three elements that must be satisfied are (1) the communication involved a transmission in interstate or foreign commerce, (2) the communication contained a threat, and (3) the threat was one to seriously injure or kidnap another person.

Although the law in question did not go into much detail about the intent *(mens rea)* or object of illegal threats, the court concluded that:

> to constitute *"a communication containing a threat"* under Section 875(c), a communication must be such that a reasonable person (1) would take the statement as a serious expression of an intention to inflict bodily harm (the mens rea), and (2) would perceive such expression as being communicated to effect some change or achieve some goal through intimidation (the actus reus).

Applying this standard, the court concluded that the second requirement was lacking. The purpose of expressing the intention to inflict bodily harm was not to intimidate or otherwise affect the victim directly but, rather, that Baker and Gonda "apparently sent e-mail messages to each other in an attempt to foster a friendship based on shared sexual fantasies."

Impact

This case illustrates some important principles in analyzing possible cases of cyberstalking. Looking at the language used in e-mailed or posted statements is not sufficient. It is necessary to consider the likely intent of the statements and whether they are communicated to the victim. If so, it is not hard to infer at least an intent to inflict emotional distress.

BOCHAN V. LA FONTAINE, 68 F. SUPP. 2D 692 (E.D. VA. 1999)

Background

The plaintiff, Stephen N. Bochan, and the defendants, Ray and Mary La Fontaine, became embroiled in a dispute over the couple's book, a work claiming to shed new light on the assassination of John F. Kennedy. As part of a series of vehement Internet newsgroup postings, Bochan posted a part of the acknowledgments for the La Fontaines' books that mentioned their children. Ray La Fontaine's reply posting included the following: "I know you like kids, Bochan, but I suggest you limit your interest to trolling in alt.sex.fetish.tinygirls and leave my children out of it." La Fontaine went on to post information that, according to La Fontaine, included postings that Bochan had made in newsgroups related to child pornography, adult pornography, and cannibal snuff (murder) films.

Bochan, a Texas resident, sued the La Fontaines and another newsgroup poster named Harris, who had made similar comments. The suit was brought in a Virginia federal district court for defamation and intentional infliction of emotional distress, claiming that the defendants had publicly accused him of being a pedophile.

Legal Issues

The defendants claimed that the court had no jurisdiction over them. The La Fontaines said they had not been in Virginia since 1993, had sold no books in Virginia, and had not engaged in promotional tours or other business in the state. Harris, owner of a computer store, said he sold computers only in New Mexico, and had made his postings through Internet service providers in New Mexico or California.

The issue, therefore, is whether someone can be sued in state court for postings made on the Internet, when the defendant has no business or personal connection to that state.

Decision

The court began by looking at analogous cases involving communications posted on computer bulletin boards. With regard to the La Fontaines, the court concluded that because the postings to the newsgroups went through America Online, whose servers were located in Virginia, the messages must have at least temporarily been stored in that state. This amounted to legal publication of the allegedly defamatory material and allowed Bochan to file his suit in a Virginia court.

In Harris's case the court ruled that because he did not send his messages through servers in Virginia, they were not published there and he was thus not subject to being sued. However, despite the fact he had not sold any computers in Virginia, Harris had a web site that advertised his products, and the site was, of course, accessible to residents of Virginia. Further, the site provided contact information and did not state any geographic limitation on purchasers.

The court considered this degree of connection to be sufficient for Harris to have met the statutory standard for jurisdiction for the suit. Further, because "the statements made by all defendants posted on the Internet concerned the presumably local activities of an individual each knew was a Virginia citizen . . . and the reputational harm resulting from defendants' actions and allegations of pedophilia and sexual deviancy, if any, has been primarily suffered in Virginia, where Bochan lives and works" the court ruled that the constitutional standard for jurisdiction was also satisfied.

Impact

This case is part of a trend that has generally established that a person can sue for defamation in his or her own state because that is where the alleged damage was experienced. Because of the global reach of the Internet it can be argued that this is the most practical way to provide recourse for victims of online defamation. However, basing part of the determination on where a computer server is located makes little sense from the point of view of Internet structure. Nevertheless, this broad view of jurisdiction means that victims of cyberstalking or online harassment may be able to have a better chance at a civil remedy. Further, the idea that any online advertising effectively means that a company is doing business in every state has implications for suits on fraud and other matters.

OASIS CORP. V. JUDD, 132 F. SUPP. 2D 612 (S.D. OHIO 2001)

Background

Dan Judd went into his burning building to try to rescue some personal memorabilia and, in particular, his pet cat and her six kittens. Judd and the Chubb Insurance Group then got into a dispute over whether the insurer was responsible for the defective cord in the Oasis water cooler that had started the fire. The insurer insisted that Judd was responsible for the value of the destroyed business records because he could have retrieved them rather than rescuing the felines. Judd then created a web site that complained of what he considered his disgraceful treatment by Chubb, as well as accusing Oasis of not being willing to admit that it had allowed defective products to be distributed. The site urged a boycott of Oasis products and provided e-mail contact information for Oasis employees. The site also included an "automatic letter generating system" that enabled users to send prewritten letters to Oasis and to media outlets with a single click.

Even though the web site was not run from a computer in Ohio, Oasis sued Judd for defamation, invasion of privacy, and trademark violation.

Legal Issues

Before the suit could proceed, the question of whether the Ohio court had jurisdiction had to be resolved. Specifically, did the web site and the alleged defamatory statements on its pages have any connection with the state of Ohio?

Decision

The court ruled that it had no jurisdiction over Judd. The web site was personal, not commercial in nature, so there was no connection via interstate commerce. Further, the effects of the alleged defamation and infringement did not take place in Ohio.

Impact

This case suggests that where personal web sites (including blogs) are concerned, suits for defamatory or other injurious material need to be brought in the plaintiff's state of residence, not the one where the web site is hosted.

STATE OF WASHINGTON V. HECKEL, 143 WASH. 2D 824 (2001)

Background

Starting in 1998 the defendant Jason Heckel began marketing his booklet *How to Profit from the Internet* by sending somewhere between 100,000 and 1,000,000 unsolicited e-mails, or spams, per week. The state of Washington then sued Heckel in federal district court, alleging that he had violated state law by (1) using false or misleading information in the subject line of his messages; (2) by attempting to disguise the origin of his messages by routing them through a string of servers; and (3) by not providing a valid return e-mail address.

Legal Issues

Heckel argued that the Washington laws in question violated the commerce clause of the U.S. Constitution by "unduly burdening interstate commerce" and thus intruding on activities that can only be regulated by Congress.

Decision

The court disagreed with Heckel. It noted that the Washington law applied to anyone who transmitted the illegal e-mail messages from a computer located in Washington to an electronic mail address within the state. It did not therefore discriminate against Heckel, who happened to be an Oregon resident. The court noted the harm that spam inflicted on service providers and users. Contrary to Heckel's assertion (and the situation in *American Library Association v. Pataki*), no real inconsistency is created with other states that have enacted similar regulations. The benefits of the law outweigh any burdens on interstate commerce.

Impact

Unlike the case in *American Library Association v. Pataki*, this is a regulation that applies only to communications where both sender and receiver are within the state. This makes it akin to a normal business regulation that does not affect people communicating in other states.

ASHCROFT V. ACLU, No. 00-1293 (2002)

Background

In *Reno v. ACLU* (1997) the Supreme Court found the Communications Decency Act (CDA) of 1996 to be unconstitutionally broad in its treatment of "indecent" and "patently offensive" material made accessible online. Congress responded by crafting a new law, the Child Online Protection Act (COPA). Unlike the CDA, the COPA limited its coverage to commercial web sites and targeted material deemed "harmful to minors." This term is defined using the Supreme Court's test from *Miller v. California*, which specifies that the material taken as a whole appeals to prurient interest as determined by "contemporary community standards." The material must also be "patently offensive" and, taken as a whole, "lacks serious literary, artistic, political, or scientific value."

Legal Issues

As soon as the COPA became law, affected business interests and libertarians challenged it on three grounds: (1) it violated the First Amendment by effectively banning constitutionally protected speech; (2) it was not the "least restrictive" way to fulfill the government's compelling interest in protecting children; and (3) the law was "substantially overbroad."

The federal district court issued an order blocking enforcement of the law, believing that it would not withstand constitutional scrutiny. The Third Circuit Court of Appeals affirmed on appeal, but found a different reason why the law was defective—its reliance on "contemporary community standards" was not viable in the context of the global Internet.

Decision

By a 5-4 majority, the Supreme Court disagreed with the circuit court's ruling that the community standards test was overbroad. However, the Court left the order blocking the law's enforcement in place, returning the case to the circuit court for consideration of the other constitutional issues.

Impact

The Supreme Court majority returned the case to the lower court in part because it did not seem to be convinced that outright prohibition of certain content on the Internet was necessary when other means (such as Web filtering software) could protect children without denying adults access. If so, the law would not be using the least restrictive means as required by strict First Amendment scrutiny. Note that in *United States v. American Library Association* the Supreme Court later upheld a law requiring that federally funded libraries employ filtering or blocking software.

ASHCROFT V. FREE SPEECH COALITION, NO. 0075 (2002)

Background

In recent years pornographers have tried to get around laws against child pornography by using computer techniques such as digital photo editing or even morphing to create images that appear to show children but are actually based on pictures of adults. Congress addressed this issue in the Child Pornography Prevention Act (CPPA) of 1996. In addition to pornographic images showing actual children, the CPPA also bans

> *any visual depiction, including any photograph, film, video, picture, or computer or computer-generated image or picture that "is, or appears to be, of a minor engaging in sexually explicit conduct," §2256(8)(B), and any sexually explicit image that is "advertised, promoted, presented, described, or distributed in such a manner that conveys the impression" it depicts "a minor engaging in sexually explicit conduct".* . . .

The opponents of the law, an adult entertainment trade group and some civil liberties groups, sued to block its enforcement.

Legal Issues

The opponents claimed that the law should be blocked because it was overbroad and deprived adults of works protected by the First Amendment and "chilled" (dissuaded) would-be producers of such material. Besides arguing that the law was not overbroad, proponents argued that it was necessary because pedophiles could use virtual child pornography to help them seduce children, and that an exploitive industry would be allowed to continue because of the difficulty in distinguishing between real and fake child images.

The district court agreed with the government that the law was not over-broad, but when the opponents appealed to the Ninth Circuit Court of Appeals, that court did find that the CPPA was overbroad because it banned material that did not involve actual children and that was not obscene under the definition promulgated in *Miller v. California*. The government then appealed in turn to the U.S. Supreme Court.

Decision

The Supreme Court agreed with the circuit court that the CPPA was impermissibly broad. The majority noted, for example, that the CPPA did not require (as *Miller* did) that images appeal to the prurient interest, nor did it use a community standard to judge whether the images were patently offensive. They also noted that the depiction of teens engaging in sexual activity might be in a socially redeeming context, such as a documentary. And unlike the situation in *U.S. v. Ferber*, the argument that child pornography had to be banned because of its direct connection to the exploitation of children did not apply to these virtual images.

The Court also rejected other government arguments. While it may be true that some pedophiles might use virtual child pornography to seduce children, the fact that something could be used for evil purposes is not sufficient to completely ban it from First Amendment protection.

Impact

There are two ways to look at the result. On the one hand, allowing virtual child pornography might help pedophiles seduce children or at least give them a legal way to indulge their harmful fantasies. On the other hand, child pornographers might be less inclined to exploit children in making their images when a legal alternative is available. As a practical matter this decision may make it harder to prosecute child pornography distributors on the Internet because of the need to prove that images involve actual children.

WASHINGTON POST NEWSWEEK INTERACTIVE CO. LLC V. GATOR CORPORATION, CIVIL ACTION 02-900-A (U.S. 2D. E.D. VIRGINIA, 2002)

Background

Gator is typical of a kind of adware that often accompanies shareware or other programs that users download and is installed along with that software.

The software monitors the user's Web activity and causes ads on related topics to be displayed on the browser screen. The plaintiffs, owners of news web sites, sought an injunction to stop Gator's software from, among other things, introducing pop-up ads while users were viewing the news sites and to prevent them from altering the display of the news sites.

Legal Issues

The plaintiffs argued that Gator is "essentially a parasite on the Web that free rides [sic] on the hard work and investments of plaintiffs and other Web site owners. In short, Gator sells advertising space on the plaintiffs' Web sites without [their] authorization and pockets the profits from such sales."

Gator claimed that by displaying pop-up windows while other windows are on the screen, Gator is simply behaving the way all programs do in the multitasking Windows operating system. Recording information about the web sites the user is surfing is presumably a matter between Gator and the users who accepted the software and not a legitimate concern of the owners of those web sites.

Decision

The U.S. District Court for the Eastern District of Virginia issued the requested injunction and required that Gator post a bond to guarantee its compliance pending a jury trial. Meanwhile, Gator sued the Interactive Advertising Bureau in a San Francisco federal district court, asking that the court rule that its product's operation is not illegal, and ordering that the bureau stop saying that it is. This suit was settled before trial.

Impact

This is primarily a case of infringement on copyrights and revenue, but if courts find against the adware and spyware makers, it may discourage use of such programs and thus reduce a risk to users' privacy and personal information. (There have also been concerns that Gator's installation mechanism could also be used to surreptitiously install other types of intrusive programs.)

The spyware program WhenU is being prosecuted under a Utah antispyware law in the ongoing case *WhenU.com, Inc. v. State of Utah*. On June 24, 2004, a Utah judge issued an injunction temporarily blocking enforcement of the law. On September 28, 2004, the court refused to lift the injunction.

The Law and Internet Predators

Carafano v. Metrosplash.com, Inc.
339 F. 3d 1119 (2003)

Background

Matchmaker.com is a commercial Internet dating service. Users post descriptive profiles of themselves and can then view the profiles of other users. The profiles include answers to a detailed questionnaire as well as pictures, but no name or other identifying information. If one user becomes interested in another, he or she can contact that person indirectly via e-mail routed through the Matchmaker service.

A user of the Matchmaker service posted a profile purporting to be from Christianne Carafano, an actress and singer better known under the stage name Chase Masterson. (This was a free profile available to new users as a trial of the service.) The profile portrayed her as being interested in one-night stands and sex with a dominant man. In violation of the service's rules, the profile also included a contact e-mail address that automatically replied to messages by providing Carafano's home address and phone number.

Carafano soon began to receive sexually explicit phone calls, as well as a fax that threatened her and her son. When Carafano's web site manager was sent an e-mail mentioning the false profile, he, following her instructions, demanded that Matchmaker delete the profile immediately. Matchmaker did so in a few days.

Carafano then sued Matchmaker's owner, Metrosplash.com, in state court, alleging invasion of privacy, misappropriation of the right of publicity, defamation, and negligence. The defendants moved to have the case transferred to federal court. The federal district court issued a summary order dismissing Carafano's suit. That court said that Matchmaker was not immune from suit because it was not a mere carrier of communications, but a publisher that had supplied part of the offending profile. The district judge went on to apply the defamation standards for public figures to Carafano. Under those standards her address was considered to be newsworthy, and Carafano would have had to show that Matchmaker was not merely negligent, but had acted with "actual malice." This interpretation of defamation law was developed to allow the media to robustly cover news and persons of public interest. Carafano was unlikely to be able to meet that burden in this case.

Carafano appealed the defamation decision. America Online, eBay, and two coalitions of online services also appealed the decision on immunity, arguing that the district court should have recognized Matchmaker's immunity as an online service provider.

95

Legal Issues

The issue raised by the group of service providers is whether Carafano's claims are barred under U.S.C. § 230(c)(1), which states that "[n]o provider or user of an interactive computer service shall be treated as the publisher or speaker of any information provided by another information content provider."

Decision

The court explained that Congress had included this provision in the Communications Decency Act of 1996 in order to "promote the free exchange of information and ideas over the Internet and to encourage voluntary monitoring for offensive or obscene material." The court cited several other cases where "interactive computer services" such as America Online were held to be immune for defamatory e-mails, even when the services did exercise some selection and editing over the material. The court noted that judges had generally recognized that given the volume of material passing through such services, it would be impractical to screen all messages closely for possible legal problems, and that requiring them to do so might well have a chilling effect on the development of the Internet.

The court also said that the fact that the profile was constructed largely based on a person's answers to questions did not mean that the service created the profile and was thus responsible for its contents. (A similar conclusion was drawn in *Gentry v. eBay, Inc.* (2001), where the court ruled that eBay's characterization of feedback as positive, neutral, or negative and its use of stars and other symbols to rate users did not make that service responsible for false or misleading statements in the underlying feedback.)

The appeals court therefore affirmed the lower court's ruling that Matchmaker could not be sued for the contents of the defamatory profile. Therefore, the court did not have to review the question of whether the defamation claims themselves were barred because Carafano was a public figure.

Impact

Following the intent of Congress, courts have given online service providers a high degree of immunity from legal claims. This means that in cases of online stalking or harassment the civil remedy is likely to be available only against the actual perpetrator.

HELEN REMSBURG V. DOCUSEARCH, NO. 2002-55, NEW HAMPSHIRE SUPREME COURT (2003)

Background

On October 15, 1999, cyberstalker Liam Youens fatally shot Amy Boyer outside her workplace. Youens had learned Boyer's place of employment after obtaining her Social Security number and other personal information by hiring DocuSearch, an online information broker that had, in turn, obtained access to Boyer's credit records by pretending to be doing a legitimate credit check.

Legal Issues

Boyer's estate sued DocuSearch, arguing that the agency was liable for subjecting Boyer to "an unreasonable risk of harm" in providing information about her to Youens. Among other issues, there was the question of whether DocuSearch committed an "intrusion against seclusion" against Boyer and whether she had a reasonable expectation of privacy that was violated by the firm's actions.

Decision

The court ruled that an information broker does have a legal duty toward someone whose information is being obtained without his or her consent. A Social Security number is something that persons have an expectation will be private, and an information broker is liable for damages that might be caused by revealing it without permission.

Impact

Information brokers are largely unregulated. Some provide information that may be useful to cyberstalkers and identity thieves. Holding the brokers legally liable for releasing certain personal information may at least deter legitimate information brokers and allow for recovery of damages against illegitimate ones.

UNITED STATES V. AMERICAN LIBRARY ASSOCIATION
NO. 02361 (2003)

Background

Concerned about reports that children were often using computers in public libraries to access pornography, Congress passed the Children's Internet Protection Act (CIPA). This law required that libraries that received federal library technology and E-rate funding must install Web-blocking software. Such programs are designed to prevent users from viewing web sites, images, or other material deemed to be offensive, such as for sexual content.

The American Library Association and other groups concerned with free speech and access to information sued to block enforcement of the law.

Legal Issues

Opponents of the law argued that forcing libraries to use filtering software amounted to a content-based restriction that is incompatible with the First

Amendment. Although Congress has a compelling interest in preventing children from being exposed to harmful material such as adult or child pornography, this cannot be done at the expense of core First Amendment rights. The district court agreed with this analysis and enjoined the government from enforcing the law. The government appealed to the U.S. Supreme Court.

The Supreme Court's opinion began by noting that Congress "has wide latitude to attach conditions to the receipt of federal assistance to further its policy objectives." However, Congress cannot use the threat of withholding funding to induce a state or local authority to violate the U.S. Constitution. The question here, then, was whether CIPA did so.

Decision

The Supreme Court ruled that libraries did not have a constitutional obligation to carry all Internet sites. Just as libraries can select which books to put on their shelves (and exclude pornographic materials, perhaps), they are also free to select which web sites may be accessed on their computers. The government is simply helping libraries fulfill their traditional role in deciding what to offer. Justice Kennedy noted that libraries could disable the filtering software if an adult requested it. Therefore, there is little burden compared to the government's compelling interest in protecting children from harmful material. Justice Steven Breyer wrote a concurring opinion, but he took a somewhat different approach, suggesting that the use of the filtering software was the "best fit" to the need to both safeguard adults' rights and protect children.

Three justices dissented, with justices David Souter and Ruth Bader Ginsburg joining in one of the dissents. They questioned the lack of guidelines for unblocking Internet access at adults' request, noting that the district court had found that some libraries believed such requests might take days to fill and that many library personnel would not know how to control the software. Further, the statute says only that libraries "may" unblock access, and "only for bona fide research or other lawful purposes." Further, the blocking software would, because of its indiscriminate operation, inevitably deprive adults of hundreds of thousands of web sites that they might otherwise be able to access. The dissenting justices also questioned the majority's comparing Web filtering with the traditional process by which libraries select what they consider to be suitable materials. While the latter is driven mainly by limits on available money, space, and other resources, there is no money to be saved by blocking web sites. (Indeed, the software itself represents an expense.) Also, the dissent noted that library acquisition represents thoughtful decision making on the part of trained librarians, while the software takes a necessarily mechanical approach.

Impact

Courts have generally rejected outright censorship as a way to keep harmful materials from children. However, courts give a wider latitude to Congress using the power of the purse to get its way. The debate over the shortcomings of Web filtering software remains vigorous. Some libraries have gone so far as to reject the federal funding rather than install blocking software, which they view as an abdication of their duty to provide unfettered access to materials.

UNITED STATES OF AMERICA V. CHANCE REARDEN NO. 02-50311 (9TH CIRC. 2003)

Background

The defendant, Chance Rearden, was convicted of delivering child pornography over the Internet in violation of the Child Pornography Prevention Act of 1996. However, in *Ashcroft v. Free Speech Coalition* (2002), the U.S. Supreme Court declared unconstitutional the law's provision banning virtual images that did not involve actual children. As a result, a conviction would require a sufficient showing that the defendant had used images of actual children.

Legal Issues

Rearden's appeal raised the issue of whether a sufficient showing of the use of actual children had been made at trial.

Decision

The Court noted that an expert witness, an employee of a visual effects studio, had testified that in his opinion the images transmitted by Rearden had not been manipulated in any manner. They had neither been composited (combined or superimposed) or morphed (digitally transformed by creating intermediate images). Rearden's attorney had argued that this nevertheless did not prove that real children were involved, but the Court found this argument to be unpersuasive. Rearden's conviction was therefore upheld.

Impact

In his argument Rearden had also cited congressional concern about the growing sophistication of digital graphics techniques and that it may soon be very difficult or even impossible to distinguish between real and artificial images. Although this court did not find that to be relevant to the current situation, it may mean that eventually some form of independent evidence will be needed to prove that actual children were involved in the creation of child pornography.

UNITED STATES OF AMERICA V. ANTHONY F. MURRELL, NO. 03-12582 (11TH CIRC., MAY 4, 2004)

Background

The defendant, Anthony Murrell, arranged what he thought was to be a sexual encounter with a minor, but the person he was actually talking to in the America Online chat room was an undercover detective. Murrell was convicted of attempting to have sex with a minor.

Legal Issues

On appeal, the defendant argued that being convicted under 18 U.S.C. section 2422(b) required that he spoke directly to a minor or at least someone he believed to be a minor. However, he actually communicated only with the detective who was purporting to be the minor's mother. The question is whether, nevertheless, the intent to persuade or entice a minor to have sex was sufficient for conviction and an enhanced sentence.

Decision

The law in question states that:

> *Whoever, using the mail or any facility or means of interstate or foreign commerce, . . . knowingly persuades, induces, entices, or coerces any individual who has not attained the age of 18 years, to engage in prostitution or any sexual activity for which any person can be charged with a criminal offense, or attempts to do so, shall be fined [and imprisoned].*

The defendant, Murrell, was convicted of attempt, since there never was an actual minor involved. In another case, *United States v. Root*, the same court had earlier upheld a conviction where the defendant communicated directly with a person he believed to be a minor, but was actually an undercover detective. In Murrell's case he argued that the circumstances were different because he communicated only with a person he believed to be an adult who might serve as facilitator or intermediary for the desired encounter with the minor.

The court, however, said that this distinction is irrelevant. A conviction for attempt requires only a "specific intent" to engage in the criminal activity and that the defendant took a "substantial step" toward commission of the offense. In this case Murrell's expressing his desires online and his arranging and going to a meeting with the purported mother of the minor are quite sufficient for the conviction on attempt. The court therefore affirmed Murrell's conviction and sentence.

Impact

The use of undercover detectives online is one of the most effective ways to combat Internet sexual predators. This decision upholds the practice by focusing on the alleged perpetrator's intent and actions, not on whether someone could be actually victimized. Of course, detectives must still be careful to avoid crossing the line between allowing perpetrators to further their criminal intent and engaging in entrapment.

CHAPTER 3

CHRONOLOGY

This chapter presents a chronology of important events relating to Internet predators as well as relevant developments in general computer crime. Note that while the network that became the Internet was not implemented until the 1970s and was not widely available to the public until the 1990s, related forms of computer crime appeared in earlier contexts such as electronic banking systems, online bulletin boards, and newsgroups.

1960s

- Banking becomes increasingly dependent on electronic systems and the use of credit cards grows, giving new opportunities for information crime and fraud.
- The first self-identified hackers appear at the Massachusetts Institute of Technology. Their focus is on obsessive exploration of computer systems and software, not on criminal activity.

1970

- The Credit Card Liability Act is enacted. It limits cardholder's liability for charges on lost or stolen credit cards to $50. However, the law does not address the other costs and impacts of the crime that will become known as identity theft.
- Another tool that will help consumers in the future is provided by the Fair Credit Reporting Act, which requires credit reporting agencies to provide certain reports and notifications to consumers.

1971

- A practice called phone phreaking is publicized in *Esquire* magazine. Its first practitioner, John Draper ("Captain Crunch"), discovered that a toy whistle could produce long-distance dialing codes. Phone phreakers become adept at manipulating communications and users through social engineering.

Chronology

1974

- The Fair Credit Billing Act allows consumers to dispute credit charges and suspend their payment until an investigation is completed.

1975

- John Postel, an early architect of the e-mail system, warns that a technical malfunction or user misbehavior could lead to large floods of unwanted e-mail.

1976

- Congress passes tax reform legislation that authorizes state agencies to use Social Security numbers for identification purposes. As this practice is taken up by private companies for identifying financial accounts, the numbers will become prime targets for identity thieves.

1977

- The Fair Debt Collection Practices Act becomes law. It prevents harassment, threats, or other high-pressure tactics by collection agencies and perhaps will make life a little easier for victims of identity theft.

1978

- Recognizing the growing importance of computerized financial systems, Congress passes the Electronic Fund Transfer Act. It requires that customers receive receipts for such transactions, and tightens security, such as through the use of PINs (personal identification numbers).
- The first electronic bulletin board services (BBSs) are developed, using early microcomputers. Some hackers begin to use them to exchange stolen credit card information.

1984

- The magazine *2600* gives voice to the growing hacker community. It discusses system vulnerabilities but also provides a place to debate security and the appropriateness of various hacking techniques.

1986

- Congress passes the first law that directly addresses computer crime. The Computer Fraud and Abuse Act makes it a felony to access a "federal interest" computer without authorization, as well as to maliciously damage systems or data.

1988

- Robert Morris, a graduate student in computer science at Cornell University, launches an Internet worm program. Because of a programming error, it spreads far faster than expected and causes downtime and resource costs to Internet servers. Morris is eventually arrested, tried, convicted, and sentenced to a $10,000 fine and community service. The incident reveals both the growing importance of the Internet and its vulnerability.

1989

- Actress Rebecca Schaeffer is murdered by Robert Bardo. It is the first known case of a homicide by a stalker, although the Internet was not involved.

1990

- Responding to the murder of Rebecca Schaeffer, California becomes the first state to pass a law against stalking. By the end of the decade most states will have followed suit.
- Following the reported theft of confidential AT&T documents from servers, the Secret Service launches the first major federal crackdown on hackers, Operation Sundevil. Although the charges are misdirected and overblown, public awareness and concern about the hacker threat grows.

1991

- Phil Zimmermann releases Pretty Good Privacy (PGP), a program that allows ordinary computer users to send encrypted messages and files and better protect their private information.
- The Department of Justice establishes its Computer Crime Unit.

1993

- Fugitive hacker Kevin Poulsen hacks his way into the phone systems for radio contests, winning two Porsches, $20,000, and various other prizes.
- *March 5:* For the first time, federal agents execute search warrants involving suspected child pornography stored in digital form on personal computers. The raids, called Operation Longarm, result from the discovery of a Denmark-based pornography ring that had an international clientele. Thirty-five suspects in 22 U.S. states are arrested and subsequently convicted.
- *May:* FBI agents and Prince George's County, Maryland, police detectives discover that two suspects have allegedly been using computers to

transmit pornographic pictures to minors and, in some cases, have lured them into sexual activity.

1994

- Canter and Siegel, an immigration-law firm, floods Internet newsgroups with advertisements for their services. This is widely considered to be the birth of spam and raises questions about abuse of online services.
- An e-mail hoax about a nonexistent e-mail virus called Good Times spreads rapidly, showing how easy it is to trick thousands of computer users.
- First Virtual Bank is established. It is the first Internet-only financial institution.

1995

- The U.S. Secret Service and the Drug Enforcement Agency (DEA) obtain the first Internet wiretap to gather evidence on illegal cloning of cell phone service.
- The first macro virus spreads by taking advantage of the scripting capability of Microsoft Word. Many similar viruses soon target vulnerable applications programs.
- Responding to earlier discoveries of pedophile activity on the Internet, the FBI develops the Innocent Images National Initiative. Its purpose is to bring together evidence of Internet-based child pornography and molestation to discern patterns and to track down perpetrators.
- Curtis Sliwa, founder of the volunteer anticrime group Guardian Angels, establishes an online version called CyberAngels. By 2004 about 9,000 members in 74 nations will help track down online harassers and pedophiles.
- Fugitive hacker Kevin Mitnick is finally tracked down by federal agents in Raleigh, South Carolina. He is charged with stealing 20,000 credit card numbers, although there is no proof he actually used them. The delay of his trial for several years (while he remains in prison) outrages many hackers and civil libertarians. After accepting a plea bargain, Mitnick will be released in 2000 after serving almost five years in prison.
- *March:* Russian hacker Vladimir Levin is charged with heading a hacker gang that broke into Citibank computers, stole customer account information, then diverted at least several million dollars in electronic funds transfers. After several years of extradition battles, Levin will finally plead guilty to reduced charges and serve a three-year sentence.
- *July:* A *Time* magazine cover study on cyberporn unleashes a national debate on what to do about the spread of pornography in the online world.

Critics argue that studies showing massive amounts of online smut are poorly designed and suggest the problem is exaggerated. However, there will soon be a congressional response in the form of new laws seeking to control adult and child pornography and to protect children online.

1996

- Congress passes the Communications Decency Act in an attempt to crack down on online distribution of child pornography. It is immediately challenged by the American Civil Liberties Union and other groups that believe it infringes on the free speech rights of adults.
- Hacker attacks against service providers increase. The Public Access Networks Corporation in New York is a major victim.
- The Department of Justice promotes its Computer Crime Unit to a full-fledged division called the Computer Crime and Intellectual Property Section (CCIPS).
- The Netherlands, Norway, Belgium, and the United Kingdom all establish hotlines for reporting child pornography found on the Internet.

1997

- Cybertips, the first child pornography reporting hotline in the United States, is established.
- U.S. Customs agents assist the New York state attorney general in setting up a sting to catch suspects involved in sharing child pornography online and, sometimes, in actual child molestation. By October, 31 defendants have been convicted.
- *February:* The Federal Trade Commission (FTC) wins a court order to shut down a web site that purports to be a porn site. Visitors belatedly discovered that the free site's downloaded software surreptitiously directed their computer's modem to a phone number in Moldova, in the former Soviet Union. Some 38,000 people incur thousands of dollars in long-distance charges.
- *March:* The FTC has its first of a series of surf days, in which it finds web sites that make dubious claims and then warns them that they may be in violation of the law. The first surf day deals with fraudulent business opportunities.
- *June 26:* The U.S. Supreme Court strikes down the Communications Decency Act, ruling that the Internet deserves full First Amendment protection.

1998

- *April:* In response to months of cyberstalking by the Woodside Literary Agency, writer Jayne Hitchcock testifies before the Maryland legislature.

This leads to the state passing a law making e-mail harassment a misdemeanor. California and New Hampshire soon pass similar laws.

- *September:* In a sting called Operation Smartcard.net, U.S. Customs agents set up a web site purporting to offer "smartcards" providing access to the DirectTV satellite service. About 3,500 cards are ordered by dealers and individuals, and 11 dealers are arrested the following year. Five defendants are convicted, but they receive relatively short sentences.

1999

- Gary Dellapenta is sentenced to six years in prison for cyberstalking a North Hollywood, California, woman. He had posted ads under her name inviting men to break into her house to enact a supposed home-invasion rape fantasy.
- Eight nations in the European Union form InHope, a cooperative initiative to fight child pornography on the Internet.
- *February 17:* The New York state attorney general wins a default judgment against Woodside Literary Agency for false advertising, deceptive business practices, fraud, and harassment (including e-mail and other online venues).
- *March:* A Georgetown law school student along with his mother and two fellow students use an Internet site called Fast-Trades.com to pump up the values of four inexpensive microcap stocks by recommending that online investors buy shares. According to the SEC indictment, the group made about $345,000 on the scheme.
- *April:* A stock manipulator creates a link to a phony Bloomberg stock news page in order to fool investors into thinking that PairGain Technologies, Inc., a California company, was to be bought for $1 billion by an Israeli firm. He hoped to be able to unload his PairGain stock at pumped-up prices, but he is traced by investigators despite his attempt to conceal his true Internet address.
- *July:* Charles Gary Rogers pleads guilty to transmitting obscene material. He had posted offers for sex purportedly from his neighbor's nine-year-old daughter. The girl's family endured more than two years of calls from men seeking sex. Rogers had made his postings in response to the girl's having scrawled "Hello" on his driveway in chalk.
- *August:* An Australian student is convicted of sending an e-mail death threat to tennis player Chanda Rubin. He receives a fine of $250 (Australian) and is required to perform 100 hours of community service.
- *September:* In Operation Landslide, federal officials raid a Fort Worth, Texas–based, Internet child pornography operation. One hundred and twenty of the heaviest users of the site are arrested. Names of European users are forwarded to Interpol, and more than 1,200 of them

are arrested. Among them is rock star Pete Townshend, who claims he had been researching the site for a book. Townshend is not charged.

- **October:** Amy Boyer, a 20-year-old college student, is murdered in a parking lot. Investigation reveals that she had been stalked online for several years by Liam Youens, a fellow student. Youens had used the Internet to obtain Boyer's personal information and had recounted his obsession with her in an online diary. It is the first known cyberstalking murder.

- **December:** A hacker breaks into the computer of CD Universe, an online music store, and obtains 300,000 customer credit card numbers. He threatens to reveal the numbers unless he is paid $100,000. Rebuffed, he posts 25,000 numbers on a web site that is then shut down by the FBI.

2000

- **March:** The United Nations Educational, Scientific, and Cultural Organization (UNESCO) and other organizations host the Kids International Summit in New York. As a result. the Wired Kids web site is launched in an effort to educate children and their parents about safe Internet use.

- **April:** The California legislature proclaims Child Internet Safety Week. The resolution had been promoted by a group called The Children's Internet, which plans a variety of educational events and programs.

- **May:** The Justice Department announces the formation of the Internet Fraud Complaint Center. The new agency will collect reports and work with victims of a variety of Internet-based scams and frauds.

- **May 15:** The Group of Eight nations in Europe meet to discuss a new cybercrime treaty that would require uniform laws and penalties for hacking, computer fraud, and online child pornography. There would also be greater coordination of the activities of police agencies.

- **June:** Sonya Furlow pleads guilty to three counts of mail fraud. She had defrauded at least 44 couples by promising to arrange adoptions for them involving fictitious birth mothers. She is believed to have pocketed at least $200,000. She will receive a sentence of nearly four years in prison.

- **August 23:** Three men are arrested by British police for using fraudulent electronic applications to get loans and credit cards from Egg PLC, an online bank. The bank had used tracking software to trace their activities.

- **September:** The Securities and Exchange Commission (SEC) settles its civil case against Jonathan Lebed. Starting at age 13, Lebed had used false claims on Internet message boards to pump up the values of cheap stocks. He is forced to repay $285,000 but may be able to keep $500,000 of his gains.

- **October:** The U.S. Customs Service steps up its efforts to fight computer crime, establishing the Cybersmuggling Center. It will focus on detecting and transmission of child pornography into the United States from foreign Internet sites.

- *December:* Mark Jakob pleads guilty to having issued a phony press release to drive down the value of Emulex stock that he had sold short. The release claimed that the company was under SEC investigation, its chief executive officer (CEO) was about to resign, and that the balance sheet would show a loss rather than a profit.

2001

- *February 21:* An online Nigerian money scam letter leads to the murder of the Nigerian consul in Prague. The accused shooter, a Czech pensioner who had fallen for the scheme, had wanted restitution from Nigeria.
- *August:* A federal undercover operation leads to the arrest of 100 Internet users who, for a monthly fee, had been accessing sites with names such as Cyber Lolita and Child Rape.
- *September:* Authorities in the United States and Costa Rica make arrests and begin to unravel an online Ponzi investment scheme called Tri-West. Since 1999 the scheme had netted about $58 million by promising high returns but paying off only the first few investors.
- *December:* A plan is announced to coordinate hotlines in European countries where users can report child pornography on the Internet. The tips would be combined with those gathered by efforts in the United States.
- *December:* The SEC files stock manipulation charges against Spectrum Brands, a New York firm that is accused of using e-mail messages to tout an ineffective device for killing anthrax and other microbes in the wake of the anthrax attacks.

2002

- The Federal Trade Commission announces that it is developing software that would scan for online messages that are often characteristic of scams. However, critics view the program as a threat to privacy.
- *January:* Some 150,000 Web surfers respond to an enticing site touting the stock of McWhortle Enterprises, supposedly a manufacturer of biohazard detectors. In reality the site is a fake created by the SEC and other government agencies. After clicking, users are treated to a warning about investment scams.
- *February:* Ford Credit Corporation discovers that unauthorized credit reports are being obtained. A months-long investigation gradually unravels an identity theft ring that has obtained credit backgrounds of more

than 30,000 people and used them to make fraudulent bank withdrawals and get loans.

- *February 21:* Pennsylvania governor Mark Schweiker signs the first state law that requires Internet service providers to shut down web sites that contain child pornography.
- *March 18:* Coordinated raids on suspected child pornography users result in 231 homes and places of business being searched and 86 arrests. The federal sting, called Operation Candyman, had used a fake porn site to lure the suspects. Twenty-seven suspects eventually confess to molesting children. Suspects include clergy members and a teacher's aide.
- *April 16:* The U.S. Supreme Court overturns the ban on virtual child pornography in the Child Pornography Prevention Act of 1996. By a 6-3 majority, the Court rules that the law is too broad and infringes on adults' First Amendment rights to free speech and artistic expression.
- *April 19:* The European Union issues a framework calling for a minimum sentence of one year in prison for computer intrusions or attacks that cause significant damage or expenses to businesses. Individual countries can provide for additional penalties.
- *May:* Two suspects are charged with the Dynamic Duo hacking incidents in which dozens of government web sites were defaced, allegedly to point out their lax security.
- *May 24:* A U.S. district court in Pennsylvania orders that web site mousetrapper John Zuccarini cease operations and pay a fine of more than $1.8 million. Zuccarini had created thousands of web sites designed to catch mistyped requests for popular sites. The unfortunate users were bombarded with pop-up ads (earning revenue for Zuccarini) and often prevented from closing or leaving the mousetrap site.
- *August 9:* U.S. Customs officials announce arrests of an alleged international pornography ring involving 10 Americans and 10 Europeans. They claim 45 children had been victimized by the group, which exchanged photos of the children over the Internet.
- *October:* Dwayne McGrath of Baton Rouge, Louisiana, is arrested for cyberstalking and making threats against the members and host of an Internet chat room.
- *October 29:* John E. Robinson, Sr., is convicted of the murder of three women whom he had lured to his home via Internet chat rooms where he used the screen name Slavemaster. He receives two life sentences and one death sentence. He will later plead guilty to five additional murders.
- *November:* Diana Napolis is arrested for making online criminal threats against actress Jennifer Love Hewitt. (Earlier, movie director Steven Spielberg had obtained a restraining order against Napolis, alleging she

was stalking him.) In March of next year her case will be suspended when she is found mentally incompetent to stand trial.

- *December:* South Carolina opens the first statewide center devoted exclusively to the forensic investigation of computer and other high tech crimes.
- *December:* President Bush signs a bill that adds a kids domain to the Internet. It can be used only for sites and services deemed to be safe for children.

2003

- eBay reaches $24 billion in sales, and auction fraud continues to account for about half of all online fraud according to the Internet Fraud Complaint Center.
- *January 21:* Kevin Mitnick finally completes probation, allowing him to log onto the Internet for the first time in eight years. He will remake his career as a security consultant and author who warns computer users about hacker tricks and deceptions.
- *February 18:* The New Hampshire Supreme Court rules that information brokers and private investigators can be held liable for the "foreseeable harms" involved in selling someone's personal information.
- *March 6:* The federal appeals court for the Third Circuit overturns some provisions of the Child Online Protection Act. The court notes that the community standards criterion for obscenity cannot be applied to the Internet, a medium that is not restricted by geography.
- *March 7:* A federal judge in New York City rules that entering an e-mail address into a Web form does not give probable cause of obtaining a search warrant for child pornography because there is no proof that pornography was actually received by the suspects. The ruling may threaten convictions in some online sting operations.
- *June:* The U.S. Justice Department announces a series of arrests in which 135 people are being held for online crimes, including investment scams, fake online banks, and dating services. Some $17 million in funds are also seized.
- *June 23:* The U.S. Supreme Court rules that a federal statute requiring that libraries that receive certain federal funds install Web filtering software to protect children from harmful material is constitutional. Civil libertarians complain that the software also blocks material that adults are entitled to access.
- *July 23:* The Federal Trade Commission announces its first successful court action for phishing. The perpetrator, a 17-year-old boy, sent e-mails

claiming to be from the America Online billing center. He agrees to pay back $3,500 he had stolen and also agrees to never again send spam.

- **August 26:** Amazon.com announces that it is suing 11 online marketers for sending e-mails that use false sender addresses purporting to originate from Amazon.com.
- **October:** Another federal effort, coordinated by 34 U.S. attorneys offices, the FBI, the FTC, the Secret Service, and other agencies, called Operation Cyber Sweep, results in 125 indictments for identity theft, computer intrusion, and other offenses with more than 125,000 victims altogether and a total loss of more than $100 million.

2004

- **March:** The first state law banning spyware programs goes into effect in Utah. However, one of the affected online companies succeeds in getting a district court to issue an injunction blocking its enforcement.
- **March 23:** In what is believed to be a legal first, an employee at an insurance company is charged under federal wiretapping statutes with installing a hardware device to capture keyboard information that is being entered by fellow workers.
- **April:** EarthLink becomes the first Internet service provider to offer blocking not only for spam but for phishing e-mails as well. The free software will also detect attempts to install spyware.
- **May 14:** Federal officials announce 65 arrests as the result of more than 1,000 investigations into the use of Internet file-sharing software for distributing child pornography.
- **May 27:** Howard Carmack of Buffalo, New York, is sentenced to a term of $3 \frac{1}{2}$ to 7 years in prison for sending 825 million spam messages using 300 forged e-mail accounts. He is also subject to a $16.5 million civil judgment on behalf of Internet service provider EarthLink.
- **June:** The FTC decides not to create a do-not-spam list similar to the do-not-call list for telephone solicitors. Critics argue that such a list would simply provide spammers with a source of guaranteed genuine e-mail addresses.
- **June:** The SPY Act (Securely Protect Yourself Against Cyber Trespass) clears the House Energy and Commerce Committee. It would require user notification before installation of spyware and would impose hefty civil penalties for violations.
- **July 15:** President George W. Bush signs the Identity Theft Penalty Enhancement Act into law. The legislation adds two years to prison sentences for offenders who used stolen credit cards or other personal information.

- *August 4:* A federal grand jury in Los Angeles indicts five Americans and a Romanian on charges of fraudulently ordering more than $10 million in computer equipment. About half the orders were stopped before they were shipped.
- *September:* The congressional session ends without the Senate acting on any of the pending antispyware legislation.
- *October:* A survey by America Online and the National Cyber Security Alliance finds that 77 percent of respondents reported that they felt safe from online threats such as viruses and hacker intrusions. However, inspection of their computers found that about two-thirds used outdated antivirus software files, two-thirds lacked protective firewalls, and about 80 percent unknowingly harbored spyware.

2005

- *January:* Consumers Union and other groups warn about fraudulent charitable solicitations in the wake of the December tsunami disaster in Asia.
- *January:* Microsoft begins to offer Windows users free software for detecting and removing spyware and other harmful programs.
- *January 11:* The Federal Trade Commission announces that it has won court orders to block six companies from sending pornography-related spam. The e-mails had violated the provisions of the new CAN-SPAM law because they were not clearly marked or identified.
- *February:* The Federal Trade Commission releases its 2004 annual report on fraud and identity theft complaints. The data shows a continuing rise in incidents, as well as a continuing shift from traditional mail and phone fraud to Internet-based fraud, particularly fraudulent e-mail.
- *February:* ChoicePoint, the largest U.S. data broker, reveals that it had sold personal information on about 145,000 consumers to identity thieves who had posed as a legitimate business. The company offers to help potential victims, but state and federal legislators are demanding tough new regulations on selling such information.
- *March 24:* The Federal Reserve Board tells banks that they should notify customers "as soon as possible" if their financial information has been stolen or improperly accessed.

CHAPTER 4

BIOGRAPHICAL LISTING

This chapter provides brief biographical sketches of some of the more significant figures in recent Internet predator cases. They include hackers and other predators, victims, and advocates—some figures represent a combination of these roles.

Abraham Jacob Alkhabaz, poster of violent stories that posed legal questions about the nature of threats. Also known as Jake Baker, Alkhabaz wrote detailed stories about the rape and murder of women and posted them to Internet discussion groups. He also shared his stories via e-mail with a friend. One story used the name of one of his fellow students as the victim. Although Alkhabaz had not had any personal contact with the student and claimed her name was only used because it rhymed with other words in the stories, Baker was charged under federal law with making interstate threats to injure another person. The court ruled, however, that the stories did not amount to an actual threat against the student and were thus protected by the First Amendment. (Possible defamation and invasion of privacy issues would have had to have been raised in a civil trial.)

Cynthia Armistead, cyberstalking victim. Beginning in 1996 Armistead became involved in an online argument with a man named Richard Hillyard. After receiving a series of messages that she believed were threatening, Armistead complained to Hillyard's Internet service provider. However, according to Armistead the situation escalated when solicitations for prostitution were posted in her name by someone using the name Dick Coward, leading to her receiving sexually explicit messages. Badgered as well by obscene, harassing phone calls, Armistead and her family moved three times in a single year. Armistead tried to get the police involved, but they resisted until she received an e-mail message whose sender said he had actually followed her. Hillyard was arrested and tried on charges of making harassing phone calls and stalking; however, he was acquitted on the first charge and the second was later dismissed. In turn

Hillyard has maintained a web site in which he disputes Armistead's charges and insists that she is actually stalking him. This early cyberstalking case illustrates the difficulty in prosecuting and determining responsibility in many such cases.

Franz Konstantin Baehring, convicted and unusually manipulative online pedophile. Using the online name Kon, Baehring wooed 15-year-old Lindsay Shamrock during 2000 by e-mail, letters, and eventually phone calls. Shamrock's mother tried to break off the contact by taking the computer keyboard with her when she left for work. She also contacted the FBI, but was told they could not really help her. Later in the year Shamrock disappeared from her home near Tampa, Florida. Detective Sergeant Gary Klinger of the local police missing persons unit analyzed the e-mail and discovered that Kon was actually Baehring, a German citizen, who insisted to Shamrock's mother that he, too, was concerned about her whereabouts. Eventually, however, Baehring was discovered to be with Shamrock in Thessaloniki, Greece. Investigation of coconspirators suggested that Baehring was part of a child pornography ring. Baehring was convicted in Greece, receiving a sentence of eight years that was likely to be reduced to three years before parole. Baehring reportedly continued to harass Shamrock's family from jail.

Gary Dellapenta, first cyberstalker convicted under California law. Dellapenta, a 50-year-old security guard, impersonated a woman in an online chat room, describing "her" fantasies of being raped and providing her phone number and address. The messages asked for men willing to participate in "her" fantasies. When the woman being impersonated posted messages saying that the earlier postings were a hoax, Dellapenta continued to impersonate her, posting messages saying that her denial was part of the fantasy. The woman was never physically attacked but suffered great stress from the contacts she received for more than a year. Dellapenta was arrested and charged under a new California law with stalking, using a computer to commit fraud, deceive, or extort, and solicitation to commit rape. He was sentenced to six years in prison.

Sonya Furlow, operator of an extensive online adoption scam. Under the name Tender Hearts Adoption Services, Furlow used a well-designed web site and e-mail to lead couples to believe that she could arrange for them to legally adopt a child. Typically, she would repeatedly ask for money to help the supposed birth mother with various difficulties, only to eventually tell the couples that the mother had changed her mind about the adoption. (In reality, there was never a birth mother.) Furlow was convicted of defrauding 43 couples of a total of $200,000.

Vasily Gorshkov and Alexi Ivanov, hackers who demonstrated the ability to steal credit card information on a large scale. The two natives of

Chelyabinsk, Russia, moved to the state of Washington and worked with hackers in Russia to steal at least 1 million credit card numbers while launching numerous attacks on business networks, including PayPal and the Central National Bank in Waco, Texas. One common tactic was to break into a business's computer, steal sensitive customer information, and then demand payment from the business in exchange for not revealing it. Although they had gone back to Russia, in November 2001 Gorshkov and Ivanov were lured back to Seattle by a supposed job interview, arrested by the FBI, and charged with more than 20 counts of computer-related theft, extortion, and fraud. Gorshkov received a sentence of three years and was ordered to pay $700,000 restitution. Ivanov, who pleaded guilty, awaits sentencing. The hackers became something like folk heroes among many young Russians, who believed that the FBI had used unfair entrapment tactics. At any rate, their case revealed both the international scope of hacking and computer attacks and the vulnerability of businesses to online extortion.

Johan Helsingus, developer of a controversial anonymous remailing service. The service, called anon.penet.fi, allowed users to strip the original address headers from e-mail and send it anonymously. A number of human rights and civil liberties organizations have said that such a service is necessary for allowing people under oppressive conditions to safely publicize human rights abuses. However, Helsingus ran up against the court system in Finland when the Church of Scientology complained that an unknown person was using the remailing service to post secret publications belonging to the church. A judge ordered Helsingus to release the actual e-mail address of the person. Instead, Helsingus shut down the service in August 1996. Helsingus was also accused by a British tabloid newspaper of having allowed his service to be used to transmit child pornography; however Finnish police found no evidence of this, and Helsingus had actually blocked the sending of e-mail attachments through his service in early 1995. Helsingus became an advocate for Internet privacy rights and urged that better ways be found to protect them.

Jayne Hitchcock, online harassment victim who became a writer and advocate for cybercrime issues. Hitchcock's involvement with cyberstalking began in January 1996 when she responded to a spam ad posted by the Woodside Literary Agency in the Usenet newsgroup misc.writing. Hitchcock phoned the agency and sent it a book proposal. The agency responded with enthusiasm, but asked for a $75 reading fee, generally not a practice of legitimate agencies. Hitchcock then began to correspond with other members of the newsgroup, sharing stories of alleged sleazy practices by the agency, and testing them by sending them especially atrocious writing, which was always received with praise and a request for the

$75 fee. Hitchcock then began to be harassed online in several ways. Her e-mail account was "mail bombed" with thousands of messages in an attempt to shut it down. Worse, someone posted messages in her name in sex-related discussion groups, in which "she" requested partners to help her satisfy her sexual fantasies. Hitchcock also discovered that she had been subscribed to magazines and CD clubs. Hitchcock began to organize a group to fight online harassment. In turn, Ursula Sprachman (co-owner of Woodside) filed charges claiming that Hitchcock's HELP Fund (established to pay legal expenses) was fraudulent. The accusation was dismissed as being without merit. As suit and countersuit dragged on, Sprachman and co-owner James Leonard were charged by U.S. postal inspectors with conspiracy to commit mail fraud and perjury. Leonard received eight months in prison plus three years probation; Sprachman, who was in poor health, received only probation. The New York attorney general also sued Woodside and won a settlement requiring that clients be reimbursed. The Woodside case was widely publicized and illustrates many typical forms of online harassment. Hitchcock went on to write the book *Net Crimes & Misdemeanors* and to found the organization Working to Halt Online Abuse (WHOA).

Jonathan Lebed, teenage Internet stock scammer. Starting at age 14, Lebed began to frequent investment-related online message boards. He bought some inexpensive stock and began to promote it heavily, posting messages saying the stocks were greatly undervalued and offering bogus reasons why they should soon go up in price, such as high expected revenues or secret merger negotiations. After investors who believed the hype pushed up the stock price, Lebed sold the shares and pocketed the profit. (This technique is called pump and dump.) After being sued by the Securities and Exchange Commission, Lebed agreed to repay $285,000—but according to some sources he had actually made closer to $800,000. The case showed that age was no barrier to cybercriminals and that markets were surprisingly vulnerable to online manipulation.

Vladimir Levin, dubbed the first Internet bank robber. Levin, a mathematics graduate student at the Technological University in St. Petersburg, Russia, broke into the Cash Manager system in Citibank. He was able to change electronic funds transfers so the money would be diverted into accounts he had set up around the world. Levin and his coconspirators are believed to have stolen at least $3.7 million in this way. When bank customers began to report losses, one of Levin's accounts aroused the suspicions of London's Scotland Yard. Levin was arrested in London and fought extradition to the United States for 30 months, but he was finally charged in New York. He struck a plea bargain for three years in prison and $240,015 restitution to Citibank. The case shook confidence in the banking community and made banks rush to improve security for their computer systems.

Kevin Mitnick, notorious hacker who became a cause célèbre and then a security expert. Mitnick began his criminal career as a phone phreak, using codes to manipulate phone services and to make free long-distance calls. In 1983 he moved on to computer hacking, breaking into an unclassified Pentagon computer system. (By this time the earlier image of hackers as clever if obsessive programmers had begun to be replaced by that of hackers as destructive criminals who broke into computer systems.) Still a juvenile, Mitnick received a six-month sentence in what was essentially a reform school. Undeterred, he continued to break into computers. His 1989 computer fraud conviction landed him in federal prison for a year. Mitnick went legit for a short time, but soon resumed hacking. In 1992 he became a fugitive. In 1994 he launched an attack against Tsutomu Shimomura, a well-known computer security expert. By mid-1995 investigators had traced Mitnick's activities, including the online stashes where Mitnick had left stolen information. They drew an electronic noose around Mitnick, monitoring his online activities, including his stealing of computer program source codes from Apple Computer and a trove of 20,000 credit card numbers (which he apparently never actually tried to use). Shimomura and other investigators then used special tracking equipment to find the fugitive Mitnick in his Raleigh, North Carolina, apartment. Mitnick was arrested and faced numerous state and federal charges involving illegal computer access and fraud. Mitnick had a considerable number of defenders among the more politically oriented hackers and libertarians, who protested his being held in detention while his trial was delayed for nearly three years and noted that he had not profited financially from his hacking. "Free Kevin Mitnick" signs appeared on many sites and at hacker meetings and rallies. Mitnick eventually accepted a plea bargain with a sentence of 68 months for all charges; he was released in January 21, 2000, after serving about five years of his sentence. Mitnick began to speak and write about computer security: His 2002 book *The Art of Deception* provides a sobering portrait of how hackers routinely trick people into revealing information and providing access to sensitive computer systems.

Diana Napolis, bizarre cyberstalker. Using the name Curio, Napolis stalked a number of people online. She believed that children were being subjected to satanic ritual abuse and that there was a conspiracy to cover up or discredit these cases. One of Napolis's targets was Carol Hopkins, a former school administrator and member of a San Diego County grand jury that had criticized social workers for removing children from their homes based upon false ritual abuse allegations. Napolis posted messages alleging that Hopkins was herself a child molester and had tried to protect other molesters. Hopkins eventually went into hiding to escape the harassment. Napolis also targeted Elizabeth Loftus, a well-known psychologist who had criticized the idea that child abuse victims had repressed memories that could be recovered. Loftus argued that such memories were unreliable and easily manipulated to provide false evidence against accused abusers. Eventually, however, computer expert Michelle Devereaux (who once believed that she was also a victim of ritual abuse) tracked down Napolis's computer activities. Napolis was arrested in 2000 at a computer lab at San Diego State University. No charges were filed at the time, but in 2002 she was charged with stalking and making death threats against actress Jennifer Love Hewitt, having accused her and director Steven Spielberg of being part of a satanic conspiracy. In March 2003 Napolis was committed to a state mental hospital for three years or until she was ruled fit to stand trial.

Jay Nelson, convicted Internet auction fraudster. Thirty-four-year-old Nelson of Gilsum, New Hampshire, conducted hundreds of auctions on eBay and Yahoo! in which he received payment from winning bidders but failed to deliver the merchandise. He also created fake user names and used them to post positive feedback on his auctions, giving users the impression that most customers were satisfied with their transactions. Nelson created numerous PayPal and bank accounts and shuffled money back and forth to try to disguise its origin. Nelson was eventually tracked down and arrested by postal inspectors. In July 2002 U.S. attorney Tom Colantuano announced a plea bargain in which Nelson pleaded guilty to charges of mail fraud, wire fraud, money laundering, and identity fraud. He was sentenced to six and a half years in prison for defrauding approximately 1,700 victims.

Kevin Poulsen, hacker and fraudster. Like Mitnick, the other infamous Kevin of the hacker world, Poulsen began as a phone phreak, but in 1981 he obtained an early personal computer and began to participate in underground hacker online bulletin boards. He was soon breaking into a variety of university and government computers, including those of the Lawrence Livermore Lab, the White Sands Proving Grounds, and the nuclear lab at Los Alamos. (He did not, however, steal any classified information.) A talented programmer, Poulsen was unable to hold onto his job with defense contractor SRI because of his all-consuming passion for hacking. Like Mitnick, Poulsen became a fugitive. Together with two friends, Poulsen was able to use his ability to manipulate telephone switches to ensure that he won radio call-in contests, scoring $22,000 in cash, trips to Hawaii, and two $50,000 Porsches. Poulsen also began to interfere with law enforcement efforts, breaking into the National Crime

Information Center and even alerting the subjects of federal wiretaps. Poulsen was arrested on June 21, 1991, and charged with a long list of felonies ranging from espionage and computer fraud to obstruction of justice. In a plea bargain, the espionage count was dropped, and Poulsen agreed to a 51-month prison term and agreed to stay away from computers after his release. Today the apparently reformed Poulsen writes and lectures on computer security.

John Edward Robinson, cyberspace's first serial killer, known online as the Slavemaster. A native of Cicero, Illinois, Robinson began life as an exemplary student and Eagle Scout. Married and with good job prospects, Robinson inexplicably turned to crime, first embezzling $33,000 while working as a lab technician for a doctor. He was put on probation and got another job with a television rental company, but was fired for stealing merchandise. He continued his career of embezzlement and swindling, usually getting only probation and otherwise slipping through the cracks of the system. By the late 1970s Robinson had apparently reformed, winning plaudits as a community activist for his work with the handicapped. However, he soon returned to crime, this time moving in a more sinister direction. He is suspected to have murdered an employee, Paula Godfrey, who had broken contact with her family and mysteriously disappeared. Robinson pretended to be part of a firm providing outreach and resources to unwed mothers and lured his second murder victim, 19-year-old Lisa Stasi. Robinson also created a prostitution ring specializing in sado-masochism. He also continued his criminal activities while awaiting sentencing on a fraud charge. In prison Robinson again fooled officials into thinking he was a good candidate for rehabilitation. After release he wooed two more women, Beverly Bonner and Sheila Faith, who both disappeared. Robinson then turned to the Internet in his search for victims, running fraud schemes and finding Izabel Lewicka, a Purdue University freshman who agreed to become his slave and was murdered. Robinson's last known murder victim is Suzette Trouten, a Detroit nurse. Authorities finally caught up with Robinson. In 2002 he faced three murder charges in Kansas and three more in Missouri. In 2003 Robinson was tried in Kansas for the murders of Trouten, Lewicka, and Stasi and received two death sentences and one life term. He then pleaded guilty to five more murders in Missouri.

Rebecca Schaeffer, actress whose murder inspired antistalking legislation. Schaeffer was stalked and murdered in 1989 by Robert Bardo. Even in the days before the World Wide Web, Bardo had been able to obtain a great deal of information about Schaeffer, including getting her home address from motor vehicle department records. He killed Schaeffer after entering her home under the pretext of delivering flowers. Bardo was arrested and prosecuted by Marcia Clark, who later became famous for the O. J. Simpson murder case. Schaefer's case led to a great deal of publicity about the danger of stalking, particularly for celebrities, and led both to anti-stalking laws and laws restricting access to personal information. Bardo was sentenced to life in prison without possibility of parole.

Scott W. Tyree, kidnapper who used the Internet to find his victim. When 13-year-old Alicia Kozakiewicz disappeared, investigators combed through her computer and discovered she had been carrying on an online relationship with someone named Scott. When the story broke in the media, an undisclosed informant told the FBI that someone named Scott had told him in online correspondence that he was going to Pittsburgh to pick up a girl and bring her to his home. Shortly thereafter, Scott had sent a webcam picture showing a girl who was identified as Kozakiewicz. The FBI then used Internet Service Provider records to identify Scott as Scott Tyree. Agents raided his house and recovered the girl, who was in re-straints but uninjured. Tyree was arrested on charges of abduction and transporting a minor across state lines for sexual purposes. He was sen-tenced to nearly 20 years in prison.

Liam Youens, first cyberstalker-murderer. Youens became obsessed with Amy Boyer, a 20-year-old dental hygiene student. Besides physically fol-lowing her, Youens used the Internet to find Boyer's Social Security num-ber and work address. He also posted a Web diary in which he chronicled his growing obsession, details of the stalking, and eventually, his plans to murder Boyer. Despite the web site being online for at least two years, no one reported it to the police. Boyer eventually carried out his plan, shoot-ing Boyer as she drove home from work. The murder publicized the growing problem of cyberstalking and the ease with which stalkers could obtain information via the Internet.

John Zuccarini, Internet mousetrapper. A resident of Andalusia, Pennsyl-vania, Zuccarini took advantage of the structure of the Internet to create fraudulent web sites. The sites used addresses that were almost the same as those of popular web sites for celebrities, such as pop singer Britney Spears and tennis star Anna Kournikova. Web surfers who accidentally navigated to the sites found that their browser was trapped and they were unable to get away from the site. Meanwhile the screen filled with pop-up ads, for which Zuccarini earned as much as $1 million a year in rev-enue. Zuccarini was sued by many owners of the legitimate sites that had been spoofed. Finally the Federal Trade Commission sued and won a court order forbidding Zuccarini from diverting Web users or subjecting them to unwanted advertising.

CHAPTER 5

GLOSSARY

The following legal, technical, and other terms are important for understanding the operation of Internet predators and the investigative and legal measures used to pursue them.

acceptable use policy   Rules that specify how a computer system or service is to be used. Most Internet service providers, businesses, workplaces, and universities have such policies.

anonymity   The ability to communicate or engage in transactions without being identified. This can provide privacy protection but also allows criminals to operate more freely and makes them harder to catch.

anonymous remailer   A service through which one can route e-mail in such a way that one's originating address is removed. Use of remailers can protect privacy but can also make it harder to track down authors of harassing e-mail.

attachment   An image or other file that accompanies an e-mail message. Attachments can be used to spread computer viruses.

authentication   The process of verifying the identity and access rights of a person to an online system.

back door   A way for intruders to surreptitiously access a computer system by taking advantage of a security vulnerability. Viruses and Trojan programs can install back doors.

blacklist   In antispam and Web filtering programs, a list of senders or addresses whose e-mails or sites are to be blocked and not displayed to the user.

blog (weblog)   An online journal, usually updated regularly.

broadband   Always-on, high-volume Internet connections, such as those provided via DSL phone lines or cable.

bulletin board system (BBS)   Text-based online message systems popular before the advent of the World Wide Web in the early 1990s.

business opportunity scheme   A common type of Internet fraud in which e-mails offer recipients the chance to make large profits for minimal effort, perhaps working at home. An up-front fee is demanded, and what is provided is usually worthless or at least greatly overpriced.

cache A temporary storage area on a computer containing frequently accessed files, such as Web pages. Information in a Web cache can be targeted by hackers.

censorware A general, somewhat pejorative term for software that controls Web access on the basis of content. Censorware is typically used to prevent children from browsing web sites that feature sexually explicit material or language. See also **filtering.**

certificate A digital code deposited with a third-party service that authenticates a web site, the author of software, or some other entity.

chat Interactive, real-time online messaging available from many providers such as America Online and Yahoo!

chat room An online area set up for chat, sometimes on a particular subject.

child pornography Pornography that features children in sexual or suggestive poses or activities. It is illegal to create, distribute, or possess child pornography, although there is some dispute about virtual child pornography that does not show actual children.

civil law Law involving the settling of suits that seek damages or court orders, in which no criminal penalties are involved.

cookies Small files used to identify an Internet user in order to customize the display or accumulate information about browsing.

cracker A person who breaks into computer systems for destructive or other criminal purposes. Sometimes distinguished from a classic hacker, who emphasizes the gaining of knowledge about systems.

cybercrime Crime carried out through (or through the aid of) computers, the Internet, and online services.

cybercriminal Perpetrator of crime involving computers.

cyberspace The online world as experienced by users. The term was first used in science fiction writing in the early 1980s.

cyberstalking Obsessive pursuit and harassment of a person using online information and services.

digital signature A way to use cryptography to verify the identity of an online correspondent, such as in a credit card transaction. Organizations such as VeriSign provide this service.

domain A subset of the Internet, identified by suffixes such as .com or .gov.

domain name system (DNS) The service that translates Internet names—for instance, www.well.com—into numeric addresses, such as 206.14.209.10.

e-commerce Electronic commerce; the sale of goods or services online, usually through web sites.

electronic funds transfer (EFT)   The processing of banking or credit transactions through online systems, such as transferring money from one account to another.

e-mail client   A program (such as Microsoft Outlook or Eudora) that allows users to send and receive e-mail through a mail server.

encryption   The transformation of data (such as e-mail) into a form that cannot be read without reversing the process using the appropriate key.

escrow   A service that provides an intermediary between buyer and seller (particularly in online auctions). Payment is made to the escrow service, which holds the money until delivery of the product is confirmed.

feedback   A system used in some online auctions and other marketplaces where participants in a transaction can post ratings of one another's performance. Reviewing a prospective seller's feedback is a useful (but not foolproof) way to determine if the seller is legitimate.

filtering   Automatic inspection of e-mail or web sites in order to block material that is considered objectionable or dangerous, such as fraudulent offers, viruses, or pornographic or violent content.

financial institution fraud   Fraud using misrepresentation to gain access to money or credit. It includes fraudulent applications for credit or debit cards under a false identity and fraudulent access to a checking or savings account.

finger   A program that can be used to reveal the name and login time of a user of an online service.

firewall   A program and/or hardware device that inspects Internet packets and can block and alert users to possible attacks involving viruses, worms, and Trojan programs. More sophisticated firewalls also examine outgoing packets that might contain sensitive information.

flame   A hostile online post (such as in a chat room or newsgroup) that uses vehement or insulting language to attack other persons. Repeated flaming can be a form of harassment.

419   Another name for the Nigerian money letter scam. The number refers to the relevant section of the Nigerian penal code.

hacker   Originally, a highly skilled (if rather obsessed) programmer who sought to understand every nuance of computer systems or software in order to get them to do new and interesting things. Later the term shifted in the public mind to mean people who break into computers to damage them or to steal information.

harassment   Repeated annoying or tormenting of a person. Online harassment typically takes the form of unwanted e-mails, instant messages, or news postings.

headers   Lines of text showing the sender, routing, and other information about an e-mail message.

history   The record of sites visited that is kept by a Web browser. It can be used by investigators (or concerned parents) to discover past online activity.

hoax   An untrue but persuasive story spread through e-mail or other means. Hoaxes can range from relatively benign urban legends to false claims that the recipient has been infected by a computer virus.

identity theft   The criminal use of another person's identity, usually obtained by stealing or otherwise obtaining key information such as a Social Security or credit card number. The most common use is to conduct fraudulent credit card or banking transactions, but stolen identities have also been used to conceal other criminal activity.

indecency   Material that appeals to prurient (sexual) interest but does not meet the legal definition of obscenity. Adults are legally allowed to possess indecent material.

information broker   A business that provides information about persons for a fee. Some brokers provide only information that can be legitimately obtained from public sources. Others, however, sell private personal information such as credit reports.

instant messaging (IM)   Real-time interactive text conversation between two individuals using software with services such as America Online, Yahoo!, or ICQ, among others. It is distinguished from chat in that the latter usually features multiple participants.

Internet   The worldwide network formed by computers connecting using the TCP/IP protocol. Services carried over the network include e-mail, newsgroups, and the World Wide Web.

Internet bank   A bank that does business only on the Internet.

Internet service provider (ISP)   A company or other organization that provides access to the Internet, usually for a fee. Investigation of online crime often involves obtaining information from ISPs about account holders and communications.

IP address   The numeric Internet protocol address that uniquely identifies a connection to a particular Internet location—for example, 106.14.209.10.

jurisdiction   The determination of which court should hear a given case. Also, a particular legal entity such as a county or state.

keylogger   A program that records a user's keystrokes and stores them for later retrieval. A keylogger can be surreptitiously installed by hackers or spyware programs, and the log can then be examined for access codes, credit card numbers, and so on.

local area network (LAN)   A network connecting computers in an office, school, home, or other site. Once an intruder gains access to one machine on the network, it is often easy to access the others. Most LANs now use Internet protocols, so they are also called intranets.

mail bombing   The sending of large quantities of duplicate e-mail messages to an address in order to shut down or disrupt the mail server.

mail server   The program that stores, forwards, or provides access to e-mail messages. The storage of e-mail makes it vulnerable to hackers and potentially available to investigators.

malware   A general term for harmful or annoying software, including viruses, worms, and spyware.

monitoring software   Programs that allow someone (such as a parent or employer) to monitor users' activities on the Internet, such as the web sites they visit, the materials they download, or even the keystrokes typed.

multilevel marketing (MLM)   A scheme in which participants receive a product they can sell to new participants, with the original seller receiving a commission on subsequent sales by the new participants. The legality of MLM depends on certain details such as the viability of the product and the commission structure.

newsgroup   A topical area in the Usenet service in which users can post or reply to messages. Some newsgroups are prone to flames (vehement attacks) or even harassment and threats.

Nigerian money letter scam   Originally sent by paper mail but now often a form of spam e-mail, these letters typically purport to be from a Nigerian official who needs help in transferring a large sum in illicit funds out of the country. In exchange for providing the use of his or her bank account, the victim is promised a portion of the money. The scammers demand upfront payments or use the account information to drain the victim's funds. Variants of this scam have purported to be from other countries as well.

obscenity   According to the Supreme Court, material is obscene if the average person, applying contemporary community standards and viewing the material as a whole, would find (1) that the work appeals predominantly to prurient interest; (2) that it depicts or describes sexual conduct in a patently offensive way; and (3) that it lacks serious literary, artistic, political, or scientific value. Obscene material can be subject to legal sanctions, but the courts have ruled that adults have the right to possess material that is merely indecent. See also **indecency.**

online banking   The ability to access bank accounts via web sites.

online scams   A variety of dubious or fraudulent products or services offered via e-mail or web sites.

packet   A unit of data sent over the Internet. It includes headers and a sequential number so it can be sent to the destination using one of many possible routes and then assembled with other packets to form a complete e-mail message, graphic, or other file.

parental controls   Options offered by Internet service providers to block access to sites considered to be unsuitable for children.

pedophile   A person whose only or primary object of sexual interest is children.

pedophilia   Sexual attraction to children.

phishing   The use of deceptive e-mail to trick victims into providing credit card numbers or other sensitive information. For example, a fraudster can send e-mail claiming to be from eBay or PayPal and say that its account-holder information needs to be verified. See also **spoofing.**

post   To send a message to an online forum such as a newsgroup. Also, such a message.

pretexting   The practice of obtaining information about an individual under false pretenses. For example, a private investigator may claim to represent a government or law enforcement agency. See also **social engineering.**

Pretty Good Privacy (PGP)   A public-domain encryption tool that can be used to render e-mail messages or other files unreadable except by the sender and recipient.

profile   A description of an online user's background and interests, as supplied by the user to a service. Also, a description of the likely personal characteristics of the perpetrator of a crime under investigation.

pump and dump   An investment scam in which chat rooms, newsgroups, or web sites are used to promote an inexpensive stock. When the demand pushes up the price, the scammers then sell, or dump, the stock and make a profit.

pyramid scheme   An investment scam in which high returns are offered and are sometimes paid to early investors, using funds obtained from later investors. However it soon becomes impossible to find enough new investors to keep up the payments, and the scheme collapses. Also called a Ponzi scheme after Charles Ponzi, who invented it in the 1920s.

screen name   A name chosen by users of some online services. It may or may not be related to the user's real name.

securities fraud   Fraud involving stocks or other investment vehicles.

server   A computer (or program running on a computer) that provides a particular service; for example, Web servers display Web pages, and e-mail servers handle mail messages. Because of their importance and their need to contain important information, servers are frequent targets of hackers.

Secure Socket Layer (SSL, Secure Server)   This is software used to encrypt information (such as credit card details) for an online transaction. It is often indicated by https: at the beginning of the Web page address or by a small padlock icon at the bottom of the browser window.

sexual predator   A person who commits sexually violent or abusive acts such as rape or child molestation.

shill bidding   A form of auction fraud in which a seller, using alternate accounts or accomplices, drives up the price by bidding on his or her own item.

social engineering   Hacker term for techniques used to manipulate people into revealing sensitive information (such as passwords). See also **pretexting** and **spoofing.**

spam   Unsolicited e-mail, usually sent in large batches and featuring advertisements or offers of a dubious nature.

spoofing   Assuming a false identity online, including forging addresses to make e-mail look like it is coming from a different person, and creating a web site that looks similar to that of a legitimate business. See also **phishing.**

spyware   Software, usually included in another program, that surreptitiously retrieves information from the user's computer and transfers it to a remote location.

terms of service (TOS)   The rules imposed by an Internet service provider or a service (such as Yahoo! or eBay) on its users.

Trojan   Named for the Trojan horse of Greek myth, a disguised program that looks useful or at least harmless but can be used to gain control of the system and perhaps steal information.

uniform resource locator (URL)   The complete address specifying how to reach a site on the Internet—for example, http://www.MySite.com/index.html. Note that the prefix http: does not need to be used with most browsers.

unsolicited commercial e-mail (UCE)   a more formal term for what is commonly known as spam.

user name   The unique identifier for a user of an online service. Typically a user accesses the service by supplying the user name and a previously chosen password.

virtual child pornography   Images that purport to be of children engaged in sexual poses or activity. However, the images are supposedly digitally altered from adult models or from innocent pictures of children.

virus   A program that can modify other programs or files by copying instructions into them. When the target program or operating system is run, the virus code is executed instead of or in addition to the original code. The effects of this execution could include the further copying of the virus code to other files or systems, the stealing and transmission of information, or deletion of files or entire disks. Viruses have also been used to spread fraudulent e-mail messages.

webcam   A camera that transmits images over the Internet. Webcams are often used by online pornography services and have sometimes been used to send images of child abuse to pedophiles.

Glossary

whitelist A list of acceptable web sites or e-mail senders, for use with filtering programs. See also **blacklist.**

whois A program that accesses a database containing contact and registration information about web sites. It can be used to find out more about the origin of e-mail messages or other communications.

PART II

GUIDE TO FURTHER RESEARCH

CHAPTER 6

How to Research Cybercrime Issues

This chapter presents a guide to resources and techniques for students and others who are researching topics relating to the activity of Internet predators. This topic has many facets, so the researcher will need to become familiar with a variety of different fields. These include criminology and the criminal justice system, the structure and operation of the Internet, computer security techniques and software, electronic commerce, and consumer protection and education.

Not surprisingly, given the nature of Internet crime, researchers will want to turn to the World Wide Web first in their quest for background information, news, and links to other resources. Computer and Internet crime is a rapidly changing field: For example, before 2003 Phish was only the name of a musical group, not a way to trick millions of e-mail users into revealing credit card numbers and other information. New forms of computer attack are developed seemingly every week, and legal developments are also rapid as courts and legislatures struggle to adapt to changing threats. Only the Web is fast enough to keep up with these developments.

WEB RESOURCES

Many web sites offer news, document libraries, and links on topics related to computer crime in general and Internet predators in particular. This survey will begin with the most general resources and then look at key topic areas.

General Sites

Researching computer crime requires a broad understanding of trends in Internet use. This has been the ongoing project of the Pew Internet and

American Life Project at http://www.pewinternet.org. The organization conducts numerous extensive surveys and studies of Internet users.

Turning specifically to the area of computer crime, a major federal source is the U.S. Department of Justice. Criminal Justice Division. Computer Crime and Intellectual Property Section at http://www.cybercrime.gov provides news, guidance for consumers and business, explains how to report incidents, and offers links to laws and legal issues such as those involving electronic commerce and the use of encryption.

Other federal agencies with computer crime-related activities include:

- Federal Bureau of Investigation (http://www.fbi.gov)
- U.S. Customs/Border Protection (http://www.customs.gov)
- U.S. Secret Service (http://www.ustreas.gov/usss/index.shtml)
- U.S. Postal Inspection Service (http://www.usps.com/postalinspectors)
- U.S. Food and Drug Administration (http://www.fda.gov)

There are also a number of private organizations that provide useful resources. The High Tech Crime Consortium at http://www.hightechcrimecops. org/links.htm#Computer_Crime provides links on a variety of types of computer crime, forensics, and legal issues. *Computerworld* magazine's Cybercrime Knowledge Center offers links to cybercrime-related news stories at http://www.computerworld.com/securitytopics/security/cybercrime/news. Taking a broader view, the World Justice Information Network at http://www.wjin.net/index.php provides stories and links to crime, cases, laws, and related events around the world. Searching the site with a few well-chosen keywords can yield considerable material on computer crime and fraud.

FRAUD AND IDENTITY THEFT

The Federal Trade Commission at http://www.ftc.gov is the major federal agency protecting consumers against fraudulent advertising and scams, whether offline or online. To find relevant resources, click on For Consumers, then E-Commerce and the Internet.

Internet Schemes, Scams and Frauds at http://www.crimes-of-persuasion. com/Crimes/Delivered/internet.htm presents news and articles about a variety of Internet scams, including phishing, one of the newest threats to Internet users.

Scambusters.org at http://www.scambusters.org/ is one of the best-written and easiest-to-use sites for consumers who want to learn about the latest in scams, virus threats, phishing, and other online dangers. Another interesting listing of scams and hoaxes by type can be found at Cyber Criminals Most Wanted at http://www.ccmostwanted.com/topics/sc/scams.htm

Unlike fraud, Internet hoaxes do not usually cause financial loss to their victims, but they can distract users or just waste time. The site Snopes. com at http://www.snopes.com categorizes hoaxes, tall tales, and half-truths by topic, making it easy to check the veracity of commonly recurring stories.

Readers who think they might be immune to the blandishments of online scammers might want to visit McWhortle Enterprises at http://www. mcwhortle.com People who are enticed by this supposed investment opportunity and click for more information will be told that this is actually a fake site put up by the Federal Trade Commission as a demonstration of online scamming tactics.

The Corporate Crime Reporter at http://www.corporatecrimereporter. com/index.html focuses on white collar crime, much of which now involves computers. While much of this crime involves insiders stealing from their company, it can also result in consumer information being stolen and diverted for identity theft.

The Anti-Phishing Working Group at www.antiphishing.org provides relevant news reports, statistics, and links to other organizations. There is even an archive of actual phishing messages to consult in case one is uncertain about an e-mail.

Because protecting privacy is closely related to minimizing risks of being victimized on the Internet, the Consumer Privacy Guide at http://www. consumerprivacyguide.org/ is a useful resource. It includes legal information, how-to guides, a section for kids and privacy, and other links.

Consumer groups are naturally an important ally in the fight against online fraud and to protect consumer rights, including privacy. Many organizations provide evaluations of companies, consumer protection tips, and news and advisories. Some examples include:

- Better Business Bureau (http://www.bbb.org)
- *Consumer Reports* (http://www.consumerreports.org)
- Consumer Sentinel (http://www.consumer.gov/sentinel)

ONLINE STALKING AND HARASSMENT

Founded by writer and cyberstalking victim Jayne Hitchcock, WHOA (Working to Halt Online Abuse) at http://www.haltabuse.org provides information and statistics on cyberstalking.

Another useful source is Cyber-Stalking.net at http://www.cyber-stalking. net. It focuses on stalking involving adult victims and perpetrators.

The National Cyber Security Alliance at http://www.staysafeonline. info/index.adp gears its efforts toward helping users (including older children and adults) protect themselves in cyberspace from threats such as viruses, phishing, and loss of privacy.

EXPLOITATION OF CHILDREN

A variety of sites deal with online crimes and dangers facing children, as well as providing education and resources for kids and parents.

Some background information and statistics on children and their activities can be found at a site maintained by the Federal Interagency Forum on Child and Family Statistics at http://www.childstats.gov. This web site provides a variety of statistics on American children and families, useful for context in studying the risks of the Web and other online services for young people.

The Crimes Against Children Research Center at http://www.unh.edu/ ccrc provides research reports and seeks to improve the reporting of crimes against children.

NetSmartz at http://www.netsmartz.org uses interactive activities and games to help children learn how to stay safe online. It is a joint effort of the National Center for Missing and Exploited Children and the Boys and Girls Clubs of America.

WiredSafety at https://www.wiredsafety.org involves several volunteer efforts to provide education and resources for parents, teachers, and children so they will have safer and better online experiences. The "Teenangels" program trains teens to help their peers who may be getting into trouble online.

The angelic focus continues at the CyberAngels site at http://www. cyberangels.com. This group, a program of the well-known Guardian Angels crime victim's advocacy group, provides both online and offline educational programs and resources.

Cybersmart! Curriculum at http://www.cybersmart.org/home provides lesson plans and training for teachers and activities for students. The focus is on safe Internet use, security, and critical thinking for children, families, and schools.

GetNetWise TV at http://www.getnetwise.org/gnwtv uses video to provide accessible education about the Internet for children and parents. Their broadcasts are archived and available for download from the web site.

The Children's Internet at http://www.childrensinternet.com/home. html is an example of the attempt to create safe havens for children online. It provides carefully monitored e-mail, chat, games, and thousands of pre-screened good web sites. A similar approach is found in the "kid friendly" domain of http://www.kids.us, established by federal law in 2002.

COMPUTER SECURITY

The United States Computer Emergency Readiness Team (US-Cert) at http://www.us-cert.gov is a public-private partnership engaged in understanding and reducing cyber threats, issuing timely threat warnings, and coordinating incident response activities. The site offers a variety of guidelines for dealing with personal or business computer security problems.

The term *CERT* is also used by other organizations. One prominent group that also provides numerous resources is the CERT Coordination Center based at Carnegie Mellon University. Its main site is at http://www.cert.org.

A collection of important works on computer security can be found at the Archive of Information Security. Its web site is at http://www.aracnet.com/~kea.

Turning to current opinions and news, the Computer Hacker section at www.NewsTrove.com offers links to relevant current articles focusing on hacker attacks and security issues and measures.

OTHER TECHNICAL RESOURCES

General-interest computer magazines and web sites will also prove useful, especially for reviewing the latest products and industry initiatives. Some examples of these sites include:

- *ComputerWorld* (http://www.computerworld.com)
- *InformationWeek* (http://www.informationweek.com)
- *InfoWorld* (http://www.infoworld.com)
- *PC Magazine* (http://www.pcmag.com)

There are also portals that offer extensive product reviews, free software, or low-cost shareware. They are a good place to compare and shop for security products such as spam filters and antivirus programs.

- CNet (http://www.cnet.com)
- Shareware.com (http://www.shareware.com)
- Tucows.com (http://www.tucows.com)
- ZDNet (http://www.zdnet.com)

If one has the technical background to pursue computer science resources, two very extensive portals provide access to journals, abstracts, and other resources. Note that membership is required for some resources.

- Association for Computing Machinery (http://www.acm.org)
- Institute of Electrical and Electronics Engineers (http://www.ieee.org)

LEGAL ISSUES

Cyberspace law is a rapidly expanding field that is still being defined. Below are some useful web sites.

FindLaw's Cyberspace Law section at http://www.findlaw.com/01topics/ 10cyberspace/computercrimes/sites.html provides numerous links to resources that provide papers and cases dealing with topics such as service provider liability, stalking and harassment, Internet censorship, free speech, defamation, intellectual property, and privacy.

Netlitigation at http://www.unc.edu/courses/2004spring/law/357c/001/ projects/eva/internetfraud/Identity Theft.htm is another useful resource. It, too, is divided into similar topic areas.

It can be hard to track down state laws relating to computer crime. The National Council of State Legislatures provides a list of cyberstalking laws at http://www.ncsl.org/programs/lis/CIP/stalk99.htm and a list of identity theft laws at http://www.ncsl.org/programs/lis/privacy/idt-statutes.htm. Another list of identity theft laws can be found at the University of North Carolina at http://www.unc.edu/courses/2004spring/law/357c/001/projects/ eva/internetfraud/Identity Theft.htm.

Many law schools are also developing programs focusing on cyberspace law. A good example of such a site is provided by the University of Dayton School of Law's Law on the Digital Frontier at http://cybercrimes.net/ index.html.

ADVOCACY GROUPS

The many intersections of computer crime, privacy, and free expression have given rise to concerns from several important civil liberties groups. The Electronic Frontier Foundation (EFF) at http://www.eff.org focuses on free expression and privacy issues. It provides current news and considerable case law, including extensive archives.

The Electronic Privacy Information Center (EPIC) at http://www.epic. org is, as the name suggests, focused on privacy issues. It also offers extensive resources, plus an e-mail newsletter.

The Privacy Rights Clearinghouse at http://www.privacyrights.org offers similar content. However, it is perhaps more focused on advocacy.

The Center for Democracy and Technology at http://www.cdt.org focuses on many of the same issues as EFF and EPIC, but takes more of a public policy approach.

Finally, the American Civil Liberties Union, the oldest U.S. civil liberties advocacy group, also takes a strong interest in privacy and expression rights in cyberspace. At www.aclu.org, see the links under Free Speech and Privacy and Technology.

THINK TANKS

So-called think tanks do research and public policy advocacy from a variety of ideologies and political viewpoints. Here are some examples of such organizations that have had input into issues relating to computer crime, Internet regulation, and related issues.

- Brookings Institution (http://www.brookings.org)
- Cato Institute (http://www.cato.org)
- Heritage Foundation (http://www.heritage.org)
- Hoover Institute (http://www.hoover.stanford.edu)
- Rand Corporation (http://www.rand.org)

NEWS RESOURCES

Turning from Web resource sites to other types of resources, news, both online and offline, is always important to researchers. While the more specialized or technically oriented sources (such as computer industry magazines and portals) are more likely to have detailed, accurate information about computer crimes, general news services offer breaking news.

The major broadcast and cable networks, news (wire) services, most newspapers, and many magazines have web sites that include news stories and links to additional information. For breaking news the following sites are also useful:

Associated Press (AP) wire (http://wire.ap.org/public_pages/WirePortal.
  pcgi/us_portal.html)
Cable News Network (CNN) (www.cnn.com)
New York Times (www.nytimes.com)
Reuters (www.reuters.com)

Time (www.time.com)
Wall Street Journal (http://online.wsj.com/public/us)
Washington Post (http://www.washingtonpost.com)

Yahoo! maintains a large set of links to many newspapers that have web sites or online editions at http://dir.yahoo.com/News_and_Media/Newspapers/Web_Directories.

Another useful site for tracking down recent news stories is Google News at http://news.google.com. The site assembles news automatically into headlines and sections. While the results can sometimes be a bit confusing, they are usually well organized. Users who make it their browser's home page will find it an easy way to keep in touch with news throughout the day.

FINDING MORE ON THE WEB

Although the resource sites mentioned earlier provide a convenient way to view a wide variety of information, it will eventually be necessary for the researcher to look for information or views elsewhere. The two main approaches to Web research are the portal and the search engine.

WEB PORTALS

A Web guide or index is a site that offers what amounts to a structured, hierarchical outline of subject areas. This enables the researcher to zero in on a particular aspect of a subject and find links to web sites for further exploration. The links are compiled and updated by a staff of researchers.

The best known (and largest) Web index is Yahoo! at www.yahoo.com. The home page gives the top-level list of topics, and the researcher simply clicks to follow them down to more specific areas. Because of the many issues involved with Internet predators and crimes, there are several different paths that can be taken to the same destinations. One path is: Society and Culture/Crime/Types of Crime/Computer and Internet Crime, with subtopics such as Child Pornography, Cyberstalking, Hacking, and Internet Fraud.

In addition to following Yahoo!'s outline-like structure, there is also a search box into which the researcher can type one or more keywords and receive a list of matching categories and sites.

Web indexes such as Yahoo! have two major advantages over undirected surfing. First, the structured hierarchy of topics makes it easy to find a particular topic or subtopic and then explore its links. Second, Yahoo! does not make an attempt to compile every possible link on the Internet (a task that is virtually impossible, given the size of the Web). Rather, sites are evaluated for usefulness and quality by Yahoo!'s indexers. This means that the researcher has a better chance of finding more substantial and accurate information. The disadvantage of Web indexes is the flip side of their selectivity: The researcher is dependent on the indexer's judgment for determining what sites are worth exploring.

SEARCH ENGINES

Search engines take a very different approach to finding materials on the Web. Instead of organizing topically in a top-down fashion, search engines work their way from the bottom up, scanning through Web documents and indexing them. There are hundreds of search engines, but some of the most widely used include:

- AltaVista (www.altavista.com)
- Excite (www.excite.com)
- Google (www.google.com)
- Hotbot (www.hotbot.com)
- Lycos (www.lycos.com)
- Northern Light (www.northernlight.com/news.html)
- WebCrawler (www.WebCrawler.com)

Search engines are generally easy to use by employing the same sorts of keywords that work in library catalogs. There are a variety of Web search tutorials available online (try entering "web search tutorial" in a search engine to find some). A good one is published by Bright Planet at http://www. brightplanet.com/deepcontent/tutorials/search/index.asp.

Here are a few basic rules for using search engines:

- When looking for something specific, use the most specific term or phrase. For example, when looking for information about identity theft, use that specific term. (Depending on the search engine, you may need to enclose it in quotes for it to be matched as a phrase.)
- When looking for a general topic that might be expressed using several different words or phrases, use several descriptive words (nouns are more reliable than verbs)—for example, online stalking cyberstalking (Most engines will automatically put pages that match all three terms first on the results list.)

- Use wildcards when a desired word may have more than one ending. For example, ident* matches both *identity* and *identification.*

- Most search engines support Boolean *(and, or, not)* operators that can be used to broaden or narrow a search.

- Use AND to narrow a search. For example, internet and abuse will match only pages that have both terms.

- Use OR to broaden a search: fraud or scam will match any page that has either term, and since these terms are often used interchangeably, this type of search is necessary to retrieve the widest range of results.

- Use NOT to exclude unwanted results: stalking not children should mostly find articles about stalking not involving children.

Since each search engine indexes somewhat differently and offers somewhat different ways of searching, it is a good idea to use several different search engines, especially for a general query.

Several metasearch programs automate the process of submitting a query to multiple search engines. These include Metacrawler at www.metacrawler. com and SurfWax at www.surfwax.com. Metasearch engines tend to have two drawbacks: They may overwhelm the researcher with results (and insufficiently eliminate duplicates), and they often do not use some of the more popular search engines (such as Google or Northern Light).

There are also search utilities that can be run from the researcher's own computer rather than through a web site. A good example is Copernic, available at www.copernic.com.

FINDING ORGANIZATIONS AND PEOPLE

Chapter 8 of this book provides a list of organizations that are involved with various aspects of computer crime and Internet predation, but new organizations emerge now and then. Many of the resource sites listed earlier will have links to organizations, as will Yahoo! and the other general Web portals.

If such sites do not yield the name of a specific organization, the name can be given to a search engine. Generally, the best approach is to put the name of the organization in quotation marks, such as "Internet Society."

Another approach is to take a guess at the organization's likely Web address. For example, the American Civil Liberties Union is commonly known by the acronym ACLU, so it is not a surprise that the organization's web site is at www.aclu.org. (Note that noncommercial organization sites normally use the .org suffix, government agencies use .gov, educational institutions use .edu, and businesses use .com.) This technique can save time, but does not always work. In particular, watch out for spoof sites that mimic or parody organizational sites. Such a site might, for example, have the same name as that of a government agency but end in .org instead of gov. (Such sites may be of interest in themselves as forms of criticism or dissent.)

There are several ways to find a person on the Internet:

- Put the person's name (in quotation marks) in a search engine and possibly find that person's home page on the Internet.
- Contact the person's employer (such as a university for an academic, or a corporation for an executive or technical professional). Most such organizations have Web pages that include a searchable faculty or employee directory.
- Try one of the people-finder services, such as Yahoo! People Search at http://people.yahoo.com or BigFoot at www.bigfoot.com. This may yield contact information such as e-mail address, postal address, or phone number.

Of course, these and other techniques can also be used to find and exploit sensitive information about people. They should only be used for legitimate purposes such as finding and contacting the author of a paper.

PRINT SOURCES

As useful as the Web is for quickly finding information and the latest news, in-depth research still sometimes requires trips to the library or bookstore. Getting the most out of the library requires the use of bibliographic tools and resources. *Bibliographic resources* is a general term referring to catalogs, indexes, bibliographies, and other guides that identify the books, periodical articles, and other printed resources that deal with a particular subject. They are essential tools for the researcher.

LIBRARY CATALOGS

Many library catalogs can now be searched online. Access to the largest library catalog, that of the Library of Congress, is available at http://catalog. loc.gov. This page includes a guide to using the catalog and both basic and advanced catalog searches.

Yahoo! offers a categorized listing of libraries at http://dir.yahoo.com/ Reference/Libraries. Of course, for materials available at a local public or university library, that institution will be the most convenient source.

Most catalogs can be searched in at least the following ways:

- An author search is most useful if you know or suspect that a person has written a number of works of interest. However, it may fail if the person's exact name is unknown. (Cross-references are intended to deal with this problem but cannot cover all possible variations.)
- A title search is best if the exact title of the book is known. Generally, only the first few words of the title are needed, excluding initial articles (a, an, the). This search will fail without the exact title.
- A keyword search will match words found anywhere in the title. It is thus broader and more flexible than a title search, although it may still fail if some keywords are not present.
- A subject search will find all works that have been assigned that subject heading by the library. The big advantage is that it does not depend on certain words being in the title. However, using a subject search requires knowledge of the appropriate subject headings (see below).

SUBJECT HEADINGS

The following selection of Library of Congress subject headings reflects the diversity of topics involved with computer crime and abuse.

For general background:

Computer Networks
Computers (includes many subheadings)
Crime
Criminology (includes many subheadings)
Electronic commerce
Internet (includes many subheadings)
Internet Culture
Internet Industry
Internet Users
Online Information Services
Online Information Services Industry
Telecommunications—Law and Legislation

For general questions of computer crimes and security, see:

Computer Crimes
Computer Hackers
Computer Networks—Access Control
Computers—Access Control
Computer Security

Computer Viruses
Cryptography
Database Security
Data Encryption
Data Protection
Electronic Data Processing Departments—Security Measures
Internet Domain Names
Internet Safety Measures

For fraud, identity theft, and related crimes:

Electronic Trading of Securities
Identity Theft
Internet and Older People
Internet Auctions
Internet Banking
Internet Fraud
Internet Gambling
Internet Marketing

For cyberstalking:

Harassment
Internet and Women
Intimidation
Online Chat Groups
Online Dating
Online Etiquette
Sexual Harassment
Stalking

For exploitation or protection of children and related issues:

Child Molesters
Women Child Molesters
Teenage Child Molesters
Internet Access for Library Users
Internet Abduction Prevention
Internet and Children
Internet and Teenagers
Internet Censorship
Internet Pornography

For other legal issues:

Censorship
Defamation
Freedom of Information
Freedom of Speech
Intellectual Property
Open Source Software
Privacy, Right of

Note that many headings can have subdivisions. In addition to United States and other geographical subdivisions, also look for subheadings such as:

Government Policy
Law and Legislation
Moral and Ethical Aspects

Once the record for a book or other item is found, it is a good idea to see what additional subject headings and name headings have been assigned. These in turn can be used for further searching.

AN ALTERNATIVE: BOOKSTORE CATALOGS

Many people have discovered that online bookstores such as Amazon.com at www.amazon.com and Barnes & Noble at www.barnesandnoble.com are convenient ways to shop for books. A less-known benefit of online bookstore catalogs is that they often include publisher's information, book reviews, and reader's comments about a given title. They can thus serve as a form of annotated bibliography.

Amazon has recently added a feature called "search inside the book" that applies to an increasing proportion of available titles. By default, this feature means a standard search will also retrieve books that contain the keyword or phrase somewhere in their text. This can be a mixed blessing—it can help one find obscure topics that might not otherwise be indexed, but it can also retrieve many irrelevant titles. If that happens, one can try the advanced search with more specific criteria or try Barnes & Noble instead.

BIBLIOGRAPHIES, INDEXES, AND DATABASES

Bibliographies in various forms provide a convenient way to find books, periodical articles, and other materials. How far to go back in one's reading depends, of course, on one's research topic and goals. Obviously, material about Internet crime is not likely to be found much earlier than the mid-1990s, while references to various forms of computer-related crime and fraud go back considerably further.

Popular and scholarly articles can be accessed through periodical indexes that provide citations and abstracts. Abstracts are brief summaries of articles or papers. They are usually compiled and indexed—originally in bound volumes, but increasingly available online.

Some relevant indexes likely to be available in academic or large public libraries include:

- ACM Guide to Computing Literature (http://portal.acm.org/guide.cfm)
- Applied Science and Technology Index (http://www.hwwilson.com/Databases/applieds.htm)
- Applied Social Sciences Indexes and Abstracts (http://www.isd.salford.ac.uk/publica/eisnotes/assia.pdf)
- Computer and Information Systems Abstracts (http://www.csa.com/csa/factsheets/computer.shtml)
- Computing Reviews (http://www.reviews.com)
- Criminal Justice Abstracts (http://www.ncjrs.org)
- Criminal Justice Periodical Index (http://libraries.uta.edu/dillard/subfiles/crimperi.htm)
- Psychological Abstracts (http://library.kumc.edu/tipsheets/print/psychabs.htm)
- Reader's Guide to Periodical Literature (http://www.hwwilson.com/Databases/Readersg.htm)
- Social Sciences Index (http://www.hwwilson.com/Databases/socsci.htm)
- Sociological Abstracts (http://www.csa.com/csa/factsheets/socioabs.shtml)
- Wilson Business Abstracts (http://www.hwwilson.com/newDDs/WB.htm)

The Web addresses refer to guides or summaries of the indexes available from the publisher or a library. Most researchers will want to search indexes online. Generally, however, they can be accessed only through a library, not via the Internet (except on a college campus). A university reference librarian may be able to help.

There is also a good general index that has unrestricted search access. UnCover Web at http://www.ingenta.com contains brief descriptions of about 13 million documents from about 26,000 journals in seemingly every subject area. Copies of complete documents can be ordered with a credit card, or they may be obtainable for free at a local library.

ONLINE GENERAL PERIODICAL INDEXES

Most public libraries subscribe to database services such as InfoTrac and EBSCO that index articles from hundreds of general-interest periodicals (and some moderately specialized ones). The database can be searched by author or by words in the title, subject headings, and sometimes words found anywhere in the article text. Depending on the database used, hits in the database can result in just a bibliographical description (author, title, pages, periodical name, issue date, and so on), a description plus an abstract (a paragraph summarizing the contents of the article), or the full text of the article itself. Before using such an index, it is a good idea to view the list of newspapers and magazines covered and determine the years of coverage.

Many libraries provide dial-in, Internet, or telnet access to their periodical databases as an option in their catalog menu. However, licensing restrictions usually mean that only researchers who have a library card for that particular library can access the database (usually by typing in their name and card number). Researchers can check with local public or school libraries to see what databases are available.

Periodicals not indexed by InfoTrac or another index (or for which only abstracts rather than complete text are available), may be found online. Most publications have their own web sites. Some scholarly publications are putting all or most of their articles online. Popular publications tend to offer only a limited selection of articles. Major newspapers typically offer current and recent articles (up to a week old, perhaps) for free and provide an archive from which articles can be purchased for a few dollars.

PERIODICALS

Relevant specialized periodicals can be found in general university libraries or departmental libraries (good departments to check are computer science, criminology, psychology, public policy, and sociology). Medical and legal libraries are also a possibility, although such materials may be too technical or specialized for most researchers.

Some examples of periodical or serial titles (with Web addresses where available) include:

- Communications of the ACM (http://www.acm.org/pubs/cacm)
- Computer Security Journal
- Computer Security Update (http://www.marketresearch.com)
- Computers & Security (http://www.sciencedirect.com)
- Crime and Justice: A Review of Research

- Crime & Justice International: Worldwide News and Trends
- Criminal Victimization in the U.S. (Statistics) (http://www.ojp.usdoj.gov/bjs/abstract/cvusst.htm)
- Criminology
- Cybercrime Law Report (http://west.thomson.com/product/37005124/product.asp)
- E-Commerce Law & Strategy (http://www.lawcatalog.com)
- E-Commerce Law Report (http://www.e-comlaw.com)
- Information Management & Computer Security
- International Criminal Justice Review (http://www.gsu.edu/~wwwicj)
- Internet Industry Magazine (http://www.internetindustry.com)
- Journal of Computer Security (http://www.isse.gmu.edu/~csis/faculty/jocs.html)
- Journal of Criminal Law and Criminology (http://www.press.uillinois.edu/journals/jclc.html)
- Journal of Interpersonal Violence (http://www.sagepub.com/journal.aspx?pid=108)
- Journal of Research in Crime and Delinquency (http://www.sagepub.com/journal.aspx?pid=145)
- The Online Reporter (http://www.onlinereporter.com)
- Proceedings of the IEEE (http://www.ieee.org)
- Violence Against Women (http://www.sagepub.com/journal.aspx?pid=93)
- Virus Bulletin (http://www.virusbtn.com)
- White Collar Crime Fighter (http://www.wccfighter.com)
- White Collar Crime Reporter (http://west.thomson.com/product/40213538/product.asp)

LEGAL RESEARCH

It is important for researchers to be able to obtain the text and summary of laws and court decisions relating to Internet crime. Because of the specialized terminology of the law, legal research can be more difficult to master than bibliographical or general research tools. Fortunately, the Internet has also come to the rescue in this area, offering a variety of ways to look up laws and court cases without having to pore through huge bound volumes in law libraries (which may not be easily accessible to the general public, anyway).

FINDING LAWS AND REGULATIONS

When federal legislation is passed, it eventually becomes part of the U.S. Code, a massive legal compendium. The U.S. Code can be searched online in several locations, but the easiest site to use is probably that of Cornell Law School at www4.law.cornell.edu/uscode. The fastest way to retrieve a law is by its title and section citation, but phrases and keywords can also be used.

A good shortcut to researching legal issues is to check the various general resource and advocacy web sites listed at the beginning of this chapter. Many of these organizations regularly summarize or compile recent cases and documents.

KEEPING UP WITH LEGISLATIVE DEVELOPMENTS

The Library of Congress Thomas web site at http://thomas.loc.gov includes files summarizing legislation by the number of the Congress (each two-year session of Congress has a consecutive number: For example, the 109th Congress will be in session in 2005 and 2006). Legislation can be searched for by the name of its sponsor(s), the bill number, or by topical keywords. (Laws that have been passed can be looked up under their Public Law number.)

For example, selecting the 106th Congress and typing the words "identity theft" into the search box will retrieve a number of bills pertaining to that subject. Clicking on the highlighted bill number brings up a display that includes the bill's status and text as well as further details, including sponsors, committee action, and amendments.

FINDING COURT DECISIONS

The U.S. Supreme Court and state courts make important decisions every year that determine how the laws are interpreted. Like laws, legal decisions are organized using a system of citations. The general form is: *Party1 v. Party2 volume reporter* [optional start page] *(court, year)*.

Here are some examples:

Brandenburg v. Ohio, 395 U.S. 444 (1969)

Here the parties are Brandenburg (the defendant who is appealing his case from a state court) and the state of Ohio. The case is in volume 395 of the *Supreme Court Reports*, beginning at page 444, and the case was decided in 1969. (For the Supreme Court, the name of the court is omitted.)

Fierro v. Gomez 77 F.3d 301 (9th Cir. 1996).

Here the case is in the Ninth U.S. Circuit Court of Appeals, decided in 1996.

A state court decision can generally be identified because it includes the state's name. For example, in *State v. Torrance*, 473 S.E.2d. 703, S.C. (1996) S.E. refers to the appeals district, and S.C. to South Carolina.

Once the jurisdiction for the case has been determined, the researcher can then go to a number of places on the Internet to find cases by citation and sometimes by the names of the parties or by subject keywords. Some of the most useful sites are:

- The Legal Information Institute at http://supct.law.cornell.edu/supct has all U.S. Supreme Court decisions since 1990 plus 610 of the "most important" historic decisions.
- Washlaw Web at www.washlaw.edu lists a variety of courts (including states) and legal topics, making it a good jumping-off place for many sorts of legal research. However, the actual accessibility of state court opinions (and the formats in which they are provided) varies widely.

LEXIS AND WESTLAW

Lexis and Westlaw are commercial legal databases that have extensive information, including an elaborate system of notes, legal subject headings, and ways to show relationships between cases. These services are too expensive for use by most individual researchers, but they are available through some university or corporate libraries.

MORE HELP ON LEGAL RESEARCH

For more information on conducting legal research, see the Legal Research FAQ at www.cis.ohio-state.edu/hypertext/faq/usenet/law/research/top.html. After a certain point, however, the researcher who lacks formal legal training may need to consult with or rely on the efforts of professional researchers or academics in the field.

EVALUATING WEB SOURCES

Thanks to the Web there is more information available from more sources than ever before. There is also a greater diversity of voices, since any person or group with a computer and Internet service can put up a web site—in some cases, a site that looks as polished and professional as that of an established and well-funded group. One benefit is that dissenting views can be found in abundance. However, as can be seen in the reports of online fraud, scams, and phishing, the Web is also inundated with deliberate misinformation and deception as well as hoaxes, urban legends, and well-meaning but incorrect accounts.

Thus the student or researcher must not let the attractions of the Web override the need for the same kind of critical thinking that would be applied to printed materials. Further, the nature of the Web means that the researcher should take extra care to try to verify facts and to understand the possible biases of each source. Some good questions to ask include:

- Who is responsible for this web site?
- What is the background or reputation of the person or group?
- Does the person or group have a stated objective or agenda?
- What biases might this person or group have?
- Do a number of high-quality sites link to this one?
- What is the source given for a particular fact? Does that source actually say what is quoted? Where did *they* get that information?

Using a good variety of the tools and resources that have been highlighted here will help ensure that the results of research are balanced and comprehensive.

CHAPTER 7

ANNOTATED BIBLIOGRAPHY

This chapter presents a selection of books, articles, and Web documents relating to Internet predators and the response to their crimes. The bibliography uses three levels: major topics, aspects of the topic, and types of materials.

The works in the first topical section, "Computer Crime Background," deal with background material and issues that are common to all the types of Internet predation discussed in this book.

The works in the second section, "Online Frauds and Scams," cover the various ways in which criminals have sought to separate Internet users from their money.

The works in the third section, "Information and Identity Theft," focus on criminal activity that aims to obtain personal account, credit card, or other identifying information in order to assume a person's identity and gain unlawful access to funds or credit.

The works in the fourth section, "Online Stalking and Harassment," deal with cyberstalking, the obsessive pursuit or harassment of a victim through personal information gained on the Internet and using e-mail or online communications services.

The works in the final section, "Sexual Exploitation of Children," involve pedophiles or child molesters who pursue their victims online as well as with the creators and distributors of child pornography.

Each topical section is further divided as appropriate into sections for the following aspects:

- Introductions, General Discussion, and Examples
- Regulation, Investigation, Enforcement, and Legal Issues
- Technical Threats, Issues, and Measures
- Education and Assistance

Finally, each of these subsections is divided by type of material:

- books
- articles and papers
- Web documents

COMPUTER CRIME BACKGROUND

REFERENCE WORKS

Books

Clemens, Martin, and Bernadette Schelle. *Cybercrime: A Reference Handbook.* Santa Barbara, Calif.: ABC-CLIO, 2004. Covers a broad range of computer crimes and threats from hacking to espionage and cyberterrorism. Includes overview, biographies, and bibliographies.

Newton, Michael. *The Encyclopedia of High-Tech Crime and Crime-Fighting.* New York: Checkmark Books, 2004. A comprehensive A–Z guide covering topics such as cyberstalking, devices, hackers and other high-tech criminals, infamous computer viruses, the use of DNA evidence to exonerate or convict people, and more. Includes a glossary.

Norrgard, Lee E., and Julia M. Norrgard. *Consumer Fraud: A Reference Handbook.* Santa Barbara, Calif.: ABC-CLIO, 1998. This reference provides a good if somewhat dated overview of types of consumer fraud (including limited coverage of Internet fraud) plus a chronology, biographies, and discussion of relevant laws. There is also a bibliography and a directory of organizations

Articles and Papers

Fink, Kenneth. "Criminology Web Sites: An Annotated 'Webliography.'" *Searcher,* vol. 11, September 2003. Also available online. URL: http://www.infotoday.com/searcher/sep03/fink.shtml. In-depth study of Internet predators and computer-related crime. Requires familiarity with principles of criminology and the general resources available in the field. This web site bibliography includes annotated links to government and law enforcement web sites, private companies, U.S. and foreign associations, policy think tanks, journals and online databases, and educational resources.

Web Documents

"Annotated Stalking Bibliography." Stalking Resource Center. Available online. URL: http://www.ncvc.org/src/main.aspx?dbID=DB_Annotated_

Stalking_Bibliography344. Downloaded on August 30, 2004. A listing of books and articles on stalking (does not focus on cyberstalking). Includes introductions, behavioral studies, and example cases. The most recent material cited appears to be from 2001.

"Computer Crime and Security." Library of Congress, Science Reference Services. Available online. URL: http://www.loc.gov/rr/scitech/tracerbullets/compcrimetb.html Posted on June 22, 2004. Part of the Tracer Bullets Online series, this is a research guide and bibliography that includes such resources as books, conference proceedings, government publications, technical reports, bibliographies, journals, and additional Web links. Gives good basic guidance, but references only go up to the early 1990s.

Harrison, Jon, Editor. "Criminal Justice Resources: CyberCrime." Michigan State University Libraries. Available online. URL: http://www.lib.msu.edu/harris23/crimjust/cybercri.htm. Updated on June 23, 2004. Provides Web resources, information about organizations, links to selected articles and publications, and information about telephone hotlines.

Lee, J. A. N. "Computer Crime—Bibliography." Virginia Polytechnic Institute and State University, Computer Science Department. Available online. URL: http://courses.cs.vt.edu/~cs3604/lib/Crime/bibliography.html. Updated on October 24, 2001. A list of articles, reports, and Web links relating to computer crime, covering the years 1997 to 2001.

Pacifici, Sabrini. "Annotated Bibliography of Resources on Identity Theft." BeSpacific.com Available online. URL: http://www.bespacific.com/mt/resources/2003.04.07.IDTheftABATechShowbiblio.pdf. Posted in April 7, 2003. A well-organized set of links to federal agencies, federal laws, legislative action, state laws, consumer and industry resources, and news articles.

"Topic Bibliography: E-Commerce & Internet Fraud." Information Resource Center. United States Embassy, Thailand. Available online. URL: http://www.usa.or.th/services/irc/bib_inet_crime.htm. Posted on April 26, 2001. A listing of articles and reports on Internet crime, fraud, privacy issues, and related topics. Also includes U.S. legislation and resource web sites.

INTRODUCTIONS AND OVERVIEWS

Books

Baase, Sara. *A Gift of Fire: Social, Legal, and Ethical Issues for Computers and the Internet.* 2d ed. Upper Saddle River, N.J.: Pearson Education, 2003. This textbook lucidly and systematically explores the ethical and legal implications of the role of computers and the Internet in modern society.

Relevant areas discussed include speech, anonymity, privacy, hacking, the challenge of computer crime, and the inherent risks of computer systems.

Biggs, John. *Black Hat: Misfits, Criminals and Scammers in the Internet Age.* Berkeley, Calif.: APress, 2004. Written for a popular audience, this book is not just an overview or introduction but offers portraits of and interviews with actual hackers and others on the legal margins of the Internet.

Branigan, Steven. *High-Tech Crimes Revealed.* Indianapolis, Ind.: Addison-Wesley Professional, 2004. Fascinating, vivid accounts of forensic investigation into computer crime. Many of the difficulties in securing and preserving evidence are explained, as well as the frustrations involved in pursuing electronic criminals when having to deal with a cumbersome legal system. Technical details are also explained in easily understood terms.

Hafner, Katie, and John Markoff. *Cyberpunk: Outlaws and Hackers on the Computer Frontier.* Revised ed. New York: Simon & Schuster, 1995. A classic look into the world of hacking and underground computer culture at the start of the modern Internet era.

Hitchcock, Jayne. A. *Net Crimes & Misdemeanors: Outmaneuvering the Spammers Swindlers, and Stalkers Who Are Targeting You Online.* Medford, N.J.: Information Today, 2002. The author combines vivid accounts of Internet victimization with practical advice and tips for minimizing risk and getting help. In addition to scams, frauds, stalking, and the special vulnerability of children, other topics covered include ways to protect privacy and secure computer systems against attack.

Hollinger, R. C. *Crime, Deviance and the Computer.* Aldershot, U.K.: Dartmouth Publishing, 1997. The author describes the history of computer-related crime from 1946 to the 1990s. The focus is on how this type of crime emerged as a distinctive problem while perpetrators developed their own criminal subculture. Specific topics include the response of society to destructive computer hackers and the legal responses to a variety of threats, including system attacks, viruses, pornography, and fraud.

Jewkes, Yvonne, editor. *Dot.cons: Crime, Deviance and Identity on the Internet.* Portland, Ore.: William Publishing, 2003. A collection of essays that explore how Internet users test and break social boundaries. Crimes such as intrusive hacking, identity theft, and fraud are just one aspect of free-wheeling activities that can include new forms of gambling, prostitution, dating, and other activities both legal and illegal.

Joyce, Bryan H. *Internet Scams: What to Be Afraid of in Cyberspace.* Pembroke Pines, Fla.: Net Works, 2002. Looks at a variety of attacks, cons, and scams encountered by today's Internet users. Topics include viruses and other system attacks, social engineering, and surreptitious information gathering.

Lilley, Peter. *Hacked, Attacked & Abused: Digital Crime Exposed.* London: Kogan Page, 2002. A wide-ranging survey of hacking, computer crime, online frauds, information warfare, privacy, and related topics. Includes many interesting quotes and incidents. Appendixes include excerpts from computer crime laws of various nations as well as international treaties.

Loader, Brian, and Douglas Thomas. *Cybercrime: Law Enforcement, Security and Surveillance in the Information Age.* New York: Routledge, 2000. A comprehensive discussion of the legal, law enforcement, technical, and social issues arising from emerging cybercrime threats.

McWilliams, Brian S. *Spam Kings: The Real Story Behind the High-Rolling Hucksters Pushing Porn, Pills, and %*@)# Enlargements.* Sebastapol, Calif.: O'Reilly, 2004. The author, an investigative reporter, exposes the personalities and techniques behind spam, showing how some "spam kings" have made fortunes. He also explores the technical and legal battle between spammers and Internet businesses.

Platt, Charles. *Anarchy Online: Net Crime/Net Sex.* New York: HarperPrism, 1996. This is actually two books bound together with separate covers. One deals with computer crime, mainly piracy (illicit cracking and copying of commercial software). The other volume recounts the early controversy over pornography on the Internet, refuting studies that claimed the Internet was inundated with smut. It also chronicles the civil libertarians who fought against laws requiring filtering (blocking) of Web sites deemed offensive. An important historical resource for understanding the development of issues that still preoccupy Internet users today.

Power, Richard. *Tangled Web: Tales of Digital Crime from the Shadows of Cyberspace.* Upper Saddle River, N.J.: Pearson Education, 2000. Vivid, detailed narratives of the operations of hackers, criminals, private investigators, law enforcers, and security experts in the new world of online crime. A variety of conclusions are drawn about the impact and significance for the Internet and electronic commerce.

"Spammer-X." *Inside the Spam Cartel.* Rockland, Mass.: Syngress, 2004. Computer security expert Jeffrey Posluns edits the work of an anonymous author who provides fascinating details about the spam industry—and it is indeed an industry, with underground investors, hackers and spam writers often working together to harvest money from Internet users while avoiding technical and law enforcement challenges. The book is ambiguous in that it can serve simultaneously as an exposé, a resource for spam fighters, and a handbook for would-be spammers.

Spinello, Richard A., Herman T. Tavani, editors. *Readings in CyberEthics.* Sudbury, Mass.: Jones and Bartlett, 2001. An anthology of essays on important areas in the ethics and governance of cyberspace. Topics include free speech, responsibility for content, intellectual property, privacy, security, and codes of ethical conduct. Provides useful background and context for issues involving computer crime.

Sterling, Bruce. *The Hacker Crackdown: Law and Disorder on the Electronic Frontier.* New York: Bantam Books, 1992. A noted science fiction author and writer on privacy and related issues made this classic contribution to the literature of computer crime at the start of the modern Internet era. The book tells the story of the first major federal sweep against computer hackers and how it almost destroyed an innocent games company. Along the way, important First Amendment issues were raised and a new generation of cyber-libertarians organized groups such as the Electronic Frontier Foundation.

Worley, Becky. *Security Alert: Stories of Real People Protecting Themselves from Identity Theft, Scams, and Viruses.* Indianapolis, Ind.: New Riders Publishing, 2004. Through vivid anecdotes and sound advice, the author explains a variety of online threats, including identity theft, scams, viruses, stalking, and dangers for children, and suggests ways to minimize the risk of becoming a victim.

Articles and Papers

Hale, Chris. "Cybercrime: Facts & Figures Concerning This Global Dilemma." *Crime & Justice International*, vol. 18, September 2002, pp. 5–6, 24–26. Also available online. URL: http://158.135.23.21/cjcweb/college/cji/index.cfm?ID=116. This overview depicts cybercrime as a growing international problem. Describes the different types of cybercrimes, how the growth of the worldwide Internet led to a corresponding growth in the prevalence and impact of cybercrime, and why law enforcement has largely failed to come to grips with the challenge.

Mannix, Margaret, et al. "The Internet's Dark Side: Internet Crime." *U.S. News & World Report*, vol. 129, August 28, 2000, pp. 36ff. Although the figures cited are now outdated, the detailed vignettes of stalking, fraud, child solicitation, and other online crimes provide a vivid introduction to a growing problem.

Reilly, Rob. "Internet Crime: What's Hot, Statistics, Reporting Incidents." *Multimedia Schools*, vol. 9, October 2002, pp. 68ff. The author points out that scams and other online criminal activity date back to the "ancient" days of bulletin board systems in the 1980s. Today, however, Internet crime is rampant. The various types of criminal activity are described, with a guide to appropriate agencies for reporting incidents.

"Unlimited Opportunities?" *Economist*, vol. 371, May 15, 2004, pp. 18ff. Despite the downturn in the past few years, the Internet remains a source of great opportunity for starting new businesses. The cost of entry is low and the huge number of people online make it likely to attract enough like-minded people to support a specialized business. However, 2003 was also possibly the worst year on the Internet for crime, which threatens to cripple e-commerce by destroying consumer confidence. The Internet can still welcome shoppers, but the e-shops need better "locks."

Web Documents

Fallows, Deborah. "The Internet and Daily Life: Many Americans Use the Internet in Everyday Activities, but Traditional Offline Habits Still Dominate." Pew Internet & American Life Project. Available online. URL: http://www.pewinternet.org/PPF/r/131/report_display.asp. Posted on August 11, 2004. Exposure to Internet crime is related to the amount of time people spend online and the importance they attach to information found there. This report does not discuss Internet crime, but provides an overall context for the importance of the Internet. Eighty-eight percent of respondents to this survey believe the Internet now plays a role in their daily routines—about one-third of these say it plays a major role. People go online both for social (communication) reasons and to obtain information. However, the fact that the majority of daily activity is still offline means that traditional forms of fraud and other crime must not be neglected.

———. "Spam: How It Is Hurting E-mail and Degrading Life on the Internet." Pew Internet & American Life Project. Available online. URL: http://www.pewinternet.org/pdfs/PIP_Spam_Report.pdf. Posted on October 22, 2003. This survey suggests that unsolicited e-mail (spam) is making e-mail harder or less pleasant to use. About one-third of users are concerned that e-mail filtering software may be blocking wanted messages. A large majority is bothered by deceptive or dishonest content of spam (80 percent) and obscene or offensive content (76 percent).

Fox, Susannah. "Older Americans and the Internet." Pew Internet & American Life Project. Available online. URL: http://www.pewinternet.org/pdfs/PIP_Seniors_Online_2004.pdf. Posted on March 25, 2004. Senior citizens tend to be more vulnerable to fraud and related crimes, so the growing number of seniors online calls for special attention from law enforcement and consumer education agencies. As of 2004, 22 percent of Americans age 65 or over are online; although still a minority, this represents a 47 percent growth in this demographic since 2000. About two-thirds of wired seniors have sought product information online, and about half have made online purchases.

Kelley, John X. "Cybercrime—High Tech Crime." JISC Legal Information Service. Available online. URL: http://www.jisclegal.ac.uk/cybercrime/cybercrime.htm. Posted on March 25, 2002. An overview of the categories of computer crime and their prevalence, with a focus on the impact on universities and higher education. Although the legal references are to British law, there is also much general data and some data specific to the United States.

"National and State Trends in Fraud & Identity Theft." Federal Trade Commission. Identity Theft Data Clearinghouse. Available online. URL: http://www.consumer.gov/sentinel/pubs/Top10Fraud2004.pdf. Posted on February 1, 2005. Latest in a series of annual reports summarizing complaints of fraud and identity theft reported to the federal Consumer Sentinel database. More than 635,000 consumer complaints were received in 2004; 31 percent related to identity theft, the rest to fraud. Internet auctions remain the largest source of fraud complaints.

REGULATION, INVESTIGATION, ENFORCEMENT, AND LEGAL ISSUES

Books

Casey, Eoghan. *Digital Evidence and Computer Crime.* San Diego, Calif.: Academic Press, 2003. This comprehensive textbook is designed to teach principles of computer forensics (including investigative techniques and evidence handling) to law enforcers, attorneys, and technical people who may become involved in cybercrime cases. The accompanying CD includes simulated cases.

Cohen, Henry. *Freedom of Speech and Press: Exceptions to the First Amendment.* Washington, D.C.: Congressional Research Service. Also available online. URL: http://usinfo.state.gov/usa/infousa/media/files/press1.pdf. Updated August 27, 2003. Summarizes the extent of exceptions to the First Amendment's protection for speech and the press. Categories relevant to legislating against computer crime include obscenity, child pornography, defamation, speech harmful to children, and children's First Amendment rights.

Doyle, Charles. *Computer Fraud & Abuse: A Sketch of 18 U.S.C. 1030 and Related Federal Criminal Laws.* Washington, D.C.: Congressional Research Service. Also available online. URL: http://www.ipmall.info/hosted_resources/crs/RS20830_031124.pdf. Updated November 24, 2003. Summarizes federal laws protecting federal computers and private computers used in interstate commerce against trespassing or damage and criminalizing their use as instruments of fraud.

Grabosky, Peter, Russell G. Smith, and Gillian Dempsey. *Electronic Theft: Unlawful Acquisition in Cyberspace.* Cambridge, U.K.: Cambridge University Press, 2001. A study of criminal practices involving the unlawful transfer of funds in cyberspace. The Australia-based authors provide an international perspective on theft, extortion, fraud, theft of intellectual property, industrial espionage, and identity theft.

Ku, Raymond S., Michele A. Farber, and Arthur J. Cockfield. *Cyberspace Law: Cases and Materials*. New York: Aspen Publishers, 2002. This handbook is organized by topic. Each section includes introductory articles, excerpts from case decisions, and questions for further discussion. Although many of the topics deal with property rights (copyright, ownership of domain names, and so on) there is also relevant discussion of indecency and regulation of speech, use of filtering software, and the limits of user anonymity and privacy.

MacDougall, Paul R., editor. *Overview of Computer Fraud and Abuse*. Hauppauge, N.Y.: Nova Science Publishers, 2002. An overview of the federal Computer Fraud and Abuse Act, including the actions covered and penalties.

National Institute of Justice. *Forensic Examination of Digital Evidence: A Guide for Law Enforcement*. Washington, D.C.: U.S. Department of Justice, Office of Justice Programs, 2004. This small handbook for law enforcement officers would also be valuable for legal and security professionals and students who need to understand how evidence is handled in computer-related crimes. Chapter topics include policy and procedure development, evidence assessment, evidence acquisition, evidence examination, and documenting and reporting. Includes example cases and a glossary.

Nicoll, C., J. E. J. Prins, and M. J. M. Van Dellen. *Digital Anonymity and the Law: Tensions and Dimensions*. New York: Cambridge University Press, 2003. The Internet has evolved in such a way that communications and transactions can be carried out with a high degree of anonymity. The legal conflict arises from the need of law enforcement and judicial authorities to fix the identity of persons so as to be able to hold them accountable for their actions. However, laws that can be used to force persons to reveal their identity can also be used to invade privacy or chill freedom of expression. The relevant U.S. and European regulations are discussed.

Shinder, Debra Littlejohn. *Scene of the Cybercrime: Computer Forensics Handbook*. Rockland, Mass.: Syngress Publishing, 2002. Addressed to computer professionals, law enforcement personnel, and businesspeople, this book provides a comprehensive look at types of cybercrime, including fraud, information theft, and system and network attacks. Includes coverage of the national and international legal framework relevant to computer crime and describes appropriate forensic and investigatory techniques. There is also a useful introduction to computer concepts and systems that are relevant to investigators.

Smith, Marcia S. *Internet Privacy: Overview and Pending Legislation.* Washington, D.C.: Congressional Research Service. Also available online. URL: http://www.usembassy.it/pdf/other/RL31408.pdf. Updated July 6, 2004. Surveys current issues involving privacy of Internet users, including law enforcement access to online subscriber records under the USA PATRIOT Act and the growing use of intrusive spyware and adware. Includes summary of legislation pending in the 108th Congress.

———. *"Junk E-mail": An Overview of Issues and Legislation Concerning Unsolicited Commercial Electronic Mail ("Spam").* Washington, D.C.: Congressional Research Service. Also available online. URL: http://www.usembassy.fi/pdfiles/RS20037.pdf. Updated April 15, 2003. Discusses issues surrounding the regulation of spam e-mail. Proponents of regulation argue that the large flow of unsolicited mail puts an unfair burden on service providers and users. (The author gives only minimal coverage to recent observations that spam is also a major carrier for Internet fraud and scams, including phishing.) State and congressional action is also covered, including the terms of the CAN-SPAM Act.

Smith, Russell, Peter Grabosky, and Gregor Urbas. *Cyber Criminals on Trial.* New York: Cambridge University Press, 2004. A detailed look at the prosecution and sentencing of cybercriminals in the world's major legal systems. A number of high-profile cases are discussed in an attempt to determine common obstacles and effective techniques.

Spinello, Richard A. *Regulating Cyberspace: The Policies and Technologies of Control.* Westport, Conn.: Quorum Books, 2002. Laws against cybercrime must be viewed in the broader context of regulatory philosophy—what is the best way to promote security and reliability while allowing for the maximum freedom that has characterized the electronic frontier? The author opts for a decentralized approach that he says mirrors the structure of the Internet itself. Regulation should reinforce responsible behavior rather than impose mandates that may be too restrictive and inflexible.

Wall, David S., ed. *Crime and the Internet.* New York: Routledge, 2001. A collection of papers exploring how criminologists are struggling to come to terms with the growing phenomenon of cybercrime and how this type of crime fits into ongoing debates in criminology. The book's final section looks at how Internet crime challenges the criminal justice system.

Westby, Jody R., ed. *International Guide to Combating Cybercrime.* Chicago: American Bar Association, Privacy and Computer Crime Committee, Section of Science and Technology Law, 2003. A comprehensive if rather technical overview of international and national laws and legal issues relating to computer crime. Topics covered include cybercrime laws, jurisdictional issues, the impact of cybercrime on law enforcement, search and seizure in the digital domain, and cooperation between public agencies and private organizations. There is also a bibliography and list of additional resources.

Articles and Papers

Alexander, Daniel. "Policing and the Global Paradox." *FBI Law Enforcement Bulletin*, vol. 71, June 2002, pp. 6–13. Also available online. URL: http://www.fbi.gov/publications/leb/2002/june02leb.pdf. The author draws interesting parallels between the global movement of people represented by legal and illegal immigration and the global movement of money (legitimate or otherwise) in cyberspace. He notes that more communities are becoming gated or otherwise physically isolated from one another. Thus law enforcement is faced with a paradox: As crime becomes more global, victims or citizens in general may become more isolated.

Bowker, Arthur L. "The Advent of the Computer Delinquent." *FBI Law Enforcement Bulletin*, vol. 69, December 2000, pp. 7–11. Also available online. URL: http://www.fbi.gov/publications/leb/2000/dec00leb.pdf. The author suggests a number of factors that are leading to a growing amount of computer-related delinquency among teens. Today's youth have more knowledge and familiarity with computer technology than ever before. Common attitudes among young people toward pirating software and other issues suggest they are not receiving a good ethical foundation for computer use. Finally, the anonymity of the Internet makes it easy for youths to disguise their age and makes any online equivalent of a curfew impracticable. Meanwhile, investigators face legal obstacles such as lack of clear jurisdiction.

Brenner, Susan W. "U.S. Cybercrime Law: Defining Offenses." *Information Systems Frontiers*, vol. 6, June 2004, pp. 115–132. The general term *cybercrime* reflects the unique aspects of the use of computer technology to commit crimes. The law has had to respond by creating new definitions for offenses. The article surveys the different types of cybercrime and explains the relationship between federal and state laws.

Dahl, Darren. "New Liability for Hacked Companies." *Inc*, vol. 26, June 2004, p. 28. Many companies that have discovered their computers have been penetrated and customer information compromised have stonewalled and not told customers about the situation. California passed a law in 2003 requiring that such break-ins be fully disclosed, and Senator Diane Feinstein (D-Calif.) has introduced similar federal legislation.

Gilmour, Kim. "In 2001, This Man Was Given Three Years and 15m £ to Combat Organised Crime on the Internet. Two Years Later We Ask Len Hynds if it Was Time and Money Well Spent." *Internet Magazine*, May 2003, pp. 48ff. The head of Britain's National HiTech Crime Unit describes its efforts. Although online pedophiles are the most notorious cybercriminals, much of the investigatory effort is directed toward organized groups of extortionists and hackers. The unit is working with software companies to design more effective security products.

Goldsmith, Jack L. "Against Cyberanarchy." *University of Chicago Law Review*, vol. 65, 1998, pp. 1199ff. Argues that the real difficulties in regulating cyberspace should not lead a conclusion that all regulation in this realm is futile. Default laws can allow for private ordering just as the architecture of the network itself can promote desirable behavior. However, despite the fact that the global nature of the Internet can allow online operations to evade direct regulation, indirect regulation focusing on the users of such services can still be effective. Nations can negotiate the problem of spillover effects, in which one country's actions affect the Internet as a whole.

James, Barry. "Internet Crime-Fighting Plan May Open Door for Snoopers." *International Herald Tribune*, March 23, 2001, p. 25. Describes the controversial Convention on Cybercrime that is being adopted by the European Union. While proponents see the convention as providing necessary tools for going after child pornographers and hackers who work across national boundaries, critics are concerned about the law's lack of privacy protection and the outlawing of anonymity, which can help protect political dissidents. Further, provisions designed to protect copyrights may deprive disadvantaged users of access to important information.

Johnson, David R., and David Post. "Law and Borders: The Rise of Law in Cyberspace." *Stanford Law Review*, vol. 48, 1996, pp. 1367ff. Discusses how the nature of cyberspace is affecting traditional laws based upon physical geography. Sovereignty, physical effects, legitimacy, and the ability of persons to conform to the appropriate rules are all tied to the existence of physical spaces. All of these are being threatened by the lack of physical boundaries in cyberspace.

Johnston, Richard. "The Battle Against White-Collar Crime." *USA Today*, vol. 130, January 2002, pp. 36ff. The author believes that "the exponential growth of technology and the use of computers have triggered a purposeful rethinking of the tools needed by law enforcement organizations to address internet-related crime." One in three American households is a victim of white-collar crime, often involving the use of computer systems, according to a groundbreaking survey by the National White Collar Crime Center. Other organizations are also discussed, as are a variety of recommendations.

Lessig, Lawerence. "The Law of the Horse: What Cyberlaw Might Teach." *Harvard Law Review*, vol. 113, December 1999, pp. 501–46. Also available online. URL: http://www.lessig.org/content/articles/works/finalhls.pdf.

This paper responds to a challenge from a conference where a judge insisted that there was no more a law of cyberspace than there was a law of the horse. The author replies that while not all special concerns require fundamental rethinking of the law, computers and the development of cyberspace do. The architecture of cyberspace interacts with law, customary norms, and other forces to shape online behavior. For example, the attempts to protect privacy and regulate obscenity, although very different in objectives, both run up against the structure of cyberspace. In the long run, regulating that structure itself would be the most effective approach.

"Office Hours: Sleuthing in Cyberspace." *The Guardian (London)*, February 16, 2004, p. 2. Reports the growing demand for computer forensics experts who can recover traces of illicit activity and even resurrect deleted e-mail or files. Many experts work for companies that are trying to stop or prosecute employees guilty of fraud or harassment. In addition, experts are aiding authorities who need to obtain electronic evidence of suspected customers of international child pornography rings. Employers are urged to take the cybercrime threat seriously and to preserve evidence before it is too late. (Although the story is based in the United Kingdom, trends in the United States are similar.)

Podgor, Ellen S. "Computer Crimes and the USA PATRIOT Act." *Criminal Justice*, vol. 17, Summer 2002, pp. 61–69. Explains that while the USA PATRIOT Act focuses on fighting terrorism, many of the tools given to investigators and prosecutors are broadly phrased and can likely be applied to computer-related fraud, identity theft, extortion, and similar activities. Connections to money laundering can also be pursued, as can the possible link between computer crimes and financing of terrorism.

Shinder, Deborah Littlejohn. "Understanding Legal Issues." *Law and Order*, vol. 51, December 2003, pp. 38, 42–44, 49. An overview of how standard search-and-seizure law applies to computer-related evidence. For example, a laptop computer found in a vehicle search is ordinarily considered to be a closed container requiring that a warrant be obtained before any search of its contents. Possible situations where immediate search is allowed include exigent circumstances, abandoned property (trash), objects in plain view, and searches incident to an arrest.

Stewart, Christopher S. "Fighting Crime One Computer at a Time." *New York Times*, June 10, 2004, p. C5. Describes the growth in private services that investigate or seek to prevent a variety of computer crimes including identity theft, investment scams, and selling of counterfeit prescription drugs. Some example cases illustrate the resourceful if sometimes questionable tactics used by undercover officers.

———. "Online Crime Engenders New Hero: Cybersleuth." *International Herald Tribune*, June 11, 2004, p. 17. Describes how cybersleuths investigate

Internet activities ranging from spamming to investment scams and sales of bogus prescription drugs. Corporations are hiring an increasing number of tech-savvy private investigators to combat online hackers and fraudsters.

Web Documents

"Computer Crime Laws by State." National Security Institute. Available online. URL: http://nsi.org (follow links). Downloaded on August 7, 2004. A compilation of state law provisions relating to computer crime. Click on a state's link to see its laws.

"Convention on Cybercrime." Council of Europe. Available online. URL: http://conventions.coe.int/Treaty/EN/CadreListeTraites.htm. Posted on November 23, 2001. Agrees that nations will establish legislation to outlaw offenses against "the confidentiality, integrity and availability of computer data and systems." Forgery or fraud involving computer data will also be criminalized, as will copyright violations and the distribution of child pornography. Various mechanisms are established for coordinating legal proceedings among the signatory nations.

"The Electronic Frontier: The Challenge of Unlawful Conduct Involving the Use of the Internet." President's Working Group on Unlawful Conduct on the Internet. Available online. URL: http://www.usdoj.gov/criminal/cybercrime/unlawful.htm. Posted in March 2000. Report of a high-level multiagency working group that is formulating policy regarding the investigation and prosecution of Internet crime. It recommends the development of Internet-specific regulation based on general policy principles, the development of effective tools and training for legal and law enforcement agencies, cooperation with the private sector, and the development of education and tools for Internet users.

Johnson, David R. "The Unscrupulous Diner's Dilemma and Anonymity in Cyberspace." Electronic Frontier Foundation. Available online. URL: http://www.eff.org/legal/anonymity_online_johnson.article. Posted on March 4, 1994. This relatively early look at the burgeoning Internet suggests that allowing anonymous use of the Internet leads to destructive forms of group behavior, while people who are identified and can be held responsible for their behavior can form stable, trusting, productive social structures.

Levy, Paul Allen. "Legal Perils and Legal Rights of Internet Speakers: An Outline with Citations." Public Citizen. Available online. URL: http://www.citizen.org/litigation/briefs/IntFreeSpch/articles.cfm?ID=6141. Downloaded on August 19, 2004. A detailed outline with links and citations covering such issues as First Amendment protections, jurisdiction (where someone can be sued), commercial speech, liability for third-party content, the right to speak anonymously, and use or infringement of trademarks.

Rainie, Lee, and Deborah Fallows. "The Impact of CAN-SPAM Legislation." Pew Internet & American Life Project. Available online. URL:
http://www.pewinternet.org/pdfs/PIP_Data_Memo_on_Spam.pdf.
Posted in March 2004. This survey reports what most e-mail users already
suspect: Federal antispam legislation has not appreciably reduced the flow
of unsolicited e-mail into mailboxes. About one-third of users say they
have reduced e-mail use because of having to struggle with spam; about
two-thirds say that spam has made them less trusting of e-mail in general.

"Searching and Seizing Computers and Obtaining Electronic Evidence in
Criminal Investigations." United States Department of Justice. Computer Crime and Intellectual Property Section. Available online. URL:
http://www.usdoj.gov/criminal/cybercrime/s&smanual2002.htm. Posted
in July 2002. Begins by describing the general legal requirements for
search and seizure of evidence, including such issues as expectation of privacy, content, warrant requirements and exceptions, and special circumstances for locations such as workplaces. It then discusses specific
strategies and provisions relating to computers, including the Electronic
Communications Privacy Act.

"Searching and Seizing Computers and Related Electronic Evidence Issues." United States Department of Justice. Computer Crime and Intellectual Property Section. Available online. URL: http://www.usdoj.gov/
criminal/cybercrime/searching.html. Updated on December 17, 2001.
Describes federal statutes and current legal issues and provides links to
relevant documents.

"When Is an ISP Liable for the Acts of Its Subscribers?" FindLaw. Available online. URL:http://cobrands.public.findlaw.com/internet/nolo/
ency/1902780E-68C9-436B-925AC37E42F4CD71.html. Posted in 2002.
Discusses circumstances in which an Internet service provider (ISP) may
be held liable for injurious actions by its users, such as copyright violations, libel, or cyberstalking. Under a provision of the Communications
Decency Act, an ISP is not considered the publisher of defamatory materials distributed through its service. The Digital Millennium Copyright
Act shields ISPs from liability for copyright violations provided they do
not have actual knowledge of the facts of the violation, act promptly to
remove violating material, and do not profit from the activity.

TECHNICAL THREATS, ISSUES, AND MEASURES

Books

Abraham, Spencer, editor. *Cybersquatting & Consumer Protection: Ensuring
Domain Name Integrity.* Collingdale, Pa.: DIANE Publishing, 1999. A
hearing before the Senate Committee on the Judiciary regarding the

practice of registering Internet domain names intended to be confused with those of legitimate businesses. This can often be a vehicle for fraud.

Denning, Dorothy E., and Peter J. Denning, editors. *Internet Besieged: Countering Cyberspace Scofflaws.* New York: ACM Press; Reading, Mass.: Addison-Wesley, 1998. Hacking and computer security are discussed from the point of view of designing and managing the infrastructure of the Internet. Topics include hacking techniques, system vulnerabilities, the use of cryptography to secure systems, the need to secure electronic commerce, and the supporting framework of law, public policy, and industry practices.

Furnell, Steven. *Cybercrime.* Boston, Mass.: Addison-Wesley Professional, 2001. Describes the evolution of criminal activity involving computers, with an emphasis on viruses, system intrusions, and other hacking activities. The changing role and perception of the hacker and the responses of government and the media are also covered.

Kruger, Lennard G. *Internet Domain Names: Background and Policy Issues.* Washington, D.C.: Congressional Research Service. updated April 22, 2003. Also available online. URL: http://lugar.senate.gov/CRS%20reports/ Internet_Domain_Names_Background_and_Policy_Issues.pdf. Updated April 22, 2003. Because of the misuse of Internet addresses by fraudsters (as in phishing,) this review of how the Internet domain name system is administered and the current laws affecting use of Internet addresses is useful for computer crime research. Recent proposed laws involving protecting children online and securing trademarks are also discussed.

Levy, Steven. *Hackers: Heroes of the Computer Revolution.* Updated Edition. New York: Penguin Putnam, 2001. This revised edition of an engaging narrative first published in 1984 shows how hacker culture developed in the 1960s as groups of brilliant if obsessed programmers in places such as the Massachusetts Institute of Technology and Stanford University pushed early minicomputers to their limits. Disdaining authority while both competing and sharing with one another, early hackers created essential software tools and are largely responsible for today's Linux and other open source software. Only later was the term *hacker* applied to persons who used computer knowledge for criminal purposes.

Lilley, Peter. *Dot.con.* Sterling Page, Va.: Kogan Page, 2002. A computer security investigator and consultant explains how computer systems are compromised and attacked and how viruses and other means can be used in electronic crime and fraud.

Mitnick, Kevin D., and William L. Simon. *The Art of Deception: Controlling the Human Element of Security.* Indianapolis, Ind.: Wiley Publishing, 2002. Mitnick, a notorious convicted hacker turned security consultant, explains the tools of his trade to security professionals and the public at large. Contrary to popular perception, the most effective techniques involve hacking the human mind, not the computer. Mitnick explains the many social engineering tactics he used to get people to willingly provide him with the information he needed to break into computer systems.

———. *The Art of Intrusion: The Real Stories behind the Exploits of Hackers, Intruders & Deceivers*. Indianapolis: Wiley, 2005. Mitnick expands upon his earlier *The Art of Deception* (which focused mainly on social engineering) with these vivid stories about how a variety of hackers and cybercriminals obtained access and sensitive information from many businesses and agencies. While avoiding giving exact recipes to would-be intruders, Mitnick provides enough detail to be able to clearly explain how and why the exploits succeeded, and follows up with good suggestions for improving security.

Mohay, George, et al. *Computer and Intrusion Forensics*. Boston: Artech House, 2003. An overview of the technical methods used for detecting and obtaining the indirect evidence left behind in cases of computer intrusion, fraud, espionage, and other crimes. There is also discussion of the relevant national and international legal frameworks.

Prosise, Chris, Kevin Mandia, and Matt Pepe. *Incident Response and Computer Forensics*. 2d ed. New York: McGraw Hill-Osborne, 2003. A detailed guide to how to recognize that a computer system has come under attack, including how to minimize damage while gathering evidence in a form that can be used for investigation and prosecution.

Schneier, Bruce. *Secrets and Lies: Digital Security in a Networked World*. New York: Wiley, 2000. The author suggests a multilevel defense for computer systems in hardware, software, and in proper training so employees will not be deceived by hackers and scammers. This serious book is written in a lively and sometimes humorous style.

Slatalla, Michelle, and Joshua Quittner. *Masters of Deception: The Gang That Ruled Cyberspace*. New York: HarperCollins, 1995. An entertaining account of the exploits of notorious hackers of the 1990s, including Mark Abene (also known as Phiber Optik). Feuds soon led to the Masters of Deception group splitting off from the Legion of Doom. Stolen account information and credit card numbers were prized trophies for proving one's hacking prowess.

Thomas, Douglas. *Hacker Culture*. Minneapolis: Minnesota University Press, 2002. Now more than 40 years old, hacker culture encompasses many positive elements such as curiosity, a sense of play, and the ability to get the most out of emerging technology. However, the fact that some hackers engage in information and identity theft and cyberstalking means that this multifaceted look at hackers and hacking is a valuable resource for persons dealing with cybercrime. The author suggests that hackers both resist and rearrange the dominant culture, and that the image of the hacker also reflects society's fear and anxiety about technology.

Verton, Dan. *The Hacker Diaries: Confessions of Teenage Hackers.* New York: McGraw Hill–Osborne, 2002. Despite its rather lurid title, this book provides an interesting and thoughtful look at the stories of a variety of bright if troubled young people who discovered the pleasures and perils of illicit exploration of computers. Although there is a certain amount of destructive pranks and cyber-vandalism, the stories suggest little in the way of real criminality.

Wolfe, Paul, Charlie Scott, and Mike Erwin. *Anti-Spam Tool Kit.* New York: Osborne, 2004. Provides detailed discussion of antispam filtering tools (including blacklists, keyword filters, and gateway solutions such as Brightmail). There are also more technical products that require knowledge of e-mail header structure and the sendmail program. Includes CD-ROM with a variety of software.

Articles and Papers

Armstrong, H. L., and P. J. Forde. "Internet Anonymity Practices in Computer Crime." *Information Management & Computer Security*, vol. 11, October 22, 2003, pp. 209–215. Considers the role that the ability to be anonymous plays in Internet crimes such as money laundering, drug dealing, hacking, fraud, and distribution of child pornography. Because anonymity gives criminals a considerable advantage both in cooperating with one another and in committing crimes, society must determine what restrictions should be placed upon it.

Cogar, Stephen. W. "Obtaining Admissible Evidence from Computers and Internet Service Providers." *FBI Law Enforcement Bulletin*, vol. 72, July 2003, pp. 11–15. Also available online. URL: http://www.fbi.gov/publications/leb/2003/july03leb.pdf. Because computers and the Internet have become ubiquitous, they are now sources of evidence for many types of crime, both high tech and conventional. The rapidly changing nature of computer and communications technology requires investigators to keep up with technical, legal, legislative, and procedural developments. The proper requirements mandated by the Fourth Amendment must be observed in a variety of circumstances: workplace computers, home computers, computers used by more than one person, and information held by Internet service providers.

Davis, Harold E., and Robert L. Braun. "Computer Fraud: Analyzing Perpetrators and Methods." *CPA Journal*, vol. 74, July 2004, pp. 56ff. A study breaks down the computer fraud scenarios in terms of whether the perpetrator is an authorized user and the type of alteration made to the system. Other characteristics of cases are summarized, such as average time between offense and charge and average prison sentence or fine. Effects of recent federal legislation are also summarized.

Donofrio, Andrew. "Identifying the Sender of an E-mail." *Law Enforcement Technology*, vol. 31, January 2004, pp. 62, 64–66. Explains how the routing information in e-mail headers is constructed and how to use software utilities to trace the origin of messages.

Grossman, Wendy M. "Anonymous Trust." *Scientific American*, vol. 291, August 2004, pp. 20ff. Describes a proposed computer security scheme called direct anonymous attestation (DAA), which would allow computers to verify that software was certified safe before running it, without allowing the computer to itself be identified or tracked by the certification authority. This would provide security without opening a privacy loophole.

Harrison, Warren, et al. "High-tech Forensics." *Communications of the ACM*, vol. 47, no. 7 (2004) pp. 48–52. Describes how an Oregon police department has enlisted technical experts to serve as police reserve specialists. Given the financial constraints on most police departments, this is an effective way for them to acquire the necessary help in investigating complex computer-related crimes.

Lee, Dan. "Anti-Spam Plan Forged By E-Mail Firms." *San Jose Mercury News*, June 23, 2004, p. 1A. Reports that a coalition of major Internet e-mail providers is proposing technological solutions to the torrent of unsolicited e-mail (spam) currently flooding users' mail boxes. The e-mail system would be revised so it would verify that messages are actually coming from the supposed sender. Mail from unidentified senders (which presumably includes most spam) would be refused.

———. "Cyber Defenses Are on the Way." *San Jose Mercury News*, August 23, 2004, p. 2E. Describes a new program being offered by Norton/Symantec that combines antivirus protection with filters to block spam and Internet fraud. Other vendors are expected to follow suit.

Mercer, Loren D. "Computer Forensics: Characteristics and Preservation of Digital Evidence." *FBI Law Enforcement Bulletin*, vol. 72, March 2003, pp. 28–32. Available online. URL: http://www.fbi.gov/publications/leb/2003/mar03leb.pdf. Describes the challenges of dealing with evidence that is intangible (numeric codes expressed electronically) and stored in media that is often vulnerable to disruption. Copies must be mathematically validated to prove that they are an accurate representation of the original.

Piscitello, David, and Stephen Kent. "The Sad and Increasingly Deplorable State of Internet Security." *Business Communications Review*, vol. 33, February 2003, pp. 49ff. The authors argue that despite the media hype about new investigative techniques, cybersleuths, and expanded law enforcement, overall security of computer systems is poor and may indeed be getting worse. The rate of incidents of computer break-ins and viruses as well as the financial losses from fraudulent access and theft of proprietary information continues to increase. Reasons for fundamental security problems include the priority given to ease of use over security in system design and marketing, lack of user awareness of basic vulnerabilities, lack of diversity in operating systems (meaning all security eggs are in one basket), poor software engineering practices, and sloppy management. Meanwhile, the industry emphasis is on developing products that detect and respond to attacks rather than redesigning the systems themselves.

Weintraub, Arlene. "Cyber Alert: Portrait of an Ex-Hacker: A Journey into the Mind of Kevin Mitnick Shows Just How Vulnerable Companies Are to Internet Crime." *Business Week,* June 9, 2003, p. 116. Notorious hacker Kevin Mitnick is out of prison and making a new career as a security consultant and author. Mitnick's reemergence (and the value of his extensive experience with social engineering deceptions used to obtain access and information) coincides with steady growth in the number of hacking incidents. However, the wisdom of hiring reformed hackers is questioned by some experts.

Web Documents

Anderson, Kent. "Criminal Threats to Business on the Internet: A White Paper." Archive of Information Security. Available online. URL: http://www.aracnet.com/~kea/Papers/White_Paper.shtml. Revised February 1, 1999. Although written at the end of the 1990s, this overview of computer security challenges to business remains sound and useful. Businesses face an environment characterized by rapidly growing connectivity, technological complexity and change, and an ever-shortening time to bring products to market. Information resources have often conflicting requirements for availability, confidentiality, and the preservation of integrity. When crime occurs, information technology professionals must often deal with news media that misunderstand or exaggerate the threat as well as law enforcement and security experts who spend little effort on understanding the unique characteristics of computer crime. A variety of possible threats and actors against information systems are identified and categorized.

———. "Managing the Cyber Threat." Network Risk Management LLC. Available online. URL: http://www.aracnet.com/~kea/Papers/Managing%20the%20Cyber%20Threat.pdf. Posted in 2004. Argues that the pervasive connection of information resources and networks has fundamentally changed relationships between businesses, partners, customers, and government. A high degree of employee mobility and rapid technological change have brought many new risks of fraud, theft, piracy, industrial espionage, and business disruption.

Annotated Bibliography

ONLINE FRAUDS AND SCAMS

INTRODUCTIONS, GENERAL DISCUSSION, AND EXAMPLES

Books

Baines, Gary. *Nigerian Scams Revisited.* Hauppauge, N.Y.: Nova Science Publishers, 2002. A fascinating look at the decades-old money letter scams originating in Nigeria and now prevalent in e-mail form. Several ways in which they appeal to victims are discussed, including pity for the poor and the implication that the victim is sophisticated and the perpetrator a hapless "native." Includes examples of real scam letters.

Mitnz, Anne P., editor. *Web of Deception: Misinformation on the Internet.* Medford, N.J.: Information Today, 2002. Scams and hoaxes are only part of the vast quantity of intentionally misleading or just erroneous information to be found online. This survey includes hoaxes, fake web sites, bad medical information, false advertising, investment schemes, privacy threats, charity scams, and sites providing dubious legal advice. The concluding chapters offer advice for evaluating web sites and search engines and for more effective search techniques.

Newman, Graeme R., and R. V. G. Clarke. *Superhighway Robbery: Preventing E-Commerce Crime.* Portland, Ore.: Willian Publishing/International Specialized Book Service, 2003. Applies the concepts of situational crime prevention to Internet-based crime. The basic approach is to look in careful detail at the types of transactions (or stages in transactions) that give criminals opportunities, and to find ways to discourage the criminal by making the crime harder to commit, less rewarding and/or more risky.

Swierczynski, Duane. *The Complete Idiot's Guide to Frauds, Scams, and Cons.* Indianapolis, Ind.: Alpha Books, 2002. A humorous but helpful guide to a variety of frauds and cons, including the ones burgeoning on the Internet. Describes how con artists work, five types of con artists, classic American cons, and more.

Thomes, James T. *Dotcons: Con Games, Fraud & Deceit on the Internet.* San Jose, Calif.: Writers Club Press, 2000. An introduction to privacy threats, identity theft, and a variety of frauds and scams in the online world. Includes suggestions for minimizing risk.

Articles and Papers

Carbonara, Peter. "The Kid & The Con Man." *Money,* vol. 30, March 1, 2001. Tells the story of Jonathan Lebed, a 15-year-old who used Internet message boards to tout penny stocks with false rumors, enabling him to later sell the stock for a profit. His connection with convicted stock swindler Ira Monas exacerbated his offense, but it is unclear whether he knew of Monas's background.

Foster, Ed. "Phony Lotteries, Domain Name Extortion May Be the Latest Internet Con." *InfoWorld*, vol. 23, January 8, 2001, p. 71. Reports on new forms of Internet fraud, including nonexistent lotteries used to harvest e-mail addresses and the son of a Nigerian ambassador who supposedly needs help in getting a large sum of money out of the country. Another scam threatens victims with Internet addresses too similar to their own.

Howell, Donna. "Internet Auctions Still Lead FTC's Fraud Complaints." *Investor's Business Daily*, January 26, 2004, p. A06. Law enforcement and industry officials highlight the prevalence of Internet auction fraud and the measures buyers can take to protect themselves, including checking a seller's reputation and using credit cards and/or escrow services.

Kirsner, Scott. "Catch Me If You Can." *Fast Company*, August 2003, pp. 72ff. An extensive profile of convicted Internet auction fraudster Jay Nelson. He was charged with defrauding more than 1,700 victims of more than $200,000. According to postal inspectors, Nelson failed to deliver computer parts won in auctions or provided defective parts or illegal copies of software. He also used fake identities to get around being banned from eBay and Yahoo! auctions as well as to generate bogus positive feedback ratings. He was pursued and eventually arrested through the persistent efforts of postal inspector Tom Higgins.

Mannix, Margaret. "Cashing In on Fear." *U.S. News & World Report*, vol. 31, December 3, 2001, pp. 36ff. The author reports that numerous scammers are selling bogus antianthrax drugs in the wake of the anthrax scare, as well as possibly counterfeit Cipro, a legitimate antibiotic that should only be used by people who have actually been exposed to the pathogen. Meanwhile, other scammers have been e-mailing fraudulent charitable appeals supposedly on behalf of the families of victims of the September 11, 2001, terrorist attacks.

Perron, Celeste. "Online Birth-Control Scams." *Cosmopolitan*, vol. 236, p. 258. What do you call a woman who buys prescription birth control drugs on the Internet? Sometimes, a mother. The FDA issued an alert after four web sites were caught selling fake, inactive contraceptive patches.

Rockstroh, Dennis. "Foreign Lottery Scams Part of Growing Industry." *San Jose Mercury News*, April 13, 2004, p. 3B. A columnist reports receiving an e-mail saying he had won $1.5 million in something called Mega Lottery International. The e-mail was a fraud, and anyway, it is illegal for U.S. citizens to participate in foreign lotteries.

Smith, Anne Kates, and Matt Popowsky. "What Were They Thinking?" *Kiplinger's Personal Finance*, vol. 56, April 2002, pp. 94ff. Amazingly, more than 1,000 investors lost more than $1 million total buying into a sports betting scheme that promised 200 or 250 percent returns. The alleged mastermind of this classic Ponzi or pyramid scheme was 17-year-old Cole Bartiromo, using the alias Tom Manning. (Bartiromo paid restitution but would later be convicted of several other types of Internet fraud.)

Taylor, Frances Grandy. "Internet Adoption Remains a Gray Area." *Hartford Courant,* January 30, 2001, n.p. Although some Internet adoption agencies are reputable, desperate seekers of adoptions are vulnerable to deceptive services or outright scams.

Wildstrom, Stephen H. "Software Scams on Internet Time." *Business Week,* September 30, 2002, p. 26. Warns people about e-mail ads that offer name-brand software products (such as from Symantec) at prices that are literally too good to be true. The software is likely counterfeit, and credit card numbers submitted at the linked sites are at best insecure and at worst become fodder for identity theft.

Woods, Lynn, and James Ramage. "When Online Bargains Turn Sour." *Kiplinger's Personal Finance Magazine,* vol. 53, July 1999, pp. 111ff. Tells the story of an online shopper who thought she had found a travel bargain—but when Sunscapes Travel took her money, they did not actually make her reservations. The article ends with warnings about danger signs and important advice for verifying that one is dealing with a reputable company.

Web Documents

"Amazon.com Teams with New York Attorney General to Combat Email Forgeries." Amazon Investor Relations. Available online. URL: http://phx.corporate-ir.net/phoenix.zhtml?c=97664&p=IROL-NewsText&t=Regular&id=443386&. Posted on August 26, 2003. Press release giving details on legal action that has been taken by Amazon.com to seek restraining orders against companies that have sent advertising e-mails purporting to come from addresses such as Amazon.com. The company also cooperated with the New York attorney general's office in obtaining a settlement against Cyebye.com, which agreed to refrain from such practices.

Block, Marylaine. "Lies, Damned Lies, and the Internet." Available online. URL: http://marylaine.com/lies.html. Posted on April 24, 2003. The author provides background, an overview, and various links relating to types of fraud and deception on the Internet. The author is a librarian, Internet trainer, and webmaster.

Cox, Beth. "PayPal Targeted by Scam Artists." Internetnews.com. Available online. URL: http://www.internetnews.com/ec-news/article.php/1470291. Posted on September 25, 2002. An early account of the appearance of e-mail phishing messages directed at PayPal users. The messages claim that the service has lost customer data during a computer changeover and asks the user to click on a link. The link is to a fake PayPal web site that captures the data entered by the user. The growing popularity of the online payment service has made it a major target for fraud.

"Credit Repair Scam Could Lead You to Commit Fraud." Quicken.com. Available online. URL: http://www.quicken.com/cms/viewers/article/banking/39349. Some credit repair services offer to wipe out a bad credit history. They suggest the client get a new employee identification number from the Social Security Administration and essentially build a new, clean credit record around that new identity. However this file segregation is illegal and can leave the client open to criminal fraud charges.

"Credit Repair: Self-Help May Be Best." Federal Trade Commission. Available online. URL: http://www.ftc.gov/bcp/conline/pubs/credit/repair.htm. Posted February 1998. Explains that many solicitations for credit repair services promise results that they do not deliver. Bad credit cannot be magically turned into good credit, but consumers can request their reports from the three major services and make sure incorrect information is removed.

"Gifting Clubs Are Pyramid Schemes!" Better Business Bureau. Available online. URL: http://www.bbb.org/alerts/article.asp?ID=528. Explains that so-called gifting clubs that have gone under names such as The Airplane or Jacobs Ladder are just pyramid schemes in disguise. Participants are promised that if they make a gift to join the network they will soon receive gifts from later participants.

Hutton, Shawn, and Ryan Brown. "Credit Card Fraud." National White Collar Crime Center. Available online. URL: http://www.nw3c.org (request from Web form). Posted in January 2003. Summarizes various types of credit card counterfeiting and fraud, including the role of the Internet and some recent cases and developments.

"IC3 Internet Fraud—Crime Report: January 1, 2004–December 31, 2004." National White Collar Crime Center and the Federal Bureau of Investigation. Available online. URL: http://www.ifccfbi.gov/strategy/2004_IC3Report.pdf. Posted in 2005. This annual report characterizes and summarizes Internet fraud complaints, including the type of activity, victim, and alleged perpetrator.

Kesterbaum, Lawrence. "Nigerian Fraud Email Gallery: A Rich Harvest of Criminal Creativity from My (and Others') Email." Available online. URL: http://potifos.com/fraud/ index.html. Updated in 2004. A large collection of Nigerian money letter scam e-mails as well as a brief description of how senders of such e-mails try to hook recipients.

Longley, Robert. "'Operation Cyber Sweep' Nabs Online Dirtbags." About.com. Available online. URL: http://usgovinfo.about.com/b/a/044925.htm. Posted November 21, 2003. Reports the results of an ongoing sting operation that netted more than 125 alleged perpetrators of online fraud, software piracy, and fencing of stolen goods. Several have already pleaded guilty, such as Albert Mayzels, who admitted to using stolen credit card numbers to purchase more than $80,000 in electronic equipment from online retailer Outpost.com.

"Phishing Attack Trends Report." Anti-Phishing Working Group. Available online. URL: http://www.antiphishing.org/APWG_Phishing_Attack_Report-Jun2004.pdf. Posted in June 2004. Summarizes recent trends in phishing (use of deceptive e-mail messages and web sites to obtain personal information). There were 1,422 unique phishing attacks in June 2004, and the number has been growing during the year at the rate of 52 percent per month. The report also notes the most targeted companies (Citibank, eBay, U.S. Bank, and PayPal lead the list).

Sinclair, Joseph. "Be Vigilant Against EBay Buyer Fraud." Wsj.com Startup Journal. Available online. URL: http://startup.wsj.com/runbusiness/bill collect/20040812-sinclair.html Downloaded on August 13, 2004. Most publicized cases of online auction fraud involve sellers who do not deliver the goods. However, sellers can also be preyed upon by unscrupulous buyers. Sellers have to make some difficult choices. Those who ship before checks clear or are verified are risking losses, but prompt shipping builds good feedback and repeat business. A suggested compromise is to wait for check clearance only on expensive items. Credit card risks include stolen numbers and unjustified chargebacks. Often there is little remedy.

"Special BBB Investigation Confirms: Work-At-Home Deals Are 'Too Good to Be True.'" Better Business Bureau (BBB). Available online. URL: http://www.bbb.org/alerts/article.asp?ID=405. Posted on October 12, 2000. Reports the findings of Operation Job Fraud, a joint effort of the BBB and the U.S. Postal Inspection Service. Typically, work-at-home schemes appeal to people who are desperately in need of money. Although the take per victim is relatively modest, the schemes can be quite profitable for their operators. In most schemes participants are given tasks that are impossible to complete to the standards demanded or depend on getting other people to join the scheme.

"Work-At-Home Schemes: Modern Twist to Old Scams." Better Business Bureau. Available online. URL: http://www.bbb.org/alerts/article.asp?ID=436. Posted on March 25, 2003. Begins by listing some general warning signs, such as exaggeration of profitability and requirement of upfront payments. Besides losing money, participants in work-at-home schemes are likely to lose many hours of their time and may end up in legal trouble. The different types of schemes are then summarized, including at-home assembly of products, chain letters, envelope stuffing, multilevel marketing, online business opportunities, and at-home processing of medical insurance claims.

REGULATION, INVESTIGATION, ENFORCEMENT, AND LEGAL ISSUES

Books

Collins, Susan, editor. *Securities Fraud on the Internet.* Collingwood, Pa.: DIANE Publishing Co., 1999. A hearing before the Senate Committee on Governmental Affairs highlights emerging forms of online securities fraud, including use of discussion forums and chat rooms, bogus newsletters, and mass e-mails. Witnesses also discuss prevention efforts and investor education.

De Bruin, Ronald. *Consumer Trust in Electronic Commerce: Time for Best Practice.* New York: Kluwer Law International, 2002. Sets forth a detailed legal and procedural framework for building consumer trust and confidence in e-commerce. Topics include disclosure of information to consumers, online contracts, secure electronic payment systems, dispute resolution, and applicable laws. The use of a combination of law, regulation, and technical means (such as cryptography) together can provide a secure environment.

Rustad, Michael L., and Cyrus Daftary. *E-Business Legal Handbook, 2003 Edition.* Gaithersburg, Md.: Aspen Law and Business, 2002. A detailed resource for persons interested in running a business online or in exploring Internet crime, liability, and other issues from a business point of view. Topics include security, privacy, protecting intellectual property, tort liability, jurisdictional questions, and developing legally safe e-mail and Internet usage policies.

Stearns, Cliff, editor. *On-Line Fraud & Crime: Are Consumers Safe?* Collingwood, Pa.: DIANE Publishing Co., 2001. Testimony from a hearing before the Senate Energy and Commerce Committee. Witnesses include representatives of the FBI, Federal Trade Commission, U.S. Secret Service, industry, and consumer groups.

Wells, Joseph T. *The Computer and Internet Fraud Manual.* Austin, Tex.: Obsidian Publishing, 2002. As the founder and CEO of the Association of Certified Fraud Examiners and a former FBI special agent, the author is well qualified to write and lecture on the detection and prevention of computer-related fraud. This handbook begins with an outline of the legal elements of fraud and the techniques used by computer criminals. The coverage then moves on to common computer fraud schemes, fraudulent use of e-mail, hacking, and e-commerce fraud. The final sections deal with the prevention, detection, investigation, and prosecution of computer fraud.

Articles and Papers

Carney, Dan. "Online Scambusters: A Team of Lawyers at the FTC Is on the Cutting Edge of Cybersleuthing." *Business Week*, April 3, 2000, p. 66.

Reports how Federal Trade Commission (FTC) sleuths are surfing the Web for scams and even creating their own fake get-rich-quick web site—users who click on the link receive a warning about their vulnerability to scams. However, critics say the FTC's civil enforcement is weak compared to the criminal sanctions available to the FBI.

Hansell, Saul. "Junk E-mail and Fraud are Focus of Attention." *New York Times*, August 25, 2004, p. C1. Reports that federal agencies have stepped up investigations of Internet fraud, particularly e-mail scams and phishing letters. Overall, the new federal legislation regulating spam has had little effect, but the law can help when targeting specific perpetrators. Still, it appears to be an uphill battle.

Kopytoff, Verne. "Agencies Crack Down on Cyberfraud: Operation Web Snare Results In Arrests, Convictions, Justice Department Reports." *San Francisco Chronicle*, August 27, 2004, pp. C1, C6. Reports on Operation Web Snare, to date the largest and most successful federal crackdown on Internet fraud. So far there have been 103 arrests and 53 convictions. The crimes investigated victimized more than 150,000 people for an estimated total loss of $215 million.

Lee, Jennifer B. "U.S. and States Join to Fight Internet-Auction Fraud." *The New York Times*, May 1, 2003, p. C4. The Federal Trade Commission and 33 state and local law enforcement agencies are coordinating a new effort against Internet auction fraud. Fifty-one civil and criminal cases have been filed. Techniques used by auction fraudsters have become more sophisticated and include setting up phony escrow and payment services. Identity theft is also used to set up fake accounts for buying or selling.

Walker, Richard, H., and David M. Levine. "'You've Got Jail': Current Trends in Civil and Criminal Enforcement of Internet Securities Fraud." *American Criminal Law Review*, vol. 38, Summer 2001, p. 405. Describes how the Internet has changed the way investors get information and make decisions and, in turn, how it challenges regulators and prosecutors to apply rules designed more than 50 years ago. The case of teenage pump-and-dump fraudster Jonathan Lebed is used as an illustration of the variety of criteria that must be applied in deciding which cases to pursue.

Web Documents

"Background on Operation Cyber Sweep—Examples of Prosecutions." U.S. Department of Justice. Available online. URL: http://www.usdoj.gov/opa/pr/2003/November/03_crm_639.htm. Posted on November 20, 2003. Gives numerous examples of cases brought under Operation Cyber Sweep. Charges include manufacture of counterfeit checks, fraudulently labeling computer memory modules, tampering with the web site of the Arabic media organization Al Jazeera, manufacture of counterfeit music CDs and cassette tapes, online auction fraud, and a variety of other offenses.

Cooper, Beth, and Rebecca Pringle. "Online Prescriptions: A Developing Convenience or Emerging Nightmare?" Georgia State University College of Law. Available online. URL: http://gsulaw.gsu.edu/lawand/papers/fa01/davis. Posted in Fall 2002. Discusses the risks and legal issues arising from the growing number of online pharmacies (legitimate or otherwise). The risks include mislabeled packaging, counterfeit drugs, and other forms of fraud. The global nature of the Internet makes it very difficult for regulatory agencies to establish jurisdiction and to pursue cases.

Dutrow, Kelli L., and Kathryn H. Wade. "Internet Adoption: How Much Is That Baby in the Window?" Georgia State University College of Law. Available online. URL: http://gsulaw.gsu.edu/lawand/papers/su01/dutrow_wade. Posted Summer 2001. This student paper discusses recent cases involving Internet-based child adoption fraud. After discussing the general legal background for adoption, the authors look at the advantages and problems of the Internet for facilitating adoption. On the plus side, the Internet can greatly increase the chances of children and prospective parents being matched up, including special needs children who are often hard to place. On the negative side, the Internet's relative anonymity and lack of personal contact can facilitate fraud, such as demanding money to help with a pregnancy that does not exist or offering the same child to multiple adoptive parents.

"'Operation Cure. All' Wages New Battle in Ongoing War Against Internet Health Fraud." Federal Trade Commission. Available online. URL: http://www.ftc.gov/opa/2001/06/cureall.htm. Posted on June 14, 2001. Describes a coordinated effort of the FTC and the Food and Drug Administration (FDA) to crack down on health-related Internet fraud and scams. Many of these offerings involve dietary supplements that have no scientific proof of effectiveness and that may also be dangerous. By diverting people from proper medical treatments for life-threatening conditions, the fraudsters may be endangering people's lives. A variety of specific fraudulent promotions are discussed.

TECHNICAL THREATS, ISSUES, AND MEASURES

Books

Bologna, G. Jack, and Paul Shaw. *Avoiding Cyber Fraud in Small Businesses: What Auditors and Owners Need to Know.* New York: Wiley, 2000. Most computer fraud is an inside job and, especially with most businesses on the Internet, computer intrusions and information theft threaten their survival. This book is intended to advise business owners of the scope and nature of the problem so they will allocate sufficient resources to keep it in check. The other audience is auditors who need the technical knowledge to ensure they properly fulfill their responsibilities.

Essinger, James. *Internet Trust.* Upper Saddle River, N.J.: Pearson Education, 2001. The author begins by noting that consumer trust and confidence is essential to the success of an online business. However, there is a fundamental problem: how to ensure that one is dealing with a trustworthy partner in a transaction or a trustworthy third party who can provide such assurance. A variety of technical and organizational solutions are discussed, including the use of certifications and digital signatures.

Articles and Papers

Hoffman, Karen Epper. "Vendors Take Aim at Online Crooks: Neural Nets Help Combat Payment Fraud." *Bank Technology News*, vol. 14, June 2001, p. 45. Describes a number of software systems that use various techniques to identify possibly fraudulent online orders. Neural networks learn which patterns of characteristics correlate with fraud, while programs can also consult a database of rules to determine whether a transaction should be accepted, rejected, or referred for human review.

Web Documents

"ATM Fraud: Banking on Your Money." MSNBC News. Available online. URL: http://msnbc.msn.com/id/3607110/. Posted on December 11, 2003. Surprisingly, just about anyone can buy an independent ATM and sign up with a banking network. Most people do this in order to earn the transaction fees, but enterprising crooks are attaching equipment to the ATMs to record the account and PIN numbers. They can then make their own unauthorized withdrawals.

Felten, Edward W., et al. "Web Spoofing: An Internet Con Game." Princeton University Computer Science Department. Available online. URL: http://www.cs.princeton.edu/sip/pub/spoofing.html. Downloaded on December 22, 2004. Describes a demonstration of spoofing wherein users enter a fake web site that looks identical to what they were expecting, but where every user action is monitored and controlled by the spoofer. The implications for fraud are obvious but disturbing.

"How Do You Deal with Internet Fraud?" Arcticsoft.com. Available online. URL: http://www.articsoft.com/wp_internet_fraud.htm. Updated February 2, 2003. This overview distinguishes between fraud that merely uses the Internet and fraud that specifically involves Internet technology. Fraud involving Internet domain names is being addressed by stricter registration rules. However, weaknesses in the infrastructure of the Internet and the secure sockets layer (SSL) used for online transactions are subtler and harder to deal with effectively.

"What Is Web Spoofing?" University of Washington Computing & Communications. Available online. URL: http://www.washington.edu/ computing/windows/issue22/spoofing.html. Posted Winter 1999. Gives tips for determining whether a web site in the browser may be spoofed. Sometimes the actual link that pops up under the cursor will be different from what it purports to be, but sophisticated spoofers can use programs to make them match.

EDUCATION AND ASSISTANCE

Books

Alt, Betty L., and Sandra K. Wells. *Fleecing Grandma and Grandpa: Protecting Against Scams, Cons and Frauds.* Westport, Conn.: Greenwood Press, 2004. Explains the special vulnerabilities of older people to telemarketing, on-line, and other frauds, and identity theft. Describes the types of scams most often encountered and discusses ways to prevent victimization.

Bryant, Gary Paul. *Searching the Web for Health: A Guide to Finding Reliable Medical Information on the Internet.* New York: iUniverse, 2004. The best antidote to deceptive information is probably cultivating connections to reliable sources of accurate information. This guide discusses specialized medical search engines, explains search techniques, and lists more than 400 recommended portals and sites.

Dvorak, John C., Chris Prillo and Wendy Taylor. *Online! The Book.* Upper Saddle River, N.J.: Prentice-Hall, 2003. Veteran personal computer pundit John C. Dvorak and his colleagues pack a huge amount of information into this guide to the many uses of the Internet. Many of the topics covered here bear directly on computer security and online safety, including dealing with spam, blocking viruses and hackers, and safely using features such as file-sharing.

Mendelsohn, Hillary. *The Purplebook 2005: The Definitive Guide to Exceptional Online Shopping.* New York: Bantam Books, 2004. One way to avoid online shopping frauds is to become familiar with good shopping sites and how they operate. This annual guide presents and evaluates "the best" sites in 19 different consumer categories, including art and collectibles, gadgets and electronics, health and beauty, and travel and outdoors.

Web Documents

Berland, Gretchen K., et al. "Evaluation of English and Spanish Health Information on the Internet." Rand Corporation for California HealthCare Foundation. Available online. URL: http://www.rand.org/publications/ documents/interneteval. Posted in 2001. Health-related Internet fraud is a common problem. This report provides a broader context by assessing the overall accuracy of health information provided on the Web. Focusing on four conditions (breast cancer, childhood asthma, depression, and obesity) and looking at materials posted in English and in Spanish, the study concluded that overall information is accurate but incomplete; information is usually provided in a promotional (commercial) context; and most information is presented in hard-to-understand language. Spanish-language materials tended to be less complete than those in English.

"Evaluating Web Resources: A Bibliography." Lister Hill Library of the Health Sciences, University of Alabama at Birmingham. Available online. URL: http://www.uab.edu/lister/evalnet.htm. Revised September 2002. While focusing on health-related sites, this bibliography and link guide also provides some general guidance for evaluating the credibility and accuracy of web sites. It includes sections on surveys of users' approach to health information; criteria for evaluating web sites; examples of spurious sites; sites that debunk health claims; medical search engines; and evaluation sites.

Fox, Susannah, and Lee Rainie. "Vital Decisions: How Internet Users Decide What Information to Trust When They or Their Loved Ones are Sick." Pew Internet & American Life. Available online. URL: http://www.pewinternet.org/pdfs/PIP_Vital_Decisions_May2002.pdf. Posted on May 22, 2002. Reports a survey on how users search for information about their or relatives' medical conditions. As of 2002 about 73 million American adults used the Internet to find information about medical conditions, prescription drugs, weight loss plans, and other health matters. The typical search begins with use of a search engine. Information that matches what is already known or is found in more than one site is more likely to be trusted. About a third of users verify information by asking their doctor. The report also includes search tips and recommended sites provided by the Medical Library Association.

"Internet Fraud." U.S. Dept. of Justice. Available online. URL: http://www.internetfraud.usdoj.gov. Downloaded on August 31, 2004. Answers questions such as: What is Internet fraud? What are the major types of Internet fraud? What is the Department of Justice doing about Internet fraud? How should I deal with Internet fraud? The document provides a good overview and some useful links.

"Internet Fraud: How to Avoid Internet Investment Scams." U.S. Securities and Exchange Commission (SEC). Available online. URL: http://www.sec.gov/investor/pubs/cyberfraud.htm. Updated November 15, 2001. Acknowledges that the Internet can be an excellent tool for investor research but points out a number of types of Internet investment scams. Some online investment newsletters purport to be independent but actually exist to tout specific investments, without making required disclosures. Various forms of newsgroups and chat rooms can also be used for touting and the spreading of dubious information. Spam is also a popular vehicle for investment fraud. The guide goes on to suggest questions that investors should ask about any company they are interested in, and to use the SEC's EDGAR database, which lists all major companies. Several specific types of fraud are discussed, such as pump and dump.

"Play It Safe on the Internet." Better Business Bureau. Available online. URL: http://www.bbb.org/alerts/article.asp?ID=471. Posted November 19, 2003. Provides basic advice for safe Internet shopping, including not divulging personal information, making sure a merchant web site is legitimate, and carefully monitoring one's credit record and account activity.

INFORMATION AND IDENTITY THEFT

INTRODUCTIONS, GENERAL DISCUSSION, AND EXAMPLES

Books

May, David A., and James E. Headley. *Identity Theft.* New York: Peter Lang, 2004. Discusses the nature of identity theft, its legal implications, and the framework for enforcement and prosecution through the criminal justice system. Discusses federal and existing state laws and offers a model state law.

Stana, Richard. *Identity Theft: Prevalence and Cost Appear to Be Growing.* Collingdale, Pa.: DIANE Publishing, 2002. Reports on the growing costs and impacts of identity theft to consumers, the financial services industry, and to e-commerce sites that are faced with loss of confidence in the safety of online business.

Sullivan, Bob. *Your Evil Twin: Behind the Identity Theft Epidemic.* New York: Wiley, 2004. Untangles the many causes of the current identity theft epidemic. The author uses stories of real-world victims and criminals to explain how identities are stolen and exploited. He then looks at how government agencies have been slow to respond to the challenge—for example, by ending the ubiquitous use of Social Security numbers and failing to make birth certificates and driver's licenses more secure. Meanwhile, law enforcement agencies have been slow to take identity theft complaints seriously. The private sector also comes in for criticism, particularly credit card companies who put easy credit ahead of security.

Welsh, Amanda. *The Identity Theft Protection Guide: Safeguard Your Family, Protect Your Privacy, Recover a Stolen Identity.* New York: St. Martin's Griffin,

2004. An up-to-date guide on how to reduce the risk of identity theft, what to do if one's identity is stolen, how to repair damaged credit, how to deal with telemarketers and scams, and much more. Each chapter includes a quiz to help readers identify their concerns and specific tips for taking action.

Articles and Papers

Arenson, Karen W. "Students' Data on Web, and N.Y.U. on Defensive." *New York Times,* January 10, 2004, p. B1. Students whose Social Security numbers were posted on a New York University web site and later posted elsewhere on the Internet by a whistle blower are angry and concerned about their vulnerability to identity theft. The university has apologized and claims that it has removed all such information from public access.

Barlas, Pete. "'Phisher' Con Artists Stepping Up Attacks; Shoppers Undaunted." *Investor's Business Daily,* May 28, 2004, p. A04. Reports on a survey showing an explosion in the amount of phishing (use of deceptive e-mail to trick users into revealing personal information). Services such as AOL, eBay, and PayPal are responding by creating databases of the bogus web sites that the e-mails link to and providing users with a toolbar and indicator of fraudulent sites.

Claburn, Thomas. "Payback for Hackers." *InformationWeek,* August 9, 2004, p. 14. Reports on hackers who admitted that they broke into computers at Lowe's home improvement stores to steal customer credit card numbers. One was convicted for wardriving, or driving with a laptop and scanning for open wireless networks.

Crooks, Ted. "Fear of ID Theft May Do More Harm Than the Crime." *American Banker,* vol. 169, May 27, 2004. The author suggests that excessive fear of a relatively small risk of identity theft is causing many consumers to avoid buying things online or using modern payment services. The results can be a costly drag on the economy. Financial institutions must use effective procedural and technical means to protect customers' identity and privacy.

Davis, Kristin. "Targeting Kids for Identity Theft." *Kiplinger's Personal Finance,* vol. 58, January 2004, p. 20. Today children get their own Social Security numbers shortly after birth. This means that they can also become targets of identity theft. In some cases the numbers may have been stolen from a doctor's office or hospital. In other cases an estranged or troubled family member may be the culprit. Some criminals prefer children's numbers because they allow them to build a new identity virtually from scratch.

Dutta, Sunil. "Identity Theft: A Crime of Modern Times." *World and I,* vol. 18, October 2003, p. 290. An excellent overview of identity theft— what it is, how it works, what happens to victims, and what people can do to minimize its incidence and impact. The author, a sergeant with the Los Angeles Police Department, admits that until recently most law enforcement agencies were somewhere between indifferent and suspicious when approached by victims.

Lemke, Tim. "Identity Thefts Linked to Providers." *The Washington Times*, June 25, 2004, p. C10. It is little known that the majority (70 percent) of cases of identity theft are perpetrated not by outsider hackers breaking into corporate databases but by insiders—employees who have legitimate access to the system. In June 2004 an America Online employee was accused of selling more than 90 million e-mail addresses to a spammer. In more serious cases thousands of Social Security or credit card numbers have been sold by insiders for criminal use.

Mihm, Stephen. "Dumpster Diving for Your Identity." *New York Times Magazine*, December 21, 2003, p. 42. This story begins with Stephen Massey, convicted leader of one of the largest identity theft rings ever prosecuted. After his release, Massey fled parole and may have hooked up again with thieves who search trash for information that computer-savvy criminals like Massey can use for fraudulent transactions. The details of how offline and online activities are meshed into a criminal money pipeline are explored in detail. Another fraudster profiled is Kari Melton, whose methods gradually became more esoteric and high-tech.

Smoloe, Jill, et al. "Tangled Web: Police Say an E-Savvy New York City Busboy Tried to Bilk Some of America's Richest Celebs through the Internet." *People Weekly*, vol. 55, April 2, 2001, pp. 75ff. The account of an alleged fraudster named Abraham Abdallah, who used the Internet to obtain identifying information about high-profile celebrities and then used them to obtain money through bogus financial transactions. After his arrest, police found detailed dossiers on targets as well as hundreds of fake credit cards and an embossing machine.

Tedeschi, Bob. "Growing Concern About Fraud Is Pushing the Online World into Action. The Task Looms Large, Though." *New York Times*, September 8, 2003, p. C9. Report on surveys show that consumers are becoming increasingly uneasy about online security. This is spurring groups such as the Information Technology Association of America, which is helping to create a Coalition on Online Identity Theft. But while credit card issuers and others agree about the need for consumer education, many may be reluctant to share information about security techniques that they believe to be proprietary.

Web Documents

"Federal Trade Commission—Identity Theft Survey Report." Federal Trade Commission; prepared by Synovate. Available online. URL: http://

www.ftc.gov/os/2003/09/synovatereport.pdf. September 2003. A survey with statistics on the incidence of identity theft and information misuse, types of identity crimes, and consequences to victims. The survey also found a strong correlation between early discovery of an identity theft and reduction of impact to the victim.

Germain, Jack. "Identity Theft Online: Debunking the Myths." Tech-NewsWorld. Available online. URL: http://www.technewsworld.com/ perl/story/32622.html. Posted on January 17, 2004. An analyst argues that, contrary to popular opinion, the increased use of the Internet for banking and paying bills has actually reduced the overall rate of identity theft. This is because most of the information obtained by identity thieves is from offline sources such as postal mail and garbage. By eliminating paper checks and other records, online banking and payment services make less private information available to thieves. Also, consumers who track their accounts online may detect unauthorized charges much more quickly than those who rely on mailed monthly statements.

"Identity Theft: The Aftermath 2003." Identity Theft Resource Center. Available online. URL: http://www.idtheftcenter.org/idaftermath.pdf. Posted in Summer 2003. A detailed further survey of identity theft victims identified in an earlier FTC survey draws some discouraging conclusions. On the average, although victims are learning of their situation sooner, it takes an average of 600 hours of work by a victim to deal with creditors or debt collectors and fully clear his or her records and identity. Law enforcement and financial institutions have generally not improved their sensitivity and helpfulness to victims. Numerous charts summarize the detailed findings.

"Latest ID Theft Scam: Fake Job Listings." CNN.com/Technology. Available online. URL: http://www.cnn.com/2003/TECH/internet/02/28/ monster.theft.ap/index.html. Posted on March 1, 2003. Reports that the prominent online job bulletin board Monster.com is warning millions of job seekers about fake job listings that are being used to steal personal information. Enticing job offers are accompanied by forms requesting the information. Other online job services have experienced similar scams.

Salkever, Alex. "'Phishing' Is Foul on the Net; This Rapidly Growing Type of E-mail Fraud Is Particularly Dangerous Because You're Lured into Revealing Valuable Personal Info." *Business Week Online*. Available online. URL: http://www.businessweek.com/technology/content/oct2003/ tc20031021_8711_tc047.htm. Posted on October 21, 2003. The growing sophistication of phishers is highlighted when an experienced executive with an antispam company is unable to tell whether an e-mail is legitimate. The phishing threat is growing in prevalence and impact. Phishers use a variety of psychological hooks to snag users.

"Site Clues Consumers into Identity Theft." *USA Today*. Available online. URL: http://www.usatoday.com/tech/2002/06/26/identity-theft-site.htm. Posted on June 26, 2002. Reports on the unveiling of the CardCops web site, which collects information about stolen credit cards from online chat rooms and creates a database that users can access to see whether their card number has been stolen.

REGULATION, INVESTIGATION, ENFORCEMENT, AND LEGAL ISSUES

Books

Collins, Susan, editor. *Phony IDs & Credentials via the Internet: An Emerging Problem*. Collingwood, Pa.: DIANE Publishing Co., 2000. Testimony from a Senate hearing on the use of counterfeit identification documents or credentials obtained using information on the Internet.

May, David A., and James E. Headley. *Identity Theft*. New York: Peter Lang, 2004. Describes the nature of the relatively new crime of identity theft and its current legal status. Includes a survey of cases and state laws as well as discussion of technical measures for fighting the growing problem.

Articles and Papers

"Battle Against Identity Theft Continues to Heat Up." *The America's Intelligence Wire*, July 8, 2004, n.p. Reports on legislative efforts to strengthen penalties for identity theft and to coordinate the fight against cybercriminals. There is also a discussion of new software that MasterCard is using to detect web sites that are being used for phishing and frauds. Another focus is the verification of address changes for credit cards and other accounts, since they are a key element in fraudulent diversion of funds.

Berwick, Isabel. "Customers Wilt under the Burden of Proof." *Financial Times*, May 22, 2004, p. 22. Tough British rules now require new bank customers to provide two different forms of identification to verify name and address. While it is touted as a way to stop money laundering and identity theft, many banks appear to be going to extremes, provoking frustration and anger from customers. The results suggest that poorly thought out or clumsily implemented security policies could do more harm than good.

Buxbaum, Peter A. "Nine-Digit Dilemma: Reacting to the Epidemic of Identity Theft, Some States Are Curbing the Use of the Social Security Number for Identifying Customers and Employees." *Computerworld*, vol. 37, October 13, 2003, pp. 41ff. Reports that in response to identity theft concerns, about a dozen states have banned or are considering banning the use of Social Security numbers for identification. However, banks and insurance companies still have to use the numbers in filing reports with the government. Designers of computer systems are struggling to find a way to reconcile the two requirements, such as by using separate external ID numbers or encrypting the Social Security numbers in the database.

Cancelada, Gregory. "Postal Inspector Cracks Down on Identity Thieves." *St. Louis Post-Dispatch*, March 8, 2004, p. C1. Describes how the little-known postal inspection service is cracking down on identity thieves, who now account for about two-thirds of the agency's arrests. The fact that such cases often involve multiple jurisdictions makes them particularly interesting and challenging.

"Feds Want Tougher Penalties for Insider Identity Theft." *InformationWeek*, May 24, 2004, n.p. Reports that new federal legislation enhancing penalties for identity theft will especially target persons who use their positions to misuse information entrusted to them. (The bill later passed as the Identity Theft Penalty Enhancement Act.)

Feldman, Judy. "Credit Tools." *Money*, vol. 33, February 2004, p. 35. Reports that Congress gave consumers new rights in amendments to the Fair Credit Reporting Act passed in 2003. Consumers are entitled to one free credit report per year from each of the three major services, plus free access to one's credit score when applying for a mortgage. Fees for other credit reports are also capped. However, some consumer advocates are unhappy because the federal law also preempts possibly stricter state laws.

Hulme, George V. "Bills Aim to Block Spyware." *InformationWeek*, June 24, 2004, p. 79. Describes pending California and federal legislation that would require users to give consent before hidden programs are installed on their computers. However, that consent, to be effective, would have to be clearly visible rather than being buried in a user license agreement. Existing provisions of the Computer Fraud and Abuse Act also provide ammunition for going after illegal spyware.

Lemke, Tim. "Penalties Stiffened for Identity Theft; New Law Gives Harshest Sentences to Terrorists, Corporate Insiders." *The Washington Times*, July 16, 2004, p. C11. Reports on President Bush's signing of the Identity Theft Penalty Enhancement Act. The law is intended to send a deterrent message to criminals who use identity theft, making it a separate criminal count with a penalty of up to two years in prison (five years if in conjunction with a terrorist act).

Marquis, Oscar. "Who Can Be Held Liable for Identity Theft." *American Banker*, vol. 168, November 18, 2003, p. 18A. Discusses cases in which credit agencies were sued by identity theft victims for not adequately screening fraudulent applications made in their name. Courts have generally held that these institutions have no relationship with card-holders that creates a "duty of care." However, growing pressure by victims and legislators may lead to passing laws that create such duties.

Oldenburg, Don. "Identity Theft Spurs Congress, States to Action." *Washington Post*, January 28, 2003, p. C10. Also available online. URL: http://www.washingtonpost.com/ac2/wp-dyn?pagename=article&contentId=A52575-2003Jan27&notFound=true. Reports on federal and state action to curb the growing menace of identity theft. Some states still use Social Security numbers as default driver's license numbers, but consumers fearing identity theft are demanding that states at least offer alternative numbers. Federal legislation would remove Social Security numbers from most public records, government checks, and so on. Meanwhile, California has passed a law allowing consumers to request that their credit records be locked from access except when released by the individual's request. Credit agencies seem reluctant to make the service available nationally, saying that it would be cumbersome and could block the legitimate use of credit.

Stoneman, Bill. "How One Small Bank Attacked Identity Theft." *American Banker*, vol. 168, November 18, 2003, p. 5A. Reports on how a small Georgia bank developed a low-tech but effective way to deter identity theft. When a customer gives his or her name to a teller, the person's authorized signature and photo appear on a screen for easy comparison. The bank also guards customer information by not giving it to third parties, not including unnecessary identifying information on correspondence, and providing shredders for customer convenience. The bank tries to educate customers through its web site and helps identity theft victims contact the appropriate authorities.

Vjayan, Jaikumar. "One Year Later, California Identity Theft Law Remains Low-Key." *Computerworld*, vol. 38, June 7, 2004, p. 7. When California passed its 2003 anti–identity theft law, there were concerns that certain provisions would cause trouble for online companies. For example, while the law specified that sensitive customer data be encrypted, it did not specify the type or level of encryption required. It was also unclear when customer notification had to be given. Despite that, there have been no lawsuits filed against these companies. Companies have been encouraged to act more responsibly in protecting customer data.

Web Documents

Frommer, Creighton K. "Corporate Identity Fraud: Spoofing and Phishing." Georgia State University College of Law. Available online. URL: http://gsulaw.gsu.edu/lawand/papers/fa03/frommer. Posted in Fall 2003. Provides a good overview of spoofing (creating fake web sites or

Internet addresses) and phishing, the practice of using such deceptions to trick people into revealing valuable personal information such as credit card numbers. Civil and criminal cases and applicable laws are also surveyed.

Gilbert, Satonja, and Tracy Harrison-Watkins. "SPAM: Survey of State and Federal Legislation." Georgia State University College of Law. Available online. URL: http://gsulaw.gsu.edu/lawand/papers/su01/gilbert_harrison. Posted on July 16, 2001. Although spam (unsolicited e-mail) is inherently more a nuisance than a threat, it can also serve as a vehicle for fraudulent and deceptive offers. This student paper provides an overview of federal and state laws relating to unsolicited e-mail, including opt-out provisions and those aimed specifically at e-mail fraud.

"Identity Theft Statutes." National Conference of State Legislatures. Available online. URL: http://www.ncsl.org/programs/lis/privacy/idt-statutes.htm. Updated in July 2003. Lists identity theft provisions by state, giving the statutory citation, title, and penalty specified.

Mark, Roy. "Anti-Spyware Bill Clears Committee Hurdle." Internetnews.com. Available online. URL: http://www.internetnews.com/security/article.php/3373041. Posted on June 24, 2004. Reports the continuing progress of antispyware legislation in Congress. The SPY Act would prohibit keystroke logging, computer hijacking, and displaying advertising windows that cannot be closed. The user must opt in before any information is collected or transmitted.

Rusch, Jonathan J. "Identity Theft: Fact and Fiction." CNet News.com. Available online. URL: http://news.com.com/2010-1071-958328.html. Posted on September 18, 2002. The author argues against pessimism about the ability of the law and law enforcement to go after identity thieves. A 1998 federal law gives prosecutors the ammunition to go after anyone who misuses another person's means of identification in connection with any federal, state, or local felony. What is needed, however, is greater general recognition of the nature and seriousness of identity theft and thus public cooperation in safeguarding information.

Schaefer, Stephen. "Identity Theft and the Internet." Georgia State University College of Law. Available online. URL: http://gsulaw.gsu.edu/lawand/papers/fa02/schaefer. Posted in Fall 2002. Provides a good overview of the nature of identity theft, example cases, and the technical means by which it is carried out. In addition to those techniques dealing specifically with identity theft, there are many others that can be applied to theft of information, violation of privacy, and intrusion or damage to computer systems.

TECHNICAL THREATS, ISSUES, AND MEASURES

Articles and Papers

Barlas, Pete. "Anti-Phishing Group Intends to Reel in Online Identity Thieves; Crooks Use Phony Sites; Yahoo!, eBay, Even FBI Have Been Impersonated by Internet Scam Artists." *Investor's Business Daily*, March 12, 2004, p. A04. Reports that the sudden surge in deceptive e-mails (phishing) is not only costing consumers money and peace of mind but also threatening the ability of companies to communicate legitimately by e-mail. The establishment of the Anti-Phishing Working Group, with more than 200 members, including EarthLink and Wells Fargo Bank, shows that this problem is now being taken seriously by major corporations.

Bergstein, Brian. "Freeze Can Help against ID Theft." *San Jose Mercury News*, August 1, 2004, p. 1F. Describes a little known but effective procedure called a security freeze. It blocks access to a consumer's credit information unless the consumer specifically allows it, virtually inoculating a person against identity theft. However, industry observers fear that widespread use of this measure could cause considerable delay and expense to businesses and consumers.

Glanz, William. "Thieves Target Online Bankers: Thieves Record Keystrokes of Online Bank Customers." *The Washington Times*, July 5, 2004, p. C13. In addition to the growing use of phishing e-mails, cybercriminals are now exploiting a flaw in the Internet Explorer software. It allows them to display pop-up ads that secretly record the user's keystrokes, including entry of account or credit card information.

Howell, Donna. "EBay First to Reel Out Tool to Fight Phishing Onslaught." *Investor's Business Daily*, August 16, 2004, p. A05. Describes eBay's new antiphishing browser toolbar. It uses Web Caller-ID technology from Whole Security to identify the source of e-mails. The software also looks for patterns (such as convoluted Web addresses, newly registered sites, and forms that ask for personal data).

Hulme, George V. "Net Faces New Attack." *InformationWeek*, June 28, 2004, p. 20. Describes a new form of system attack in which hacked web sites infect visitors' computers with Trojan horse programs that open surreptitious channels to intruders and keyloggers, which record users' keystrokes, including account numbers and passwords.

"It's Cloak and Dagger on Many Computers, As Spyware Emerges; Raises Identity Theft Worries." *Investor's Business Daily*, June 17, 2004, p. A04. Reports on a survey that found that about one in three computers contained some form of spyware that could be used for fraud or identity theft. While many items found by spyware detection programs are innocuous cookies used for advertising research, many of the computers were infected by Trojan spyware that could actually divert information being entered by the user, such as credit card numbers.

McDougall, Paul. "Laptop Theft Puts Customer Data at Risk." *InformationWeek*, March 29, 2004, p. 32. Sometimes identity theft risks arise from ordinary physical theft. In this case GMAC Insurance is reported to have had two laptop computers stolen. As a result, the company wrote to about 200,000 customers informing them that their personal data may have been compromised. This points to the need to keep all such data on central servers, not easily stolen laptops.

Pollock, John, and James May. "Authentication Technology: Identity Theft and Account Takeover" *FBI Law Enforcement Bulletin*, vol. 71, June 2002, pp. 1–5. Also available online. URL: http://www.fbi.gov/publications/leb/2002/june02leb.pdf. Law enforcement agencies have been urged to be more proactive and helpful to victims in identity theft cases. The use of increasingly stringent authentication devices can help fight this growing crime. For example, PIN numbers could be entered to authenticate check transactions, integrating this form of payment with the electronic funds transfer (EFT) network. PINs could also be used to authenticate online (electronic commerce) transactions, and biometrics (such as fingerprints) could be used in some cases.

Udell, Jon. "Ending E-Mail Forgery." *InfoWorld*, vol. 26, April 19, 2004, pp. 52ff. While online transactions are protected by encryption (SSL or secure socket layer) and software installation can use third-party certification, there is no comparable authentication for e-mail. This may change if a proposal called Reverse Mail Exchange is adopted. The receiving mail program would query a database to determine if the mail exchange (MX) record indicates that the sending mail host is authorized.

Web Documents

Connolly, Jennifer, Colleen O'Reilly, and Darin Beffin. "Credit Card Fraud Online." Duke University School of Public Policy. Available online. URL: http://www.pubpol.duke.edu/centers/dewitt/course/internet/fraud/ccfraud.html. Downloaded on August 29, 2004. Describes techniques used by criminal hackers and others to obtain credit card information and describes countermeasures by credit card companies.

Creek, Dinah. "Police Warn on Key-Logging Spam Trojan." ZDNet UK. Available online. URL: http://uk.news.yahoo.com/040813/175/f09pp.html. Posted on August 13, 2004. Describes a new multipurpose phishing and hacking tool. Users receive an e-mail message that appears to be an invoice for an order purported to have been made by the recipient. If the recipient then follows the provided link to a fake web site, code on the site downloads a Trojan program that installs itself and records the user's keystrokes, including account numbers and passwords used at online banking sites. The user's machine can also be set up as a remote-controlled zombie that can be used to send spam.

Edelman, Benjamin. "'Spyware': Research, Testing, Legislation, and Suits." Available online. URL: http://www.benedelman.org/spyware. The author, who claims to have researched spyware issues and served as an expert witness, provides an introduction and links to current issues, research, legislation, and litigation involving software that surreptitiously obtains and transmits user information.

Festa, Paul. "IE Bug Lets Fake Sites Look Real." CNet News.com. Available online. URL: http://news.com.com/2100-7355_3-5119440.html. Updated on December 10, 2003. Reports on the discovery of a flaw in Microsoft Internet Explorer that allows phishers to display the actual address of a legitimate company in the browser's address bar while taking the user to a fake site. (Microsoft complained that the bug should have been reported to them quietly in order to allow time for creating a patch to fix it.)

Landesman, Mary. "Cayam Worm Targets eBay Users." About.com. Available online. URL: http://antivirus.about.com/cs/allabout/a/cayam.htm. Posted December 16, 2003. Describes a computer worm that uses e-mail from hijacked systems to spread a phishing message that is used in turn to get account information from unwary users. The worm also spreads through disguised files on peer-to-peer file sharing service. A similar worm has targeted PayPal users.

Moulds, Richard. "Protection against Web Site Spoofing." Out-Law.com Available online. URL: http://www.out-law.com/php/page.php?page_id= protectionagainstw1078495924&area=news. Posted on May 3, 2004. A key ingredient in phishing scams is the spoofed web site that is made to look like the real site for the company in question. The author suggests that legitimate sites can fight spoofing by not keeping online the private keys used to authenticate their digital certificates. Meanwhile, certification agencies such as VeriSign are beefing up their cryptographic protection.

EDUCATION AND ASSISTANCE

Books

Collins, Judith, and Sandra K. Hoffman. *Identity Theft—First Responder Manual for Criminal Justice Professionals, Police, Attorneys & Judges.* Flushing, N.Y.: Looseleaf Law Publications, 2003. Identity theft has been exacerbated by the inability of law enforcement and legal professionals to help identity theft victims. This handbook provides materials for training professionals to understand and properly respond to identity theft cases.

———. *Identity Theft Victims' Assistance Guide*. Flushing, N.Y.: Looseleaf Law Publications, 2003. Provides detailed, step-by-step instructions for helping identity theft victims restore their identity and credit. Topics include fixing credit and bank records and disentangling motor vehicle department and IRS records from the effects of the fraud.

Gertler, Eric. *Prying Eyes: Protect Your Privacy from People Who Sell to You, Snoop on You, or Steal from You*. New York: Random House Reference, 2004. Takes a broader view of the identity theft problem by offering ways to protect one's privacy, including controlling the use of one's Social Security number and restricting access to one's credit report. There is also a section on privacy intrusions in the workplace and background on the constitutional and legal issues surrounding privacy.

Articles and Papers

Dolan, Ken, and Dari Dolan. "New Strategies for Preventing Identity Theft." *The America's Intelligence Wire*, May 25, 2004, n.p. Two anchors for the CNN Financial Network discuss identity theft with researcher Jim Van Dyke. According to Van Dyke, studies show that stolen paper records (such as mail) are a much bigger source of identity theft problems than the Internet. Shredding can help, but that assumes the mail gets to its intended recipient in the first place. It is best to pay bills online through secure web sites. The strategy for dealing with identity theft has three parts: prevention, detection of suspicious activity, and resolution (clearing up records and credit).

Katzeff, Paul. "Protect Yourself from Identity Theft: ID Theft Is Increasing, Failure to Safeguard Your Financial Information Can Be Costly, Infuriating." *Investor's Business Daily*, July 19, 2004, p. A13. Provides succinct advice on what to do if victimized by identity theft and how to minimize risk and losses in the future. For example, credit rather than debit cards should be used for online transactions because credit cards have a $50 loss limit.

Lippert, Barbara. "Look Who's Talking: Fallon Turns Identity Theft into Entertainment for Citibank." *ADWEEK*, vol. 44, November 24, 2003. Describes the striking television ads in which identity theft is portrayed by a jarringly incongruous voice emerging from the onscreen character. "'Firewall?' she says, laughing in a horrific male voice. 'Like that could stop me! Once I got her account number, I couldn't spend it fast enough: 64-inch plasma-screen monitor, 10 4.2-megahertz wireless routers and

20,000 bucks to complete my robot. My girl robot. This is gonna be the best prom ever!'" The ads promote Citibank's identity theft protection program.

Milne, George R. "How Well Do Consumers Protect Themselves from Identity Theft?" *Journal of Consumer Affairs*, vol. 37, Winter 2003, pp. 388ff. This study assesses and compares behaviors that tend to increase or decrease the risk of identity theft. A population of students is compared to a population of nonstudents. Both groups have high compliance to some security procedures (such as not carrying PIN numbers or passwords and shredding credit card offers before throwing them in the trash). However, other measures, such as regularly checking credit reports and statements, need to be reinforced.

Web Documents

"Are the Businesses You Frequent or Work For Exposing You to an Identity Thief?" Privacy Rights Clearinghouse and Identity Theft Resource Center. Available online. URL: http://www.privacyrights.org/itrc-quiz2.htm. Downloaded on December 23, 2004. A self-scoring quiz that lists problematic practices of businesses with regard to personal information about employees, such as inappropriate uses of Social Security numbers.

"Are You at Risk for Identity Theft? Test Your 'Identity Quotient.'" Privacy Rights Clearinghouse. Available online. URL: http://www.privacyrights. org/ITquiz-interactive.htm. Updated in July 2003. An interactive questionnaire that assesses respondents' risk of identity theft.

"Consumer Advice: How to Avoid Phishing Scams." Anti-Phishing Working Group. Available online. URL: http://www.antiphishing.org/consumer_ recs.html. Downloaded on August 30, 2004. Gives tips for identifying phishing messages and cautions users to avoid following web site links in e-mail or filling out forms within the e-mail or at an unverified web site.

"Consumer Advice: What to Do If You've Given Out Your Personal Financial Information." Anti-Phishing Working Group. Available online. URL: http://www.antiphishing.org/consumer_recs2.htm. Downloaded on August 30, 2004. Gives users suggestions about what to do and whom to contact if they have been hooked by a phish message or otherwise compromised their computer system. Situations covered include users having disclosed credit or debit card numbers, bank account or eBay account numbers, or Social Security numbers. There are also suggestions for dealing with exposure to viruses or spyware that might steal personal information.

"For Parents: Keeping Kids Privacy-Safe Online." Consumer PrivacyGuide.org. Available online. URL: http://www.consumerprivacyguide.

org/kids/forparents.shtml. Downloaded on August 31, 2004. Helps parents understand the danger of children giving out personal information online and provides tips from the Federal Trade Commission, including how to identify and parse a web site's privacy policy.

"The MailFrontier Phishing IQ Test." MailFrontier.com. Available online. URL: http://survey.mailfrontier.com/survey/quiztest.html. Downloaded December 23, 2004. This quiz presents users with a series of e-mails and asks them to decide whether they are legitimate or bogus. Users will thus assess their vulnerability to phishing e-mail and get practice in identifying it.

"Preventing, Detecting and Correcting Identity Theft." Better Business Bureau. Available online. URL: http://www.newyork.bbb.org/identitytheft/index.html. Downloaded on August 28, 2004. A detailed consumer guide to identity theft: what it is and the latest scams (including services that purport to prevent identity theft!). There are resource links, suggestions for prevention, detection of problems, and what to do if one becomes a victim.

"Tips for Privacy-smart Kids!" Consumer Privacy Guide.org. Available online. URL: http://www.consumerprivacyguide.org/kids/forkids.shtml. Downloaded on August 30, 2004. In kid-friendly language, this page provides brief tips for avoiding giving too much information online. It notes that "Just like in the schoolyard, at the store or on the telephone, kids need to be careful about who they give information to."

ONLINE STALKING AND HARASSMENT

INTRODUCTIONS, GENERAL DISCUSSION, AND EXAMPLES

Books

Bocij, Paul. *Cyberstalking: Harassment in the Internet Age and How to Protect Your Family.* Westport, Conn.: Praeger, 2004. Although the title makes this sound like a how-to book aimed at the popular market, it is actually academic in tone and its assertions are buttressed by many excerpts from and summaries of studies. Subjects include the definition of cyberstalking and how it differs from physical stalking; the incidence and prevalence of cyberstalking; the characterization and motives of cyberstalkers; the victims of cyberstalking; threats to young people; and legal and law enforcement aspects of the problem.

Douglas, John E. *Anyone You Want Me to Be: A True Story of Sex and Death on the Internet.* New York: Simon & Schuster, 2004. The author, an FBI profiler, traces the lurid career of John Robinson, who went from obscurity to become known as the Slavemaster, a notorious rapist and murderer who trolled the Web for victims. He eventually was convicted for or pleaded guilty to six murders of women.

Meloy, J. Reid, editor. *The Psychology of Stalking: Clinical and Forensic Perspectives.* San Diego, Calif.: Academic Press, 2001. A definitive collection of contemporary psychological perspectives on stalkers and stalking, including legal and forensic aspects. The psychopathology of stalking is explored, as are the relationship to domestic violence and obsessive love interests (erotomania). There is also specific material on cyberstalking.

Mullen, Paul E., Michelle Pathe, and Rosemary Purcell. *Stalkers and Their Victims.* New York: Cambridge University Press, 2000. Most accessible to professionals or students with some background in psychology, this detailed handbook explains how stalking has been defined as a specific set of behaviors, types of stalking, and ways to help victims both psychologically and legally. Current theories and methodologies are also discussed.

Articles and Papers

Adam, Alison. "Cyberstalking and Internet Pornography: Gender and the Gaze." *Ethics and Information Technology*, vol. 4, issue 2 (2002), pp. 133–42. Applies feminist theory to the phenomena of cyberstalking and the presentation of online pornography. The two concepts are privacy and its invasion through the gaze in a context of gender conflict.

"Beware of Cyberstalking—The Latest Workplace Threat." *HR Focus*, vol. 77, April 2000, p. S3. As part of a special report on workplace violence, editors look at the growing threat of cyberstalking in the workplace. Typical characteristics are explained along with a list of preventive steps.

Finn, Jerry. "A Survey of Online Harassment at a University Campus." *Journal of Interpersonal Violence*, vol. 19, April 2004, pp. 468ff. Of students surveyed at the University of New Hampshire, as many as 15 percent reported receiving repeated e-mail or instant messages that "threatened, insulted, or harassed." Generally, there was no difference in the rate of such harassment among demographic groups, except that members of sexual minorities were more likely to be victimized.

Koch, Lewis Z. "Open Sources: Cyberstalking Hype." *Inter@ctive Week*, vol. 7, May 29, 2000, p. 28. Argues that cyberstalking is a rather rare crime that has been excessively hyped by the media. The studies quoted by the media have generally used very broad characterizations of stalking that yield inflated numbers.

Lichtblau, Eric. "Neo-Nazi Must Pay $1.1 Million to Activist." *Los Angeles Times*, July 21, 2000. Reports on the judgment against a white supremacist who used his web site to threaten a fair-housing activist with lynching. This is probably one of the largest amounts ever awarded for Internet-based threats.

Rich, Laura. "Click Here for Revenge." *Cosmopolitan,* vol. 228, May 2000, p. 252. A woman surfing the Web discovers that someone had created a fake site showing her naked in a digitally faked sexual position. There are an endless number of ways that someone who wants revenge for a real or imagined slight can use the Internet, as shown in this and other examples. However, it can get out of hand and become cyberstalking.

Spitzberg, B. H., and G. Hobbler. "Cyberstalking and the Technologies of Interpersonal Terrorism." *New Media & Society,* vol. 4, March 2002, pp. 71–92. Summarizes the first sociological research on cyberstalking, finding that there is a significant incidence of the phenomenon. There are relationships between cyberstalking and physical stalking patterns.

Tavani, Herman T., and Frances S. Grodzinsky. "Cyberstalking, Personal Privacy, and Moral Responsibility." *Ethics and Information Technology,* vol. 4, issue 2 (2002), pp. 123–32. Discusses cyberstalking cases (especially the murder of Amy Boyer by Liam Youens) in terms of three issues: the threat to privacy through unrestricted access to personal information, the moral and legal responsibilities of Internet service providers, and the responsibility of users to inform persons they discover to be the target of cyberstalkers.

Wood, Robert A., and Non L. Wood. "Stalking the Stalker." *FBI Law Enforcement Bulletin,* vol. 71, December 2002, pp. 1–10. An introduction to stalking including incidence statistics, characteristics of stalkers, motivations and factors that make it cease.

Web Documents

Armistead, Cynthia. "Avoiding Internet Harassment." TechnoMom's Place. Available online. URL: http://www.technomom.com/writing/avoid1. html. Updated on May 10, 2001. First of a three-part article on strategies for avoiding or minimizing harassment in chat rooms, instant messaging, and message forums. Possible techniques include the use of anonymizer sites to hide one's identity and to seek forums that are moderated or otherwise known to enforce a high degree of civility.

———. "Privacy, the Net and You." TechnoMom's Place. Available online. URL: http://www.technomom.com/writing/privacy.html. Updated on February 18, 2003. As the author points out from her and others' experiences, one way to minimize the risk of being stalked online is to preserve the privacy of one's personal information and associations. Posting information about unusual or controversial interests (such as paganism) or experiences (such as being a survivor of child sexual abuse) can open one up to harassment by people who are triggered by such topics. It is also a good idea to not identify one's employer in connection with potentially controversial postings.

Fullerton, Barbara. "CyberAge Stalking." LLRX.com. Available online. URL: http://www.llrx.com/features/cyberstalking.htm. Posted on December 22, 2003. A legal librarian provides an overview of cyberstalking with particular attention to legal aspects, including federal and state laws and cases. The article concludes with some practical advice on computer protection and dealing with potential stalkers.

Gribben, Mark. "John E. Robinson: The Slavemaster." Court TV's Crime Library. Available online. URL: http://www.crimelibrary.com/serial_killers/predators/john_robinson/2.html?sect=2. Downloaded on August 13, 2004. Tells the rather gruesome story of the sadomasochistic murderer who is often considered to be the first serial killer to find his victims via the Internet.

Hutton, Shawn, and Sandy Haantz. "Cyberstalking." National White Collar Crime Center. Available online. URL: http://www.nw3c.org (request through Web form). Describes how cyberstalking happens, characteristics and profile of perpetrators, and groups most victimized. Several cases are summarized and responses by law enforcement and online service providers are discussed.

Lyman, Jay. "When E-mail Threats Become Real." NewsFactor.com. Available online. URL: http://www.newsfactor.com/perl/story/8252.html. E-mail threats should be taken seriously when they are specific, according to an FBI spokesperson. On the other hand, some threats may not be serious, and overreaction to legally protected speech may be a problem. Opening better communication channels may help.

"Overview of Cyberstalking." Cyber-Stalking.net. Available online. URL: http://www.cyber-stalking.net/about_cyberstalking.htm. Downloaded December 23, 2004. Discusses varying definitions and characteristic behaviors. Online kooks and trolls and their harassing or annoying behavior may be similar to stalking but is usually not obsessively focused on a particular individual.

Petherick, Wayne. "Cyberstalking: Obsessional Pursuit and the Digital Criminal." Court TV's Crime Crime Library. Available online. URL: http://www.crimelibrary.com/criminology/cyberstalking. Downloaded on August 13, 2004. An accessible but detailed summary of the legal classification, typology, pathology, incidence, and other aspects of cyberstalking. Includes useful references to professional literature and other sources.

Spertus, Ellen. "Social and Technical Means for Fighting On-Line Harassment." MIT Artificial Intelligence Laboratory. Available online. URL: http://www.ai.mit.edu/people/ellens/Gender/glc. Posted on May 5, 1996.

Although this paper focuses on harassment in newsgroups rather than more recent venues such as chat rooms, it provides a useful perspective focusing on the experiences of women who have faced on-line harassment. The author concludes that while there are useful technical measures (such as moderated mailing lists and newsgroups as well as filtering programs), one of the most valuable tools for fighting harassment may be the use of freedom of speech. Victims can exercise choice in not reading unwelcome material, but they can also use their own speech to expose and perhaps embarrass their harassers.

REGULATION, INVESTIGATION, ENFORCEMENT, AND LEGAL ISSUES

Books

Collins, Matthew. *The Law of Defamation and the Internet.* New York: Oxford University Press, 2001. Discusses the principles and case law for publication of defamatory material on the Internet. Focuses on Australian and British law but includes comparative case law from the United States.

Davis, Joseph A. *Stalking Crimes and Victim Protection: Intervention, Threat Assessment, and Case Management.* Boca Raton, Fla.: CRC Press, 2001. A comprehensive collection of studies and research on the best techniques for law enforcement and other professionals dealing with stalking situations. Includes a training manual used by the San Diego Stalking Strike Force.

Kamir, Orit. *Every Breath You Take: Stalking Narratives and the Law.* Ann Arbor: University of Michigan Press, 2001. This unusual approach looks at the archetype of the stalker and stalking as portrayed in mythology and literature (including vampires, Frankenstein's monster, Jekyll and Hyde, and other monsters of 19th century horror fiction) as well as modern movies such as *Halloween.* The author argues that stalking narratives reinforce traditional gender roles and that modern stalking laws represent a moral panic. The mythologization and dehumanization of the stalker prevents proper response to the actual social phenomenon.

McCollum, Bill, editor. *Violence Against Women Act of 1999, Stalking Prevention & Victim Protection Act of 1999.* Collingwood, Pa.: DIANE Publishing Co., 1999. This hearing before the House Committee on the Judiciary contains testimony from a number of experts and advocates, including Jayne Hitchcock, a writer and victim of Internet stalking.

Articles and Papers

Ardito, Stephanie C. "Information Brokers and Cyberstalking." *Information Today*, vol. 20, May 2003, pp. 17ff. Discusses a New Hampshire Supreme

Court ruling that information brokers must exercise reasonable care in ensuring that the information sought by clients is not intended to be used for stalking. The case arose from the cyberstalking murder of Amy Boyer.

Costlow, Terry. "As Stalkers Go Online, New State Laws Try to Catch Up." *Christian Science Monitor,* September 3, 2002, p. 2. Up to 100 cases of cyberstalking are now being reported each week. Arrests have been rare so far, but one of the first cases has reached a Chicago courtroom. It involves e-mailed death threats. However, law enforcement agencies often do not understand the significance of online stalking or how to apply the law to it.

D'Ovidio, Robert, and James Doyle. "A Study on Cyberstalking: Understanding Investigative Hurdles." *The FBI Law Enforcement Bulletin,* vol. 72, March 2003, p. 10 ff. Also available online. URL: http://www.fbi.gov/publications/leb/2003/mar03leb.pdf. This study analyzes the resolution of computer-related stalking complaints by the New York City Police Department's Computer Technology and Investigation Unit. About 40 percent of the cases investigated resulted in an arrest. About 80 percent of offenders were male, and their average age was 24. E-mail and instant messaging were the most commonly used methods for communicating the harassing messages. The study identifies a number of barriers faced by investigators, including jurisdictional issues, the need for cooperation between agencies, difficulty in obtaining records from service providers that would link messages and offenders, and the use of anonymizing tools to conceal the real origin of messages.

Hitchcock, Jayne A. "Cyberstalking and Law Enforcement." *Police Chief,* vol. 70, December 2003, pp. 16–26. An introduction to cyberstalking from the point of view of law enforcement officers. Defines the crime and uses a sample case to show the danger to the victim and the difficulties involved in prosecution. For successful prosecution, investigators must establish means, specific victim, intent, and transmission or communication. Several typical types of cyberstalking behavior are described, including the perpetrator misusing electronic greeting card services or sending virus-laden e-mail. Basic procedures and techniques for investigators are also outlined, as are available resources for law enforcers and the public.

Jordan, Carol E., et al. "Stalking: Cultural, Clinical and Legal Considerations." *Brandeis Law Journal,* vol. 38, 1999–2000, pp. 513–79. This detailed examination of the crime of stalking puts the legal construction in the broader context of popular understanding of stalking, which has been greatly informed by portrayals in movies and literature.

Lamplugh, Diana, and Paul Infield. "Harmonising Anti-Stalking Laws." *The George Washington International Law Review,* vol. 34, Winter 2003, pp. 853–70. The authors believe that because stalking and cyberstalking cases sometimes involve more than one country, it is important that laws are consistent in what behavior they define as criminal.

Annotated Bibliography

Myers, R. "Anti-stalking Statutes." *Crime Victims Report*, vol. 2, 1998, pp. 67–79. Reviews state stalking laws, identifying particularly how offenders are treated after first and subsequent offenses and mental health evaluation and treatment for stalkers.

Radcliff, Deborah. "A Case of Cyberstalking: Law Enforcement Agencies Appear Powerless to Stop Electronic Harassment." *Network World*, May 29, 2000, p. 56. The author introduces a case in which a fired employee harassed a newspaper executive by impersonating him in chat rooms and signing him up for bogus subscriptions and orders. Police, attorneys, and computer forensic experts are asked for advice for cyberstalking victims. Because police consider nonviolent cyberstalking to be just a nuisance misdemeanor, they seldom investigate. Victims are often obliged to hire private investigators in hopes of finding evidence of a more serious crime or consider civil action.

Vudhiwat, Cristina. "Developing Threats: Cyberstalking and the Criminal Justice System." *Crime & Justice International*, vol. 18, September 2002, pp. 9–10, 28–29. Focuses on the legal challenges involved in prosecuting cyberstalkers. Victims are often women or children, who may be less likely to be experienced in online interaction. The traditional restraining order is often useless because of the ability of cyberstalker to remain anonymous. There is also the need of prosecutors to prove that a credible threat has been made; in less than half of cyberstalking incidents do victims report that the perpetrator directly threatened them. Legislators should focus on the effect of the action on the victim rather than the offender's specific intent or the presence of a credible threat.

Wallace, H., and K. Kelty. "Stalking and Restraining Orders: A Legal and Psychological Perspective." *Journal of Crime and Justice*, vol. 18, 1995, pp. 99–111. The authors give an overview of stalking, including psychological typology. They then evaluate the advantages and disadvantages of victims seeking restraining orders. (Orders may deter some stalkers, and violation may provide for further legal action. However, in some cases the order may enrage the stalker and lead to a greater likelihood of violence.)

Woodall, Martha. "National Conference Tackles the Growing Problem of Cyberstalking." *Knight/Ridder/Tribune News Service*, March 31, 2000, p. K7523. A conference at the University of Pennsylvania is trying to tackle cyberstalking, a problem that only an estimated 5 percent of police departments can handle. Statistics and surveys suggest a significant number of victims, mainly women.

Web Documents

"The Amy Boyer Case: Remsburg v. Docusearch." *Electronic Privacy Information Center.* Available online. URL: http://www.epic.org/privacy/boyer.

Updated on February 24, 2003. Describes a case arising from the estate of cyberstalking victim Amy Boyer. The New Hampshire Supreme Court ruled that information brokers and private investigators can be held liable if they do not take reasonable measures to ensure that data being requested is not to be used for stalking or harassment.

Haley, Jacqueline. "Anonymity of Cyberstalkers: The Cyber-Watchdog's Tough Collar." Georgia State University College of Law. Available online. URL: http://gsulaw.gsu.edu/lawand/papers/su01/haleyj. Posted Summer 2001. This student paper explores the difficulties of identifying a cyberstalker when the Internet provides a variety of means to disguise identity, including the use of multiple accounts or screen names and e-mail remailers that strip identifying information from e-mails before delivery.

Howard, Lauren. "Special Unit Created for Cyber Victims." *Leaf-Chronicle* (Clarksville, Tenn.). Available online. URL: http://www.theleafchronicle. com/news/stories/20040810/localnews/1013949.html. Posted August 10, 2004. Reports that Montgomery County in Tennessee has started what appears to be the nation's first Special Victims Unit focusing on cyberstalking and related assaults and sex crimes. The three-year pilot program is funded by a federal grant.

"How to Get a Protective Order." Aardvarc ("An Abuse, Rape, Domestic Violence And Resource Collection.") Available online. URL: http://www. aardvarc.org/dv/orders.shtml. Downloaded on August 28, 2004. Explains the general procedure for obtaining a protective or restraining order against a stalker or abuser, including how to get a permanent order. While directed primarily to women who are victims of domestic abuse, the procedures are basically the same for any victim of stalking or abuse.

Lee, Craig and Patrick Lynch. *Cyberstalking—Is It Covered by Current Anti-Stalking Laws?* Available online. URL: http://gsulaw.gsu.edu/lawand/ papers/su98/cyberstalking. Downloaded on August 11, 2004. Discusses the status of federal and state antistalking statutes as of the late 1990s. Stalking as a distinct crime emerged only in 1990, and there have been difficulties in defining stalking as a pattern of behavior in such a way as to distinguish it from constitutionally protected behaviors. Federal antistalking statutes are limited by the need to prove an actual threat.

Medlin, Amanda N. "Stalking to Cyberstalking: A Problem Caused by the Internet." Georgia State University College of Law. Available online. URL: http://gsulaw.gsu.edu/lawand/papers/fa02. Posted in December 2002. Discusses the current legal status of cyberstalking (many states have laws, but federal law is narrow and limited), current statistics about victims and stalkers, and some prominent cases. There is also discussion of law enforcement efforts, help from federal agencies, and children as cyberstalking victims.

TECHNICAL THREATS, ISSUES, AND MEASURES
Web Documents

Armistead, Cynthia. "Reading Internet Message Headers." TechnoMom's Place. Available online. URL: http://www.technomom.com/writing/headers.html. Updated on May 10, 2001. Explains how to figure out news message and e-mail headers, which can help track down the source of harassing messages. For continuation, follow the link at the end of the article.

EDUCATION AND ASSISTANCE
Books

Gross, Linden. *Surviving a Stalker: Everything You Need to Keep Yourself Safe.* New York: Marlowe & Co., 2000. Although this guidebook does not focus on cyberstalking per se, the psychological and practical needs of stalking victims are broadly applicable. Case studies and detailed guidance make this a good resource for both victims and people in the helping professions.

Proctor, Michael. *How to Stop a Stalker.* Amherst, N.Y.: Prometheus Books, 2003. An experienced police detective and consultant explains the types of stalking and gives a variety of practical steps for reducing exposure and dealing with situations. Topics include personal security, securing mail, and even essential items to have in one's car. There is also a guide to how victims can exercise their legal rights and advocate for themselves effectively in the legal system.

Snow, Robert L. *Stopping a Stalker: A Cop's Guide to Making the System Work for You.* New York: Plenum Trade, 1998. The author, a captain with the Indianapolis police department, describes the types of stalking and how to identify when one is in danger. Besides explaining how to get the police involved (and how to help them gather evidence), the author also suggests practical steps for reducing the risk of becoming a victim. These include restricting the disclosure of personal information and observing safety practices when dating.

Articles and Papers

Karp, Hal. "Angels Online." *Reader's Digest,* vol. 156, April 2000, pp.74ff. Describes the work of CyberAngels, a program of the crime victims' organization Guardian Angels. CyberAngels focuses on helping victims of online stalking.

Laughren, Jessica. "Cyberstalking Awareness and Education." University of Calgary. Available online. URL: http://www.acs.ucalgary.ca/~dabrent/380/webproj/jessica.html. Downloaded on August 28, 2004. Describes the killing of actress Rebecca Schaeffer, the case that brought the growing threat of cyberstalking to public attention. The author says that awareness and education is the key to avoiding becoming a victim of a cyberstalker. Someone who receives threatening or harassing communications needs to take it seriously, contact authorities, and document the communications as evidence of the threat. People should also consider minimizing the information they make available online and possibly use anonymous remailers for posting online messages.

EXPLOITATION OF CHILDREN ON THE INTERNET

INTRODUCTIONS, GENERAL DISCUSSION, AND EXAMPLES

Books

Arnaldo, Carlos A. *Child Abuse on the Internet: Ending the Silence.* New York: Berghahn Books, 2001. Defines and compares traditional and Internet expressions of child pornography and pedophilia. The author then presents the debate over key issues such as what forms of pornography should be illegal, how prosecutors and law enforcers can effectively pursue offenders, and what the Internet community can itself do to deal with the problem.

Baker, Leigh. *Protecting Your Children from Sexual Predators.* New York: St. Martin's Press, 2002. Describes the motivation, personality characteristics, and typical approaches used by sexual predators in approaching and molesting children. The Internet is given a prominent place, but more traditional dangers are also covered. Also covers some less familiar topics, such as female sexual predators and the molestation of children by other children.

Child Abuse—A Medical Dictionary, Bibliography and Annotated Research Guide to Internet References. San Diego, Calif.: Icon Health Publications, 2003. A reference and research handbook useful for looking up important terms, concepts, and sources relating to child abuse, including sexual abuse related to the Internet. Geared for health professionals and students in related fields.

Finkelhor, David, Kimberly J. Mitchell, and Janis Wolak. *Online Victimization: A Report on the Nation's Youth by the Crimes Against Children Research Center.* Alexandria, Va.: National Center for Missing and Exploited Children, 2000. Also available online. URL: http://www.unh.edu/ccrc/pdf/Victimization_Online_Survey.pdf. Reports on the extent of risks to children, such as unwanted sexual solicitation and approaches, unwanted sexual material, and harassing or threatening behavior. The researchers found that persons initiating contact often did not fit the stereotype of an adult male pedophile looking for victims but included youths and some females. Educating children about risks is viewed as more likely to be successful than simply telling children not to make contacts via the Internet.

Holloway, Sarah L., and Gill Valentine. *Cyberkids: Youth Identities and Communities in the On-Line World.* New York: Routledge, 2001. Provides a useful context for exploring how the Internet (and particularly aspects such as chat and games) has changed the way children learn and form relationships. Within this context it is suggested that dangers and risks have been exaggerated and that children would be served better by showing them how to become sophisticated cybercitizens.

U.S. Department of Justice. Office of Justice Programs. Office for Victims of Crime. *Internet Crimes against Children.* Washington, D.C.: OVC Bulletin, May 2001. Also available online. URL: http://www.ojp.usdoj.gov/ovc/publications/bulletins/internet_2_2001/NCJ184931.pdf. Describes the extent and nature of Internet-based crimes that victimize children. With more than 45 million children online by 2002, predators are rapidly turning to online chat rooms and other venues rather than the playground as a place to find susceptible children. Techniques used by online predators are analogous to traditional ones, but adapted to the online environment.

Articles and Papers

Dewey, Lisa. "Girls Online Feeling out of Bounds." *Camping Magazine*, vol. 75, September/October 2002, pp. 48ff. A study of teenage girls' online behavior conducted by the Girl Scout Research Institute suggests that many girls have become adept at using the computer but may have difficulty dealing with situations such as sexual harassment in chat rooms or exposure to online pornography.

Lacayo, Richard. "Caught Up in the Web: Why Was Pete Townshend Looking at Internet Child Porn?" *Time*, vol. 161, no. 4, Jan. 27, 2003, p. 51. When rock legend Pete Townshend was among the arrested users of a major Internet child pornography site, many observers sought an explanation. According to the author, Townshend's lyrics for the Who may reveal clues about his having been abused as a child, and he had apparently been researching and campaigning against child abuse. Townshend agreed to cooperate with authorities and has not been charged.

"Man Sentenced for Online Porn Fraud." *San Jose Mercury News*, May 11, 2004, p. 9A. Reports that Kenneth H. Taves of Malibu has been sentenced to more than 11 years in federal prison. He had defrauded about 900,000 credit card holders of $37.5 million by signing them up for pornographic web sites. Taves also must pay restitution that may make good some of the losses.

Miller, Bill. "Internet-based Child Porn Ring That Drew Thousands Is Uncovered." *Fort Worth Star-Telegram*, April 27, 2004, n.p. Describes how Dallas police and FBI agents uncovered and shut down online child pornography sites. They began by subpoenaing an Internet service provider and then got information from the credit card payment service used by the pornographers. Thousands of subscribers to the services may be prosecuted, although those who cooperate may be offered leniency and counseling.

Mitchell, Kimberly J., David Finkelhor, and Janis Wolak. "The Exposure of Youth to Unwanted Sexual Material on the Internet: A National Survey of Risk, Impact, and Prevention." *Youth & Society*, vol. 34, March 2003, pp. 330–58. Also available online. URL: http://www.unh.edu/ccrc/pdf/Exposure_risk.pdf. This detailed survey attempts to answer questions with important policy implications; however, the conclusions are limited and rather tentative. Children do seem to have significant exposure to unwanted sexual content online, but the extent of short-term or long-term harm from such exposure is unclear. Filtering software seems somewhat effective in reducing exposure, but other recommended measures (such as greater parental supervision) may be ineffective, although the causal relationship is uncertain.

Wolak, Janis, Kimberly J. Mitchell, and David Finkelhor. "Escaping or Connecting? Characteristics of Youth Who Form Online Relationships." *Journal of Adolescence*, vol. 26 (2003), pp. 105–19. Also available online. URL: http://www.unh.edu/ccrc/pdf/CV51.pdf. The authors examined a sample of Internet users aged 10–17. They concluded, "Girls who had high levels of conflict with parents or were highly troubled were more likely than other girls to have close online relationships, as were boys who had low levels of communication with parents or were highly troubled, compared to other boys." Of course, online relationships could be positive and age-appropriate as well as exploitative when involving adult predators.

Web Documents

"The Cyberporn Debate." eLab. Available online. URL: http://elab.vanderbilt.edu/research/topics/cyberporn. Downloaded August 10, 2004. A discussion with extensive links (some no longer active) about the controversy over Internet pornography that arose from a 1995 *Time* magazine article highlighting research by graduate student Marty Rimm. Rimm asserted that the online world was massively inundated with smut, but critics soon questioned his methodology.

Gado, Mark. "Pedophiles and Child Molesters: The Slaughter of Innocence." Court TV's Crime Library. Available online. URL: http://www. crimelibrary.com/criminal_mind/psychology/pedophiles/1.html. Downloaded on December 23, 2004. An extensive introduction to the motivations and operations of child molesters, including famous cases such as those of Richard Alan Davis (who abducted and murdered Polly Klass) and Mary Kay Letourneau, who became sexually involved with a 13-year-old boy. Other topics include the Internet and pedophilia, the media and pedophilia, pedophile statistics, what to do about suspected child molestation, and a bibliography.

Heins, Marjorie. *Not in Front of the Children: "Indecency," Censorship and the Innocence of Youth.* New York: Hill & Wang, 2002. A comprehensive history of the modern debate over whether (and how) to protect children from words and images deemed to be harmful. The discussion moves from the earliest battles over books (such as *Adventures of Huckleberry Finn*) to the latest battles over Web filtering and the V-chip. In addition to discussion of legal issues, cases, legislation, and the activities of advocacy groups there is considerable coverage of sociological and philosophical aspects. The author also suggests that excessive censorship can impair children's ability to learn how to deal with discomfiting images and ideas.

Hogg, Charles. "Pornography and the Internet in the United States." University of British Columbia, School of Library, Archival and Information Studies. Available online. URL: http://www.slais.ubc.ca/courses/libr500/fall1999/www_presentations/c_hogg/print.htm. Posted on December 5, 1999. Because of the relationship between child pornography and sexual exploitation of children online, this accessible paper provides useful general background. It begins with definitions of pornography and proceeds to ethical, feminist, and libertarian arguments for and against censorship of pornography. Finally, the legal developments are reviewed.

Hudson, David. "Cyber Smut: Protecting Kids, Preserving Freedom." Freedom Forum. Available online. URL: http://web.archive.org/web/20000815074436/http://www.freedomforum.org/speech/series/cdacontents.asp. Posted in June 1998. A six-part series of articles. Topics include the overall clash between protecting children and free speech, federal and state laws that have largely been overturned by the courts, criticism of the overbroad nature of Internet filtering software, and possible private-sector solutions. A good overview despite the lack of coverage of more recent events.

REGULATION, INVESTIGATION, ENFORCEMENT, AND LEGAL ISSUES

Books

Jenkins, Philip. *Beyond Tolerance: Child Pornography on the Internet.* New York: New York University Press, 2003. Traces the electronic and social networks that users and distributors of child pornography have developed via the Internet. The author argues that the global reach and essentially anonymous nature of the Internet have allowed offenders to operate largely beyond the reach of the law.

Smith, Marcia, and Amanda Jacobs. *Internet: Status Report on Attempts to Protect Children from Unsuitable Material on the Web.* Washington, D.C.: Congressional Research Service, 2004. Also available online. URL: http://leahy. senate.gov/issues/internet/CRSinternetprotectingchildren04.pdf. Updated January 28, 2004. Discusses the legal history of laws such as the Communications Decency Act (1996), Children's Online Protection Act (1998), and the Children's Internet Protection Act (2000). In nearly all cases the courts have overturned major portions of the legislation as being incompatible with First Amendment protections. However, the Supreme Court did uphold the constitutionality of requiring Web filtering in publicly funded libraries.

Taylor, Max, and Ethel Quayle. *Child Pornography: An Internet Crime.* New York: Brunner-Routledge, 2003. Describes how child pornography is distributed via the Internet and creates a model of the behavior and motivation of offenders so that professionals can better assess the risk of offenders progressing to actual child molestation.

U.S. Department of Justice. Federal Bureau of Investigation. *Innocent Images National Initiative.* Washington, D.C.: FBI Publications, 2003. Also available online. URL: http://www.idaho-post.org/SROs/FBI%20Publications% 20-%20Innocent%20Images%20National%20Initiative.htm. Updated September 24, 2003. Describes the Innocent Images National Initiative, an effort of the FBI's Cyber Crimes Program. This is a multiagency, coordinated national and international effort to "identify, investigate and prosecute sexual predators who use the Internet and other online services to sexually exploit children."

Articles and Papers

Aftab, Parry. "Legal Brief: When the Unthinkable Becomes a Reality." *InformationWeek*, May 12, 2003, p. 94. Explores the sticky legal problems faced by companies when child pornography is discovered on employees' computers. To minimize liability, companies need policies that clearly specify what material is unacceptable and the procedures that will be used to deal with incidents. Companies should also decide what types of offenses should be reported to law enforcement authorities.

Bagley, Christopher. "Diminishing Incidence of Internet Child Pornographic Images." *Psychological Reports,* vol. 93, August 2003, pp. 305ff. The results of a four-year sampling show a significant decline in the number of pornographic images of children posted on the Web. The author suggests that intense pressure by law enforcement and children's advocacy groups may be having an effect.

Colbey, Richard. "Jobs & Money: Internet: Visa Must Close Net on These Vile Sites." *The Guardian (London)*, October 18, 2003, p. 20. The author argues that since credit card processing is a necessity for selling things on the Internet, legally requiring credit card companies to find and cut off service to sellers of online child pornography would dry up most of these objectionable sites.

Eliscu, Jenny. "Pete Cleared on Porn Rap." *Rolling Stone,* June 12, 2003, p. 24. Four months after his arrest for viewing child pornography on the Internet, rock star Peter Townshend was let off with a warning—and his name will be placed on a sex offender registry for five years. Townshend said that he had viewed the images as part of research into his own abuse as a child.

Evans, Bob. "Kudos to Visa for Battling Pornography." *Information Week,* March 3, 2003. Also available online. URL: http://www.information-week.com/story/IWK2003030250005. The credit card company is praised for taking a proactive stance against the worldwide spread of child pornography and cooperating with law enforcement investigations. It stopped providing credit card processing services to hundreds of suspect web sites. The author has little sympathy for the libertarian Electronic Freedom Foundation (he meant the Electronic Frontier Foundation), which objects that credit card companies with their monopoly position might be able to control online content.

Fantino, Julian. "Child Pornography on the Internet: New Challenges Require New Ideas." *Police Chief,* vol. 70, December 2003, pp. 28–30. Describes a multipronged effort by Toronto police to investigate and pursue online child pornography distributors. The effort includes a pilot project for identifying specific victims of sexual abuse through interviews with child contacts of suspected molesters; partnership with Microsoft in developing new methods to investigate a suspect's computers; the hosting of an international conference on child exploitation in September 2003; and the development of an educational video.

Holland, Bill. "Congress: Support Grows." *Billboard*, vol. 115, September 20, 2003, pp. 1ff. The recording industry launches a new attack on file-sharing services on the grounds that some are used to distribute pornography. Senator Charles Schumer (Democrat–New York) has called for a federal task force to crack down on child pornography file-swapping. Other issues relating to file-sharing networks are also discussed.

Krause, Jason. "Can Anyone Stop Internet Porn?" *ABA Journal*, vol. 88, September 2002, pp. 56–61. Recounts the legal battle between Congress, which has passed a succession of laws trying to ban online material considered harmful to children, and the American Civil Liberties Union and other groups that have (mostly successfully) challenged the laws' constitutionality in the courts. The author concludes that Congress is not likely to stop trying to craft legislation acceptable to the courts.

Web Documents

Ashcroft, John. "Operation Candyman." U.S. Dept. of Justice. Available online. URL: http://www.usdoj.gov/criminal/ceos/OperationCandyman. htm. Posted on March 18, 2002. Prepared remarks by U.S. Attorney General John Ashcroft announcing the results of Operation Candyman, a more than year-long national sweep by the FBI against online child pornographers. Eighty-six persons were charged, including all 27 members of the Candyman e-group who admitted to molesting 36 children. Includes a press release with additional details.

Davis-Burke, Samantha. "Protecting Children on the Internet." Georgia State University College of Law. Available online. URL: http://gsulaw. gsu.edu/lawand/papers/fa01/davis. Posted Fall 2001. Summarizes federal, state, and foreign attempts to protect children from online pornography. There is also discussion of filters (web site blocking) and other measures.

Macmillan, Robert. "Primer: Children, The Internet and Pornography." Washingtonpost.com. Available online. URL: http://www.washington-post.com/wp-dyn/articles/A39748-2002May31.html. Posted on June 29, 2004. Describes a succession of attempts by Congress to regulate pornography on the Internet and to restrict its availability to children. Discusses the COPA (Child Online Protection Act), CIPA (Children's Internet Protection Act), and other legislation, some of which was overturned by the courts as infringing on the First Amendment rights of adults.

"Speech: Internet & First Amendment." First Amendment Center. Available online. URL: http://www.firstamendmentcenter.org/speech/internet/ faqs.aspx?id=569. Downloaded on January 13, 2005. A free speech advocacy group presents positions and explanations on a variety of issues, including virtual child pornography, community standards as applied to the

Internet, the legality of Web filtering, and the Supreme Court decision *U.S. v. ALA.*

TECHNICAL THREATS, ISSUES, AND MEASURES
Articles and Papers

Krim, Jonathan. "Pornography Prevalent on File-Sharing Services." *Washington Post*, March 13, 2003, p. E1. Reports that large numbers of pornographic images continue to be shared through online services that are more commonly associated with music downloads.

Schwartz, John. "File-Swapping Is New Route for Pornography on Internet." *New York Times*, July 28, 2001, p. A1. Describes a congressional report that warns that online file-sharing services are being increasingly used by children and teens to access pornographic images. Most existing Internet filtering programs were unable to block such files.

Web Documents

"Digital Chaperones for Kids: Which Internet Filters Protect the Best? Which Get in the Way?" ConsumerReports.org. Available online. URL: http://www.consumerreports.org/main/detailv2.jsp?CONTENT%3C%3Ecnt_id=18867&FOLDER%3C%3Efolder_id=18151&bmUID=1020221 604546. Posted in March 2001. Explains how Internet filter programs work and the different methods used to select or block content (automatic content analysis, designation of sites by human analysts, and use of content labels or ratings). There is a tradeoff between blocking all possible problem sites and also blocking appropriate ones. Various products are rated.

"Internet Blocking in Public Schools." Electronic Frontier Foundation. Available online. URL: http://www.eff.org/Censorship/Censorware/net_block_report/net_block_report.pdf. Posted on June 26, 2003. A joint study of the Electronic Frontier Foundation and the Online Policy Group determined that to a considerable extent Web blocking or filtering software "impedes the educational process by restricting access to web pages relevant to the required curriculum." Blocking keywords, or codes, were compared with topics in official curricula.

EDUCATION AND ASSISTANCE
Books

Appleman, Dan. *Always Use Protection: A Teen's Guide to Safe Computing.* Berkeley, Calif.: APress, 2004. Written somewhat in the style of popular sex education texts, this guide tries to speak to teens in accessible but not patronizing language. Dangers such as viruses, spyware, spam, scams, and online predators are put in context, and suggestions are given for dealing with them.

Brooks, Sheldon. *Everything You Need to Know About Romance and the Internet: How to Stay Safe.* New York: Rosen Publishing, 2001. This book is aimed at junior high students who are interested in meeting and perhaps dating people they meet online. It describes such features as chat rooms, private chat, discussion forums, e-mail, dating services, and personal ads. The author explains the dangers and potential problems of online relationships and explains what to do about cyberstalkers and other abusive persons. Safe procedures for meeting online acquaintances in person are stressed.

Kabay, M. E. *Cyber-Safety for Everyone: From Kids to Elders.* South Barre, Vt.: Accura Printing, 2002. Also available online. URL: http://ww2.norwich. edu/mkabay/cyberwatch.cybersafety.pdf. Provides guidance and resources for computer users of all ages in dealing with problematic aspects of the Internet. Topics include pedophiles, online dating and cybersex, hate groups, pornography, hoaxes, threats, viruses, spam, various types of frauds and scams, and identity theft.

Roddel, Victoria. *Stay Safe in Cyberspace: Cybercrime Awareness, Prevention & Safety.* Second Edition. La Belle, Fla.: Cyber Criminals Most Wanted, 2003. This introduction to online risks is written primarily for parents who may have limited computer experience. The author explains the different types of technical and human threats and gives basic advice for coping with various situations.

Rothman, Kevin F. *Coping with Dangers on the Internet: A Teen's Guide to Staying Safe Online.* New York: Rosen Publishing, 2000. A good guide for students in grades 7 and up, emphasizing common sense advice and explanations for inexperienced computer users.

Sherman, Josepha. *Internet Safety.* New York: Franklin Watts, 2003. A guide to Internet safety written for junior high readers and up. Topics include protection from viruses, guarding privacy, safe surfing and shopping online, and proper online etiquette.

Sullivan, Mike. *Safety Monitor: How to Protect Your Kids Online.* Chicago: Bonus Books, 2002. An accessible, systematic guide to building a child-safe Internet environment. Topics include talking to children and establishing an "online contract," configuring browser settings and Internet filter programs, using parental controls on America Online and other services, supervising children's Internet activity, and setting up family web sites and pages.

U.S. Department of Justice. Federal Bureau of Investigation. *A Parent's Guide to Internet Safety.* Washington, D.C.: FBI Publications, [2000]. Also available online. URL: http://www.fbi.gov/publications/pguide/pguidee. htm. This guide describes the activities of sexual predators on the Internet, discusses indications that a child may have become involved with inappropriate activities, and offers suggestions for communicating with the child, identifying problems, and seeking the assistance of appropriate agencies.

Vos MacDonald, Joan. *Cybersafety: Surfing Safely Online.* Springfield, N.J.: Enslow Publishers, 2001. Aimed at middle school students, this is a clear and attractive guide to the dangers of the Internet, including advice and even procedures for dealing with sticky situations, such as being the recipient of obscene or harassing language in a chat room.

Wolinsky, Art. *Safe Surfing on the Internet.* Berkeley Heights, N.J.: Enslow, 2003. Written for students in grades 4–8 but meaty in its content, this explores important issues in Internet use and safety, including basic rules, the controversy over legal measures protecting children from harmful Internet content, and issues involving intellectual property and plagiarism in school papers.

Articles and Papers

Parson, Matt. "Protecting Children on the Electronic Frontier: A Law Enforcement Challenge." *FBI Law Enforcement Bulletin*, vol. 69, October 2000, pp. 22–26. Also available online. URL: http://www.fbi.gov/publications/leb/2000/oct00leb.pdf. Describes Safekids, an innovative program devised by the Naval Criminal Investigative Service (NCIS) to protect the children of military families from online dangers. The Safekids program includes a compact disc with presentations for parents and children that explains dangers and offers tools to help parents protect their children. There is also an in-school presentation designed for children in grades four through nine, focusing on various scenarios and explaining how to respond to them. The Parents' Posse program gives parents instruction in Internet functions and on how to monitor or restrict children's use of problematic areas.

Web Documents

"My Agreement About Using the Internet." WiredKids.org. Available online. URL: http://www.wiredkids.org/parents/parentingonline/agreement.html. Downloaded on August 13, 2004. A sample contract in which a child agrees to follow certain rules for using the Internet and the parent agrees to help the child stay safe in cyberspace.

"Parenting Online." WiredKids.org. Available online. URL: http://www.wiredkids.org/parents/parentingonline/1.html. Downloaded on August

13, 2004. Designed for parents who may be less computer literate than their children, this guide explains how traditional advice about dealing with strangers and potentially dangerous situations can be translated into Internet terms. It explains search engines, filtering software, recommended safe sites, and ways to explain online dangers to kids. This document can also be downloaded and printed as a booklet.

"The Parents' Guide to the Information Superhighway: Rules and Tools for Families Online." The Children's Partnership. Available online. URL: http://www.childrenspartnership.org. Posted in 1998. A good basic introduction to guide parents in introducing their children to the Internet and supervising their online activities. There are also suggestions for cooperating with schools.

"Play It Safe." Bonus.com. Available online. URL: https://www.wiredsafety. org (click link). Downloaded on August 13, 2004. An interactive game that helps children recognize when they may be revealing too much personal information about themselves or their activities.

CHAPTER 8

ORGANIZATIONS AND AGENCIES

Following are listings for organizations and agencies involved with Internet predators, computer crime, computer security, and related issues. They are divided into the following categories: Federal Agencies; Fraud and Identity Theft; Cyberstalking and Crimes against Children; Academic, Technical, and Industry Groups; and Issue Advocacy Groups.

FEDERAL AGENCIES

Computer Crime and Intellectual Property Division, U.S. Department of Justice, Criminal Division
URL: www. usdoj.gov/criminal/ cybercrime
E-mail: Criminal.Division@ usdoj.gov
Phone: (202) 514-1026
U.S. Department of Justice Criminal Division (Computer Crime and Intellectual Property Section)
10th and Constitution Avenue, NW
Washington, DC 20530
This section of the Department of Justice coordinates and provides resources for federal prosecution of computer crimes. Its web site offers many resources for legal professionals and the general public.

Customs Service
URL: http://www.customs. ustreas.gov
E-mail: Web form
Phone: (202) 354-1000
U.S. Customs and Border Protection
1300 Pennsylvania Avenue, NW
Washington, DC 20229
In recent years the Customs Service has also been patrolling the nation's virtual borders. It has been involved in the investigation of virtual smuggling via the Internet, involving contraband such as child pornography.

Federal Bureau of Investigation (FBI)
URL: http://www.fbi.gov
E-mail: Web form
Phone: (202) 324-3000 (Also see Field Office listings on web site)
J. Edgar Hoover Building
935 Pennsylvania Avenue, NW
Washington, DC 20535-0001
The FBI is the premier federal criminal investigative agency, in charge of pursuing violations of more than 200 categories of federal law. These include computer-related offenses (through its Cyber Crimes Program), which as of 2004 is also temporarily continuing the work of the defunct National Infrastructure Protection Center. Investigators deal with individuals or organizations engaged in hacking/system attacks, theft of information, fraud, and online sexual predators (including child pornographers, especially through the Crimes against Children investigative program and the Innocent Images National Initiative).

Federal Trade Commission
URL: http://www.ftc.gov
E-mail: Web forms
Phone: (202) 326-2222
600 Pennsylvania Avenue, NW
Washington, DC 20580
Founded in 1914, the Federal Trade Commission has the dual mission of regulating business under federal law and educating consumers about fraud, including Internet fraud and identity theft.

See the web site's links under For Consumers, Consumer Protection, and Consumer Information.

Food and Drug Administration
URL: http://www.fda.org
E-mail: Web form
Phone: (888) 463-6332
5600 Fishers Lane
Rockville, MD 20857-0001
The Food and Drug Administration is part of the Department of Health and Human Services. It is the federal agency responsible for setting safety standards for drugs, food, food additives, cosmetics, and medical devices. In recent years the agency has become concerned with the growth of largely unregulated Internet pharmacies as well as the large number of health-related web sites and e-mails containing deceptive or fraudulent information. The web site includes a variety of consumer tips and reports as well as numerous e-mail newsletters and lists.

National Institute of Justice
URL: http://www.ojp.usdoj.gov/nij
E-mail: N/A
Phone: (202) 307-2942
810 Seventh Street, NW
Washington, DC 20531
The National Institute of Justice (NIJ) is the research arm of the U.S. Department of Justice. Its many divisions include the Electronic Crimes Program, which does research and assessment of law enforcement capabilities for dealing with computer-related crime. The

NIJ web site also provides access to the National Criminal Justice Research Service and its large abstracts database.

Postal Inspection Service
URL: http://www.usps.com/
   postalinspectors
E-mail: Web form
Telephone: Use local office
   finder on web site
222 South Riverside Plaza
Suite 1250
Chicago, IL 60606-6100
The U.S. Postal Inspection Service is charged with protecting the mails from theft, fraudulent use, or other crimes. The organization has recently publicized the danger of identity theft and the need to physically secure mailboxes and shred mail before discarding. Postal inspectors also become involved in investigating mail fraud, since many Internet-based frauds also involve the mails, such as for payments or deliveries.

Secret Service
URL: http://ustreas.gov/usss
E-mail: Web form
Phone: (202) 406-5708
U.S. Secret Service
Office of Government Liaison
   and Public Affairs
245 Murray Drive
Building 410
Washington, DC 20223
In addition to its well-known guarding of the president and other government officials, the U.S. Secret Service has historically been involved in the fight against counter-feiting. Today the agency has an important role in protecting the integrity of the computers used in interstate commerce from cyberattacks. The agency also investigates financial fraud, identity theft, and other crimes affecting the U.S. financial, banking, and telecommunications infrastructure.

**Securities and Exchange
   Commission (SEC)
Office of Investor Education
   and Assistance**
URL: http://www.sec.gov
E-mail: help@sec.gov
Phone: (202) 942-7040
450 Fifth Street, NW
Washington, DC 20549
The SEC is the primary federal agency for regulation of investments. Its main emphasis is on ensuring market integrity—for example, by discovering and prosecuting insider trading and other unfair manipulations. The agency's Internet Enforcement Division conducts surveillance for online investment fraud and investigates and prosecutes perpetrators. It also has an office of investor education and assistance.

FRAUD AND IDENTITY THEFT

**Alliance Against Fraud in
   Telemarketing and Electronic
   Commerce**
URL: http://www.fraud.org/aaft/
   aaftinfo.htm
E-mail: media@nclnet.org

Phone: (202) 835-3323
c/o National Consumers League
1701 K Street, NW
Suite 1200
Washington, DC 20006
This initiative was founded in 1989 by the National Consumers League. Its membership includes nonprofit consumer groups, educational institutions, labor unions, government consumer protection and law enforcement agencies, businesses, and trade associations. The group's members share current information on frauds and scams and develop consumer education efforts. Individuals cannot be members but can subscribe to an e-mail newsletter *Focus on Fraud.*

Anti-Phishing Working Group
URL: http://www.antiphishing.
 org
E-mail: info@anti-phishing.org
Phone: N/A
Address: N/A
The Anti-Phishing Working Group is an industry association of financial institutions, online retailers, and other businesses working to fight phishing and e-mail spoofing. Its web site provides regular reports on trends in phishing attacks, an extensive archive of the contents of actual phishing and spoof messages and sites, and a way to report phishing attacks.

**Council of Better Business
 Bureaus**
URL: http://www.bbb.org

E-mail: Web form
Phone: (703) 276-0100
4200 Wilson Boulevard
Suite 800
Arlington, VA 22203-1838
This national organization includes Better Business Bureaus in virtually every community. They provide reports on more than 2 million organizations, giving consumers an important resource in making purchasing decisions or deciding to make a donation to a charity. The BBB web site provides a variety of consumer education materials. The organization also accepts complaints online and tries to resolve them with the company involved.

Internet Fraud Complaint Center
URL: http://www.ifccfbi.gov/
 index.asp
E-mail: Web contact form
Phone: N/A
Address: N/A
A partnership between the FBI and the National White Collar Crime Center (NW3C), the Internet Fraud Complaint Center makes it easy for victims of suspected computer crimes to report the particulars, which are entered into a database that helps law enforcers detect fraud patterns and develop timely statistical data.

**National Fraud Information
 Center**
URL: http://www.fraud.org
Phone: (800) 876-7060
 (fraud hotline)

c/o National Consumers League
1701 K Street, NW,
  Suite 1200
Washington, DC 20006
An initiative by the National Consumers League to educate consumers about telemarketing and Internet fraud. The web site offers tips on common frauds and scams and has a special section for older consumers as well as a place to ask questions or report suspected fraud.

National White Collar Crime
  Center
URL: http://www.nw3c.org
E-mail: Web form
Phone: (804) 323-3563
7401 Beaufont Springs Drive
Suite 300
Richmond, VA 23225-5504
A federally funded nonprofit corporation whose membership is primarily law enforcement agencies, state regulatory bodies, and state and local prosecutors. It provides education and tools to help these professionals prosecute economic and high-tech crimes.

CYBERSTALKING AND CRIMES AGAINST CHILDREN

AntiChildPorn.org
URL: http://www.antichildporn.
  org
E-mail: Web form

Telephone: N/A
Postal address: N/A
This group monitors the Internet for child pornography sites or activities and reports them to appropriate law enforcement authorities. It also seeks to educate the public and media about the nature and dangers of child pornography and lobbies for stronger legislation.

Center for Media Literacy
URL: http:www.medialit.org
E-mail: cml@medialit.org
Phone: (310) 581-0260
3101 Ocean Park Boulevard
Suite 200
Santa Monica, CA 90405
General media and critical thinking skills are important tools for helping children avoid fraud and deception online. This nonprofit organization develops media education projects and materials and provides training and resources to teachers and others.

The Childrens' Partnership
URL: http://www.thechildrens
  partnership.org
E-mail: frontdoor@childrens
  partnership.org
Phone: (202) 429-0033
2000 P Street NW
Suite 330
Washington, DC 20036
A nonprofit, nonpartisan organization that provides public policy analysis and advocacy on behalf of children. Among their programs are efforts to promote improved Internet access and content for children.

The web site includes a Parent's Guide to the Information Super-highway.

Crimes Against Children Research Center
URL: http://www.unh.edu/ccrc/about-ccrc.html
E-mail: Kelly.foster@unh.edu
Phone: (603) 862-1888
University of New Hampshire
20 College Road
#126 Horton Social Science Center
Durham, NH 03824
Performs research into crimes and abuse against children, both offline and online, including some of the first comprehensive studies on children's exposure to sexual materials and contacts on the Internet.

CyberAngels
URL: http://www.cyberangels.com
E-mail: caexec@cyberangels.org
Phone: (610) 377-2966
Guardian Angels
CyberAngels Program
P.O. Box 3171
Allentown, PA 18106
A program of the Guardian Angels, the well-known crime-victim support and advocacy group, CyberAngels attempts to combat Internet-based child abuse, exploitation, and other crime. The group provides resources for persons who believe they are being stalked, hacked, or otherwise victimized.

Internet Content Rating Association
URL: http://www.icra.org
E-mail: Web form
Phone: (202) 331-8651
666 11th Street, NW
Suite 1100
Washington, DC 20001
This international nonprofit organization seeks to make the Internet safer for children without censorship or restrictions on the rights of adults. By filling out a questionnaire provided by the organization, web site operators provide information for a label. Filtering software can then be used with the labels to allow parents to select appropriate material for their children to view online.

National Center for Missing and Exploited Children
URL: http://www.missingkids.org
E-mail: Web form
Phone: (703) 274-3900
Hotline: (800) 843-5678
Charles B. Wang International Children's Building
699 Prince Street
Alexandria, VA 22314-3175
Established in 1984, this nonprofit organization serves as a clearinghouse of information about missing and exploited children. It also provides expert assistance to law enforcement officials and maintains the CyberTipline, which the public can use to report Internet-related child sexual exploitation.

Working to Halt Online Abuse
URL: http://www.haltabuse.org
E-mail: whoa@haltabuse.org
Phone: (561) 828-2801
c/o J. A. Hitchcock
P.O. Box 696
Dover, NH 03821-0696
Founded in 1997 by writer Jayne A. Hitchcock, this volunteer organization seeks "to fight online harassment through education of the general public, education of law enforcement personnel, and empowerment of victims." The group helps online communities develop policies to create a safer social environment.

ACADEMIC, TECHNICAL, AND INDUSTRY GROUPS

Association for Computing Machinery (ACM)
URL: http://www.acm.org
E-mail: ACMHELP@acm.org
Phone: (212) 944-1318
One Astor Plaza
1515 Broadway
17th Floor
New York, NY 10036-5701
One of the most prestigious organizations in the computer science field, the ACM provides conferences, papers, and other resources to computer scientists, software engineers, and other information professionals as well as for the general public. Members can gain access to a huge online digital library of abstracts and full-text publications. The organization's own publications often feature important articles and papers about the Internet and e-commerce infrastructure, computer security, and other subjects relevant to computer crime studies.

Business Software Alliance
URL: http://www.bsa.org
E-mail: webmaster@bsa.org
Phone: (202) 872-5500
1150 18th Street, NW
Suite 700
Washington, DC 20036
The BSA is "dedicated to promoting a safe and legal digital world." Its members are primarily commercial software developers. Although its focus seems to be primarily on antipiracy and intellectual property protection issues, it also deals with general computer and e-commerce security. The web site offers an introductory page on cybercrime.

Computer Crime Research Center
URL: http://www.crime-research.org/about
E-mail: ccrc@crime-research.org
Phone: +38 (061) 2621 472
Box 8010
Zaporozhye 95
Ukraine 69095
An independent institute "dedicated to the research of cyber crime, cyber terrorism, and other issues of computer crimes and internet fraud phenomena." Researchers are part

of a program jointly funded by the United States and Ukraine. The web site provides resources, news stories, and archives.

Computer Security Institute
URL: http://www.gocsi.com
E-mail: csimember@espcomp. com
Phone: (866) 271-8529
600 Harrison Street
San Francisco, CA 94107
This international organization provides services and training for information, computer, and network security personnel. The group sponsors two annual conferences and conducts a joint security survey with the FBI. It focuses mainly on crimes involving compromise of network and computer facilities, rather than consumer fraud and other issues affecting individuals.

IEEE Computer Society
URL: http://www.computer.org
E-mail: membership@computer. org
Phone: (202) 371-0101
1730 Massachusetts Avenue, NW
Washington, DC 20036-1992
This is the largest component of the Institute of Electrical and Electronics Engineers (IEEE). Its conferences, journals, and other resources are aimed mainly at computer and information professionals. Compared to the other leading computer society (the Assocation for Computing Machinery) the IEEE is more engineering ori-

ented, although there is considerable overlap.

Internet Society
URL: http://www.isoc.org
E-mail: isoc@isoc.org
Phone: (703) 326-9880
1775 Wiehle Avenue
Suite 102
Reston, VA 20190
The Internet Society is a professional membership organization with more than 150 organizational and 16,000 individual members in more than 180 countries. It coordinates and serves as a global clearinghouse for the influential thinkers and organizations that are shaping the structure and future of the global Internet.

National Cyber Security Partnership (NCSP)
URL: http://www.cyber partnership.com
E-mail: contact list on web site
Phone: (202) 715-1561
The NCSP is an alliance of the Business Software Alliance, the Information Technology Association of America, TechNet, and the U.S. Chamber of Commerce in partnership with various government agencies, academics, and industry experts. The group has five task forces covering awareness for home users and small business; computer security early warning; corporate governance; security across the software development life cycle; and technical standards and common criteria.

Network Abuse Clearinghouse
URL: http://abuse.net
E-mail: webmaster@abuse.net
Phone: N/A
c/o I.E.C.C.
P.O. Box 727
Trumansburg, NY 14886
Operates Abuse.net, a cooperative service that maintains a database of Internet domains and contact information to enable Internet users to know when someone is misusing their domain, such as for spamming, e-mail frauds, or spreading of viruses.

SANS Institute
URL: http://www.sans.org
E-mail: info@sans.org
Phone: (301) 654-7267
8120 Woodmont Avenue
Suite 205
Bethesda, MD 20814
The organization describes itself as "by far the largest source for information security training and certification in the word." SANS maintains a large library of documents, distributes the weekly news digest News-Bites and a weekly vulnerability digest called @Risk, and operates an early warning system called the Internet Storm Center.

SpamCon Foundation
URL: http://spamcon.org
E-mail: comments@spamcon.org
Phone: (415) 552-2557
829 14th Street
San Francisco, CA 94114
This nonprofit organization supports measures to reduce the inci-

dence of unsolicited e-mail, which imposes substantial costs on service providers, hampers worker productivity, and serves as a conduit for fraud. The web site provides information about best practices and techniques for providers and users.

ISSUE ADVOCACY GROUPS

American Civil Liberties Union (ACLU)
URL: http://www.aclu.org
E-mail: Web form
Phone: (888) 567-ACLU
125 Broad Street, 18th Floor
New York, NY 10004
The ACLU is widely considered to be the foremost U.S. civil liberties organization. It is involved in litigation and education on a wide variety of issues related to computer crime, including privacy, freedom of expression, Internet filtering, and others.

Center for Democracy and Technology
URL: http://www.cdt.org
E-mail: feedback@cdt.org
Phone: (202) 637-9800
1634 I Street NW
Suite 1100
Washington, DC 20006
This group promotes libertarian values such as free expression and privacy in issues involving the use of the Internet and other information technologies. Some of the issues

highlighted on its web site include the Children's Online Protection Act, spam, spyware, and digital authentication.

Electronic Frontier Foundation (EFF)
URL: http://www.eff.org
E-mail: information @eff.org
Phone: (415) 436-9333
454 Shotwell Street
San Francisco, CA 94110
Often described as "the ACLU of cyberspace," the EFF was founded in 1990 in response to an early federal hacker crackdown that threatened free speech by shutting down innocent web sites. Since then the group has strongly advocated for privacy protection, public access to encryption technologies, and freedom of expression, and against Internet censorship or blocking and efforts by copyright holders to overly restrict the fair use of their products.

Electronic Privacy Information Center (EPIC)
URL: http://www.epic.org
E-mail: Web form
Phone: (202) 483-1140
1718 Connecticut Avenue, NW
Suite 200
Washington, DC 20009
Established in 1994, EPIC is focused on the need to protect privacy and freedom of expression in the online world. Both issues are closely related to cybercrime issues. The web site includes reports, news, and tracking of current legislation. A free newsletter, EPIC Alert, is available.

Online Policy Group
URL: http://www.onlinepolicy.org
E-mail: support@onlinepolicy.org
Phone: (415) 826-3532
304 Winfield Street
San Francisco, CA 94110-5512
The Online Policy Group is a nonprofit organization dedicated to online policy outreach and action on issues such as access, privacy, digital defamation, and the digital divide. The group focuses on helping the Internet serve a wide variety of constituencies while protecting users' rights.

PART III

APPENDICES

APPENDIX A

STATISTICS AND TRENDS ON FRAUD AND IDENTITY THEFT

Internet fraud must be seen in the perspective of an explosion in Internet use in the United States in the first years of the new century. According to a March 2004 report from Nielsen/Netratings, more than 204 million Americans have access to the Internet at home. This is about 75 percent of the total population.

When broken down by gender or age, nearly all groups now have about the same rate of Internet access, suggesting that the Internet population is becoming saturated and the digital divide is narrowing. However, some groups such as blacks, adults without a college education, and people over age 55 are still lagging somewhat.

The following charts illustrate some significant trends in online fraud and identity theft. For perspective, they begin with an overall look at the growth in online and e-commerce activity. Succeeding charts then provide trends and snapshots of the incidence of these troubling types of Internet predation.

GROWTH IN INTERNET ACTIVITY

There has been remarkable growth in the number of Internet users participating in activities that are more likely to expose them to fraud, identity theft, or other criminal attacks. The following chart, "Growth of Online Activities, 2000–2002," shows the increase between 2000 and 2002 in the number of users who performed selected activities online.

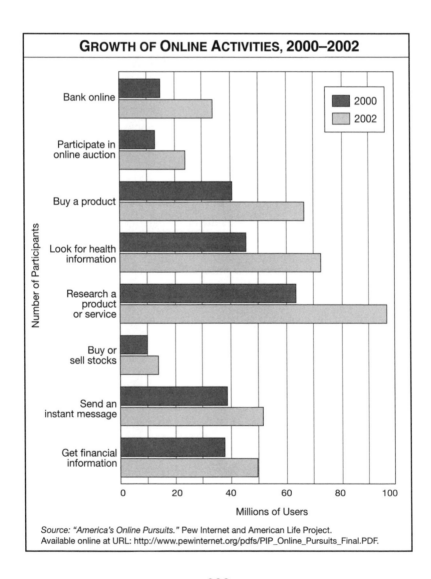

GROWTH OF ONLINE ACTIVITIES, 2000–2002

Source: *"America's Online Pursuits."* Pew Internet and American Life Project.
Available online at URL: http://www.pewinternet.org/pdfs/PIP_Online_Pursuits_Final.PDF.

Appendix A

EXPANSION OF E-COMMERCE

Another way to measure the size of the arena in which the battle against Internet fraud is being fought is to look at the overall size of the electronic commerce market. The chart "Growth in E-Commerce, 1999–2004" shows the increase in the quarterly value of goods and services sold online.

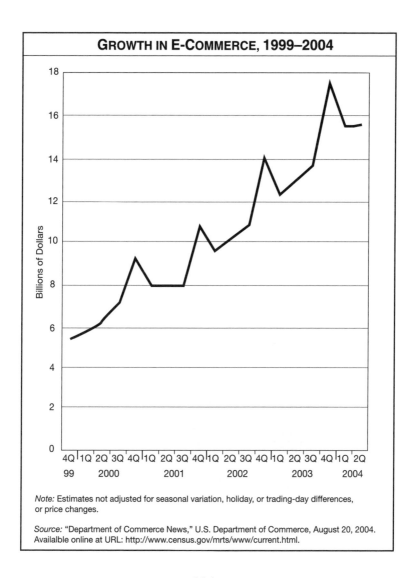

GROWTH IN E-COMMERCE, 1999–2004

Note: Estimates not adjusted for seasonal variation, holiday, or trading-day differences, or price changes.

Source: "Department of Commerce News," U.S. Department of Commerce, August 20, 2004. Availalble online at URL: http://www.census.gov/mrts/www/current.html.

GROWTH IN FRAUD AND IDENTITY THEFT COMPLAINTS

The incidence of fraud and identity theft seems to be increasing rapidly. As the chart "*Sentinel* Complaints by Calendar Year, 2002–2004" shows, the total number of complaints received by the Federal Trade Commission's (FTC) *Consumer Sentinel* increased by more than half between 2002 and 2004.

It should be noted that most experts believe that many frauds are not reported by victims for reasons ranging from fear of embarrassment to lack of confidence in law enforcement to lack of knowledge of the appropriate agency to report to. It is not known how much of the increase in complaints to the FTC represents an actual increase in the incidence of fraud and identity theft and how much might reflect increased public awareness and vigilance. It is nevertheless likely that there is a real increase in incidence.

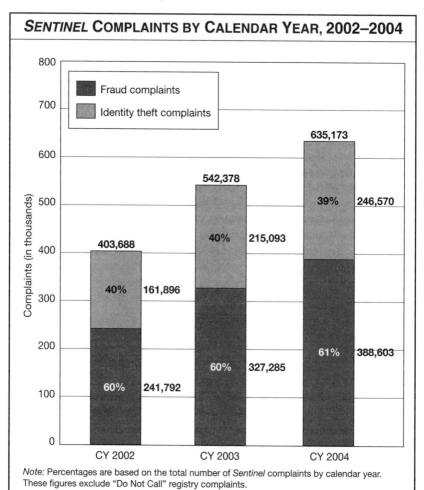

SENTINEL COMPLAINTS BY CALENDAR YEAR, 2002–2004

Note: Percentages are based on the total number of *Sentinel* complaints by calendar year. These figures exclude "Do Not Call" registry complaints.

Source: Federal Trade Commission. *National and State Trends in Identity Theft: January–December 2004*, p. 4. Available online at URL: http://www.consumer.gov/sentinel/pubs/Top10Fraud2004.pdf.

Appendix A

TYPES OF ONLINE FRAUD

There are many types of online fraud. The chart "Types of Online Frauds, January 1–December 31, 2004" gives the percentage of FTC complaints represented by various types of fraud. The largest category is identity theft, followed by Internet auctions.

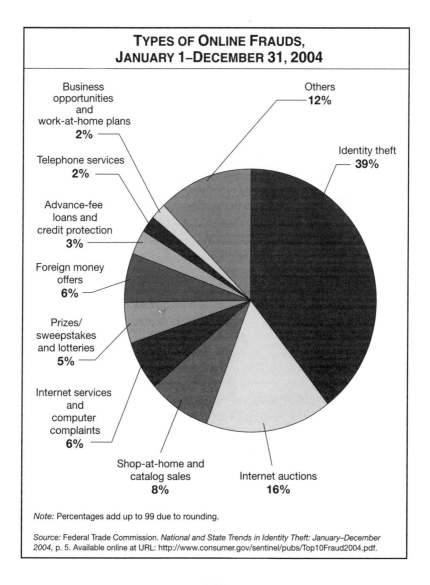

TYPES OF ONLINE FRAUDS, JANUARY 1–DECEMBER 31, 2004

Business opportunities and work-at-home plans **2%**

Telephone services **2%**

Advance-fee loans and credit protection **3%**

Foreign money offers **6%**

Prizes/ sweepstakes and lotteries **5%**

Internet services and computer complaints **6%**

Shop-at-home and catalog sales **8%**

Internet auctions **16%**

Others **12%**

Identity theft **39%**

Note: Percentages add up to 99 due to rounding.

Source: Federal Trade Commission. *National and State Trends in Identity Theft: January–December 2004*, p. 5. Available online at URL: http://www.consumer.gov/sentinel/pubs/Top10Fraud2004.pdf.

HOW FRAUD BEGINS

One important aspect of fighting online fraud is to discover its vectors, or methods in which the fraudulent content is communicated to the victim. The chart "Company's Method of Contacting Consumers, January 1– December 31, 2004" reflects fraud complaints to the FTC. The tremendous growth in spam can be seen in the fact that in 2004 e-mail outstripped web sites as the leading source of fraudulent communications although spam often includes a link to a fraudulent web site. Note, however, that the FTC *Consumer Sentinel* also covers remote offline frauds, such as through phone telemarketing or mail advertisements.

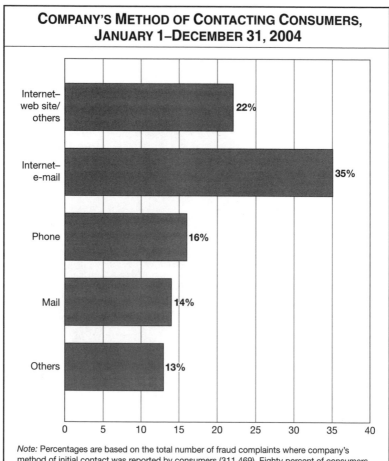

COMPANY'S METHOD OF CONTACTING CONSUMERS, JANUARY 1–DECEMBER 31, 2004

- Internet–web site/others: 22%
- Internet–e-mail: 35%
- Phone: 16%
- Mail: 14%
- Others: 13%

Note: Percentages are based on the total number of fraud complaints where company's method of initial contact was reported by consumers (311,469). Eighty percent of consumers reported this information.

Source: Federal Trade Commission. *National and State Trends in Identity Theft: January–December 2004*, p. 7. Available online at URL: http://www.consumer.gov/sentinel/pubs/Top10Fraud2004.pdf.

IDENTITY THEFT
COMPLAINTS BY AGE

As might be expected, persons under 18 account for only a tiny number of identity theft complaints because young people generally do not have access to credit cards or other payment methods most vulnerable to fraud. The incidence peaks with young adults, a group that tends to be heavy online users. Although the over-60 group accounts for only 9 percent of identity theft complaints, this figure is relatively high in proportion to this group's representation in the online population.

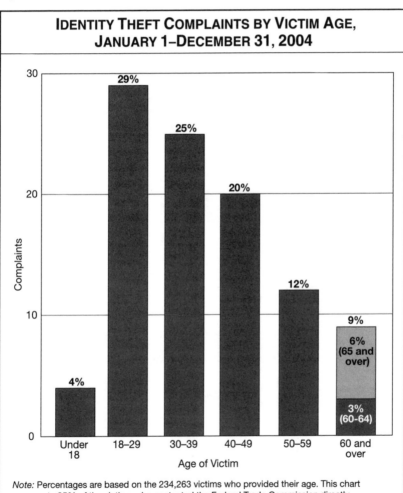

IDENTITY THEFT COMPLAINTS BY VICTIM AGE, JANUARY 1–DECEMBER 31, 2004

Note: Percentages are based on the 234,263 victims who provided their age. This chart represents 95% of the victims who contacted the Federal Trade Commission directly.

Source: Federal Trade Commission. *National and State Trends in Identity Theft: January–December 2004,* p. 11. Available online at URL: http://www.consumer.gov/sentinel/pubs/Top10Fraud2004.pdf.

HOW INFORMATION IS MISUSED

Once identity thieves obtain sensitive personal information, what do they do with it? The chart "How Information Was Misused, January 1–December 31, 2004," is based on FTC complaint data. Credit card fraud is the most common way criminals cash in, which makes sense given the availability and attractiveness of credit card numbers. Bank and utility accounts are also significantly targeted. (Note that the percentages add up to more than 100 because about 19 percent of victims experienced more than one type of identity theft.)

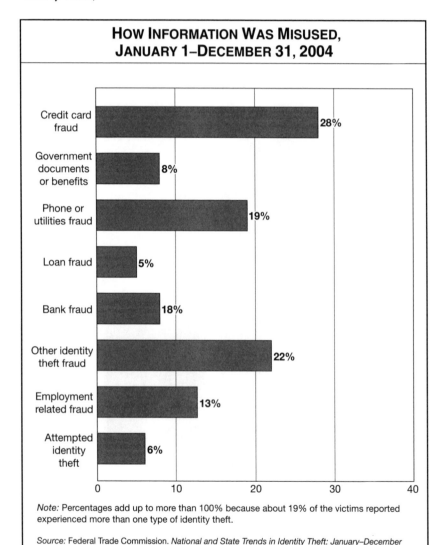

HOW INFORMATION WAS MISUSED, JANUARY 1–DECEMBER 31, 2004

- Credit card fraud: 28%
- Government documents or benefits: 8%
- Phone or utilities fraud: 19%
- Loan fraud: 5%
- Bank fraud: 18%
- Other identity theft fraud: 22%
- Employment related fraud: 13%
- Attempted identity theft: 6%

Note: Percentages add up to more than 100% because about 19% of the victims reported experienced more than one type of identity theft.

Source: Federal Trade Commission. *National and State Trends in Identity Theft: January–December 2004*, p. 10. Available online at URL: http://www.consumer.gov/sentinel/pubs/Top10Fraud2004.pdf.

WHEN DO THEY FIND OUT?

Part of the devastating effect of identity theft on its victims is the fact that weeks or even months can pass before the problem is discovered. By then, the victim's credit can be effectively ruined and he or she may be harassed by bill collectors. The chart "Length of Time to Discover Misuse" gives the percentage of the time each of three types of identity theft are discovered within a given period. Generally, credit card misuse is discovered within a month, while fraud involving the creation of new accounts often takes more than a month to be uncovered. This is because identity thieves typically create new accounts using the victim's information and a new address, so the victim never receives the account statements.

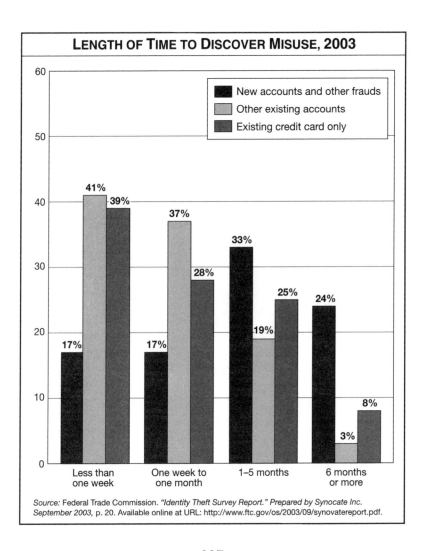

LENGTH OF TIME TO DISCOVER MISUSE, 2003

Legend:
- New accounts and other frauds
- Other existing accounts
- Existing credit card only

Less than one week: 17%, 41%, 39%
One week to one month: 17%, 37%, 28%
1–5 months: 33%, 19%, 25%
6 months or more: 24%, 3%, 8%

Source: Federal Trade Commission. *"Identity Theft Survey Report." Prepared by Synovate Inc. September 2003*, p. 20. Available online at URL: http://www.ftc.gov/os/2003/09/synovatereport.pdf.

WHO DO THEY TELL?

How—if at all—do identity theft victims report their misfortune to the authorities? The graph "Law Enforcement Contact, January 1–December 31, 2004," reveals that 61 percent of identity theft victims surveyed by the FTC did not notify any police department.

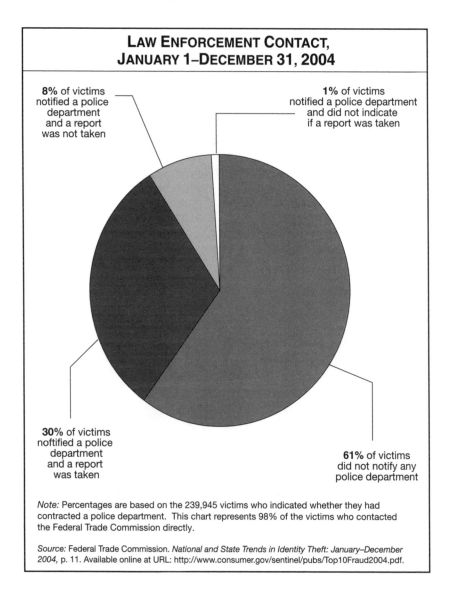

LAW ENFORCEMENT CONTACT, JANUARY 1–DECEMBER 31, 2004

8% of victims notified a police department and a report was not taken

1% of victims notified a police department and did not indicate if a report was taken

30% of victims noftified a police department and a report was taken

61% of victims did not notify any police department

Note: Percentages are based on the 239,945 victims who indicated whether they had contracted a police department. This chart represents 98% of the victims who contacted the Federal Trade Commission directly.

Source: Federal Trade Commission. *National and State Trends in Identity Theft: January–December 2004,* p. 11. Available online at URL: http://www.consumer.gov/sentinel/pubs/Top10Fraud2004.pdf.

APPENDIX B

EXAMPLES OF USER EDUCATION MATERIALS

The following four government brochures (three from the FTC and one from the FBI) are included because they illustrate the ways in which Internet users and consumers are warned about ongoing fraud, identity theft, and crimes against children. Also, much of the information is of practical use and helps expand on the topics discussed throughout this book.

The brochures included and their sources are:

Federal Trade Commission. "Dot Cons." URL: http://www.ftc.gov/bcp/conline/pubs/online/dotcons.htm

Federal Trade Commission. "How Not to Get Hooked by a 'Phishing' Scam." URL: http://www.ftc.gov/bcp/conline/pubs/alerts/phishingalrt.htm

Federal Trade Commission. "ID Theft: When Bad Things Happen to Your Good Name." URL: http://www.ftc.gov/bcp/conline/pubs/credit/idtheft.pdf

Federal Bureau of Investigation. "A Parent's Guide to Internet Safety." URL: http://www.fbi.gov/publications/pguide/pguidee.htm

DOT.CONS

DOT COM. DOT GOV. DOT NET. DOT ORG. DOT EDU. DOT MIL. DOT TV.

The Internet has spawned a whole new lexicon and brought the world to your living room, 24/7/365. And while the opportunities online for consumers are almost endless, there are some challenges, too. As in dot con.

Dot con? Dot con.
Con artists have gone high-tech, using the Internet to defraud consumers in a variety of clever ways. Whether they're using the excitement of an Internet auction to entice consumers into parting with their money, applying new technology to peddle traditional business opportunity scams, using email to reach vast numbers of people with false promises about earnings through day trading, or hijacking consumers' modems and cramming hefty long-distance charges onto their phone bills, scam artists are just a click away.

Fortunately, law enforcement is on the cyber-case. Using complaints to Consumer Sentinel, a consumer fraud database, as their guide, law enforcement officials have identified the top 10 dot cons facing consumers who surf the Internet, as well as many of the fraudsters behind them. In addition to putting many online con artists out of business, the Federal Trade Commission, the nation's chief consumer protection agency, wants consumers to know how not to get caught in their web.

According to the FTC, here's what online consumers are complaining about most:

Internet Auctions
The Bait: Shop in a "virtual marketplace" that offers a huge selection of products at great deals.
The Catch: After sending their money, consumers say they've received an item that is less valuable than promised, or, worse yet, nothing at all.
The Safety Net: When bidding through an Internet auction, particularly for a valuable item, check out the seller and insist on paying with a credit card or using an escrow service.

Internet Access Services
The Bait: Free money, simply for cashing a check.
The Catch: Consumers say they've been "trapped" into long-term contracts for Internet access or another web service, with big penalties for cancellation or early termination.

The Safety Net: If a check arrives at your home or business, read both sides carefully and look inside the envelope to find the conditions you're agreeing to if you cash the check. Read your phone bill carefully for unexpected or unauthorized charges.

Credit Card Fraud

The Bait: Surf the Internet and view adult images online for free, just for sharing your credit card number to prove you're over 18.

The Catch: Consumers say that fraudulent promoters have used their credit card numbers to run up charges on their cards.

The Safety Net: Share credit card information only when buying from a company you trust. Dispute unauthorized charges on your credit card bill by complaining to the bank that issued the card. Federal law limits your liability to $50 in charges if your card is misused.

International Modem Dialing

The Bait: Get free access to adult material and pornography by downloading a "viewer" or "dialer" computer program.

The Catch: Consumers complained about exorbitant long-distance charges on their phone bill. Through the program, their modem is disconnected, then reconnected to the Internet through an international long-distance number.

The Safety Net: Don't download any program to access a so-called "free" service without reading all the disclosures carefully for cost information. Just as important, read your phone bill carefully and challenge any charges you didn't authorize or don't understand.

Web Cramming

The Bait: Get a free custom-designed web site for a 30-day trial period, with no obligation to continue.

The Catch: Consumers say they've been charged on their telephone bills or received a separate invoice, even if they never accepted the offer or agreed to continue the service after the trial period.

The Safety Net: Review your telephone bills and challenge any charges you don't recognize.

Multilevel Marketing Plans/Pyramids

The Bait: Make money through the products and services you sell as well as those sold by the people you recruit into the program.

The Catch: Consumers say that they've bought into plans and programs, but their customers are other distributors, not the general public. Some multi-level marketing programs are actually illegal pyramid schemes. When products or services are sold only to distributors like yourself, there's no way to make money.

The Safety Net: Avoid plans that require you to recruit distributors, buy expensive inventory or commit to a minimum sales volume.

Travel and Vacation

The Bait: Get a luxurious trip with lots of "extras" at a bargain-basement price.

The Catch: Consumers say some companies deliver lower-quality accommodations and services than they've advertised or no trip at all. Others have been hit with hidden charges or additional requirements after they've paid.

The Safety Net: Get references on any travel company you're planning to do business with. Then, get details of the trip in writing, including the cancellation policy, before signing on.

Business Opportunities

The Bait: Be your own boss and earn big bucks.

The Catch: Taken in by promises about potential earnings, many consumers have invested in a "biz op" that turned out to be a "biz flop." There was no evidence to back up the earnings claims.

The Safety Net: Talk to other people who started businesses through the same company, get all the promises in writing, and study the proposed contract carefully before signing. Get an attorney or an accountant to take a look at it, too.

Investments

The Bait: Make an initial investment in a day trading system or service and you'll quickly realize huge returns.

The Catch: Big profits always mean big risk. Consumers have lost money to programs that claim to be able to predict the market with 100 percent accuracy.

The Safety Net: Check out the promoter with state and federal securities and commodities regulators, and talk to other people who invested through the program to find out what level of risk you're assuming.

Health Care Products/Services

The Bait: Items not sold through traditional suppliers are "proven" to cure serious and even fatal health problems.

The Catch: Claims for "miracle" products and treatments convince consumers that their health problems can be cured. But people with serious illnesses who put their hopes in these offers might delay getting the health care they need.

Appendix B

The Safety Net: Consult a health care professional before buying any "cure-all" that claims to treat a wide range of ailments or offers quick cures and easy solutions to serious illnesses.

Can you avoid getting caught by a scam artist working the web? Not always. But prudence pays. The FTC offers these tips to help you avoid getting caught by an offer that just may not click:

- Be wary of extravagant claims about performance or earnings potential. Get all promises in writing and review them carefully before making a payment or signing a contract.
- Read the fine print and all relevant links. Fraudulent promoters sometimes bury the disclosures they're not anxious to share by putting them in teeny-tiny type or in a place where you're unlikely see them.
- Look for a privacy policy. If you don't see one—or if you can't understand it—consider taking your business elsewhere.
- Be skeptical of any company that doesn't clearly state its name, street address and telephone number. Check it out with the local Better Business Bureau, consumer protection office or state Attorney General.

October 2000

HOW NOT TO GET HOOKED BY A 'PHISHING' SCAM

Internet scammers casting about for people's financial information have a new way to lure unsuspecting victims: They go "phishing."

Phishing is a high-tech scam that uses spam or pop-up messages to deceive you into disclosing your credit card numbers, bank account information, Social Security number, passwords, or other sensitive information.

According to the Federal Trade Commission (FTC), phishers send an email or pop-up message that claims to be from a business or organization that you deal with – for example, your Internet service provider (ISP), bank, online payment service, or even a government agency. The message usually says that you need to "update" or "validate" your account information. It might threaten some dire consequence if you don't respond. The message directs you to a Web site that looks just like a legitimate organization's site, but it isn't. The purpose of the bogus site? To trick you into divulging your personal information so the operators can steal your identity and run up bills or commit crimes in your name.

The FTC, the nation's consumer protection agency, suggests these tips to help you avoid getting hooked by a phishing scam:

If you get an email or pop-up message that asks for personal or financial information, do not reply or click on the link in the message. Legitimate companies don't ask for this information via email. If you are concerned about your account, contact the organization in the email using a telephone number you know to be genuine, or open a new Internet browser session and type in the company's correct Web address. In any case, don't cut and paste the link in the message.

Don't email personal or financial information. Email is not a secure method of transmitting personal information. If you initiate a transaction and want to provide your personal or financial information through an organization's Web site, look for indicators that the site is secure, like a lock icon on the browser's status bar or a URL for a web site that begins "https:" (the "s" stands for "secure"). Unfortunately, no indicator is foolproof; some phishers have forged security icons.

Review credit card and bank account statements as soon as you receive them to determine whether there are any unauthorized charges. If your statement is late by more than a couple of days, call your credit card company or bank to confirm your billing address and account balances.

Use anti-virus software and keep it up to date. Some phishing emails contain software that can harm your computer or track your activities on the Internet without your knowledge. Anti-virus software and a firewall can protect you from inadvertently accepting such unwanted files. Anti-virus software scans incoming communications for troublesome files. Look for anti-virus software that recognizes current viruses as well as older ones; that can effectively reverse the damage; and that updates automatically. A firewall helps make you invisible on the Internet and blocks all communications from unauthorized sources. It's especially important to run a firewall if you have a broadband connection. Finally, your operating system (like Windows or Linux) may offer free software "patches" to close holes in the system that hackers or phishers could exploit.

Be cautious about opening any attachment or downloading any files from emails you receive, regardless of who sent them.

Report suspicious activity to the FTC. If you get spam that is phishing for information, forward it to spam@uce.gov. If you believe you've been scammed, file your complaint at www.ftc.gov, and then visit the FTC's Identity Theft Web site at www.consumer.gov/idtheft to learn how to minimize your risk of damage from ID theft. Visit www.ftc.gov/spam to learn other ways to avoid email scams and deal with deceptive spam.

The FTC works for the consumer to prevent fraudulent, deceptive and unfair business practices in the marketplace and to provide information to help consumers spot, stop, and avoid them. To file a complaint or to get free information on consumer issues, visit www.ftc.gov or call toll-free, 1-877-FTC-HELP (1-877-382-4357); TTY: 1-866-653-4261. The FTC enters Internet, telemarketing, identity theft, and other fraud-related complaints into Consumer Sentinel, a secure, online database available to hundreds of civil and criminal law enforcement agencies in the U.S. and abroad.

June 2004

ID THEFT: WHEN BAD THINGS HAPPEN TO YOUR GOOD NAME

[Note: some sections have been omitted]

INTRODUCTION

My purse was stolen in December 1990. In February 1991, I started getting notices of bounced checks. About a year later, I received information that someone using my identity had defaulted on a number of lease agreements and bought a car. In 1997, I learned that someone had been working under my Social Security number for a number of years. A man had been arrested and used my SSN on his arrest sheet. There's a hit in the FBI computers for my SSN with a different name and gender. I can't get credit because of this situation. I was denied a mortgage loan, employment, credit cards, and medical care for my children. I've even had auto insurance denied, medical insurance and tuition assistance denied.

From a consumer complaint to the FTC, January 2, 2001

Appendix B

In the course of a busy day, you may write a check at the grocery store, charge tickets to a ball game, rent a car, mail your tax returns, call home on your cell phone, order new checks or apply for a credit card. Chances are you don't give these everyday transactions a second thought. But someone else may.

The 1990's spawned a new variety of crooks called identity thieves. Their stock in trade is your everyday transaction. Each transaction requires you to share personal information: your bank and credit card account numbers; your income; your Social Security number (SSN); or your name, address and phone numbers. An identity thief co-opts some piece of your personal information and appropriates it without your knowledge to commit fraud or theft. An all-too-common example is when an identity thief uses your personal information to open a credit card account in your name.

Identity theft is a serious crime. People whose identities have been stolen can spend months or years—and thousands of dollars—cleaning up the mess the thieves have made of their good name and credit record. In the meantime, victims may lose job opportunities, be refused loans for education, housing, cars, or even be arrested for crimes they didn't commit. Humiliation, anger and frustration are common feelings victims experience as they navigate the arduous process of reclaiming their identity.

Perhaps you've received your first call from a collections agent demanding payment on a loan you never took out—for a car you never bought. Maybe you've already spent a significant amount of time and money calling financial institutions, canceling accounts, struggling to regain your good name and credit. Or maybe your wallet's been stolen, or you've just heard about identity theft for the first time on the nightly news, and you'd like to know more about protecting yourself from this devastating crime. This booklet is for you.

The Federal Trade Commission (FTC), working with other government agencies and organizations, has produced this booklet to help you guard against and recover from identity theft. Can you completely prevent identity theft from occurring? Probably not, especially if someone is determined to commit the crime. But you can minimize your risk by managing your personal information wisely and cautiously.

If you've been a victim of identity theft, call the FTC's Identity Theft Hotline toll-free at **1-877-IDTHEFT (438-4338).** Counselors will take your complaint and advise you on how to deal with the credit-related problems that could result. In addition, the FTC, in conjunction with banks, credit grantors and consumer advocates, has developed the ID Theft Affidavit to help victims of ID theft restore their good names. The ID Theft Affidavit, a form that can be used to report information to many organizations, simplifies the process of disputing charges with companies where a new account was opened in your name. For a copy of the ID Theft Affidavit, scroll down to the Appendix or visit the ID Theft Web site at www.consumer.gov/idtheft.

The Hotline and Web site give you one place to report the theft to the federal government and receive helpful information. The FTC puts your information into a secure consumer fraud database where it can be used to help other law enforcement agencies and private entities in their investigations and victim assistance.

HOW IDENTITY THEFT OCCURS

My wallet was stolen in December 1998. There's been no end to the problems I've faced since then. The thieves used my identity to write checks, use a debit card, open a bank account with a line of credit, open credit accounts with several stores, obtain cell phones and run up huge bills, print fraudulent checks on a personal computer bearing my name, and more. I've spent the last two years trying to repair my credit report (a very frustrating process) and have suffered the ill effects of having a marred credit history. I've recently been denied a student loan because of inaccurate information on my credit report.

From a consumer complaint to the FTC, February 22, 2001

Despite your best efforts to manage the flow of your personal information or to keep it to yourself, skilled identity thieves may use a variety of methods—low- and hi-tech—to gain access to your data. Here are some of the ways imposters can get your personal information and take over your identity.

HOW IDENTITY THIEVES GET YOUR PERSONAL INFORMATION:

- They steal wallets and purses containing your identification and credit and bank cards.
- They steal your mail, including your bank and credit card statements, pre-approved credit offers, new checks, and tax information.
- They complete a "change of address form" to divert your mail to another location.

- They rummage through your trash, or the trash of businesses, for personal data in a practice known as "dumpster diving."
- They fraudulently obtain your credit report by posing as a landlord, employer or someone else who may have a legitimate need for, and legal right to, the information.
- They find personal information in your home.
- They use personal information you share on the Internet.
- They scam you, often through email, by posing as legitimate companies or government agencies you do business with.
- They get your information from the workplace in a practice known as "business record theft" by: stealing files out of offices where you're a customer, employee, patient or student; bribing an employee who has access to your files; or "hacking" into electronic files.

HOW IDENTITY THIEVES USE YOUR PERSONAL INFORMATION:

- They call your credit card issuer and, pretending to be you, ask to change the mailing address on your credit card account. The imposter then runs up charges on your account. Because your bills are being sent to the new address, it may take some time before you realize there's a problem.
- They open a new credit card account, using your name, date of birth and SSN. When they use the credit card and don't pay the bills, the delinquent account is reported on your credit report.
- They establish phone or wireless service in your name.
- They open a bank account in your name and write bad checks on that account.
- They file for bankruptcy under your name to avoid paying debts they've incurred under your name, or to avoid eviction.
- They counterfeit checks or debit cards, and drain your bank account.
- They buy cars by taking out auto loans in your name.
- They give your name to the police during an arrest. If they're released from police custody, but don't show up for their court date, an arrest warrant is issued in your name.

Minimize Your Risk

I'm tired of the hours I've spent on the phone and all the faxing I've had to do. When will it be over?

From a consumer complaint to the FTC, March 13, 2001

Tomorrow is Sunday so we won't get any notices, but I'm not looking forward to Monday's mail.

From a consumer complaint to the FTC, November 13, 2001

While you probably can't prevent identity theft entirely, you can minimize your risk. By managing your personal information wisely, cautiously and with an awareness of the issue, you can help guard against identity theft.

WHAT YOU CAN DO TODAY

- **Order a copy of your credit report from each of the three major credit bureaus.** Your credit report contains information on where you work and live, the credit accounts that have been opened in your name, how you pay your bills and whether you've been sued, arrested or filed for bankruptcy. Make sure it's accurate and includes only those activities you've authorized. By law, credit bureaus can charge you no more than $9 for a copy of your credit report. See "Credit Reports," below, for details about removing fraudulent and inaccurate information from your credit report.

- **Place passwords on your credit card, bank and phone accounts.** Avoid using easily available information like your mother's maiden name, your birth date, the last four digits of your SSN or your phone number, or a series of consecutive numbers. When opening new accounts, you may find that many businesses still have a line on their applications for your mother's maiden name. Use a password instead.

- **Secure personal information in your home,** especially if you have roommates, employ outside help or are having service work done in your home.

- **Ask about information security procedures in your workplace.** Find out who has access to your personal information and verify that records are kept in a secure location. Ask about the disposal procedures for those records as well.

- Order a copy of your credit report from each of the three major credit bureaus once a year. By checking your report on a regular basis you can catch mistakes and fraud before they wreak havoc on your personal finances. Don't underestimate the importance of this step. One of the most common ways that consumers find out that they're victims of identity theft is when they try to make a major purchase, like a house or a car. The deal can be lost or delayed while the credit report mess is straightened out. Knowing what's in your credit report allows you to fix problems before they jeopardize a major financial transaction.

CREDIT BUREAUS

Equifax—www.equifax.com
To order your report, call: 800-685-1111
To report fraud, call: 800-525-6285
TDD 800-255-0056 and write:
P.O. Box 740241, Atlanta, GA 30374-0241

Experian—www.experian.com
To order your report, call: 888-EXPERIAN (397-3742)
To report fraud, call: 888-EXPERIAN (397-3742)
TDD 800-972-0322 and write:
P.O. Box 9532, Allen TX 75013

TransUnion—www.transunion.com
To order your report, call: 800-888-4213
To report fraud, call: 800-680-7289
TDD 877-553-7803; fax: 714-447-6034; email:
fvad@transunion.com or write: Fraud Victim Assistance
Department, P.O. Box 6790, Fullerton, CA 92834-6790

Maintaining Vigilance
Order a copy of your report from each of the three major credit bureaus once a year. By checking your report on a regular basis you can catch mistakes and fraud before they wreak havoc on your personal finances. Don't underestimate the importance of this step. One of the most common ways that consumers find out that they're victims of identity theft is when they try to make a major purchase, like a house or a car. The deal can be lost or delayed while the credit report mess is straightened out. Knowing what's in your credit report allows you fix problems before they jeopardize a major financial transaction.

- Don't give out personal information on the phone, through the mail or over the Internet unless you've initiated the contact or are sure you know who you're dealing with. Identity thieves may pose as representatives of banks, Internet service providers (ISPs) and even government agencies to get you to reveal your SSN, mother's maiden name, account numbers and other identifying information. Before you share any personal information, confirm that you are dealing with a legitimate organization. You can check the organization's Web site as many companies post scam alerts when their name is used improperly, or you can call customer service using the number listed on your account statement or in the telephone book.

- Guard your mail and trash from theft.

  Deposit outgoing mail in post office collection boxes or at your local post office, rather than in an unsecured mailbox. Promptly remove mail from your mailbox. If you're planning to be away from home and can't pick up your mail, call the U.S. Postal Service at 1-800-275-8777 to request a vacation hold. The Postal Service will hold your mail at your local post office until you can pick it up or are home to receive it.

  To thwart an identity thief who may pick through your trash or recycling bins to capture your personal information, tear or shred your charge receipts, copies of credit applications, insurance forms, physician statements, checks and bank statements, expired charge cards that you're discarding, and credit offers you get in the mail.

- Before revealing any personally identifying information (for example, on an application), find out how it will be used and secured, and whether it will be shared with others. Ask if you have a choice about the use of your information. Can you choose to have it kept confidential?

- Don't carry your SSN card; leave it in a secure place.

- Give your SSN only when absolutely necessary. Ask to use other types of identifiers when possible. If your state uses your SSN as your driver's license number, ask to substitute another number.

- Carry only the identification information and the number of credit and debit cards that you'll actually need.

A SPECIAL WORD ABOUT SOCIAL SECURITY NUMBERS

Your employer and financial institution will likely need your SSN for wage and tax reporting purposes. Other businesses may ask you for your SSN to do a credit check, like when you apply for a loan, rent an apartment, or sign up for utilities. Sometimes, however, they simply want your SSN for general record keeping. You don't have to give a business your SSN just because they ask for it. If someone asks for your SSN, ask the following questions:

- Why do you need my SSN?
- How will my SSN be used?
- What law requires me to give you my SSN?
- What will happen if I don't give you my SSN?

Sometimes a business may not provide you with the service or benefit you're seeking if you don't provide your SSN. Getting answers to these questions will help you decide whether you want to share your SSN with the business. Remember—the decision is yours.

- Pay attention to your billing cycles. Follow up with creditors if your bills don't arrive on time. A missing credit card bill could mean an identity thief has taken over your account and changed your billing address to cover his tracks.

- Be wary of promotional scams. Identity thieves may use phony offers to get you to give them your personal information.

- Keep your purse or wallet in a safe place at work.

THE DOORS AND WINDOWS ARE LOCKED, BUT . . .

You may be careful about locking your doors and windows, and keeping your personal papers in a secure place. But, depending on what you use your personal computer for, an identity thief may not need to set foot in your house to steal your personal information. SSNs, financial records, tax returns, birth dates, and bank account numbers may be stored in your computer—a goldmine to an identity thief. The following tips can help you keep your computer and your personal information safe.

- Update your virus protection software regularly, or when a new virus alert is announced. Computer viruses can have a variety of damaging effects, including introducing program code that causes your computer to send out files or other stored information. Be on the alert for security repairs and patches that you can download from your operating system's Web site.

- Do not download files sent to you by strangers or click on hyperlinks from people you don't know. Opening a file could expose your system to a computer virus or a program that could hijack your modem.

- Use a firewall program, especially if you use a high-speed Internet connection like cable, DSL or T-1, which leaves your computer connected to the Internet 24 hours a day. The firewall program will allow you to stop uninvited guests from accessing your computer. Without it, hackers can take over your computer and access your personal information stored on it or use it to commit other crimes.

- Use a secure browser—software that encrypts or scrambles information you send over the Internet—to guard the security of your online transactions. Be sure your browser has the most up-to-date encryption capabilities by using the latest version available from the manufacturer. You also can download some browsers for free over the Internet. When submitting information, look for the "lock" icon on the browser's status bar to be sure your information is secure during transmission.

- Try not to store financial information on your laptop unless absolutely necessary. If you do, use a strong password—a combination of letters (upper and lowers case), numbers and symbols. Don't use an automatic log-in feature which saves your user name and password so you don't have to enter them each time you log-in or enter a site. And always log off when you're finished. That way, if your laptop gets stolen, it's harder for the thief to access your personal information.

- Before you dispose of a computer, delete personal information. Deleting files using the keyboard or mouse commands may not be enough because the files may stay on the computer's hard drive, where they may be easily retrieved. Use a "wipe" utility program to overwrite the entire hard drive. It makes the files unrecoverable. For more information, see *Clearing Information From Your Computer's Hard Drive* (www.hq.nasa.gov/office/oig/hq/harddrive.pdf) from the National Aeronautics and Space Administration (NASA).

- Look for Web site privacy policies. They answer questions about maintaining accuracy, access, security, and control of personal information collected by the site, as well as how information will be used, and whether it will be provided to third parties. If you don't see a privacy policy, consider surfing elsewhere.

For more information, see *Site-Seeing on the Internet: A Traveler's Guide to Cyberspace* from the FTC at www.ftc.gov.

CHOOSING TO SHARE YOUR PERSONAL INFORMATION—OR NOT

In November 2000, I found out that someone used my information to obtain a cell phone. Since then, I've been living a nightmare. My credit report is a mess. It's a full-time job to investigate and correct the information.

From a consumer complaint to the FTC, April 3, 2001

Our economy generates an enormous amount of data. Most users of that information are from honest businesses—getting and giving legitimate information. Despite the benefits of the information age, some consumers may want to limit the amount of personal information they share. And they can: More organizations are offering people choices about how their personal information is used. For example, many feature an "opt-out" choice that limits the information shared with others or used for promotional purposes. When you "opt-out," you may cut down on the number of unsolicited telemarketing calls, promotional mail and spam emails that you receive. Learn more about the options you have for protecting your personal information by contacting the following organizations.

Appendix B

CREDIT BUREAUS
Pre-Screened Credit Offers

If you receive pre-screened credit card offers in the mail (namely, those based upon your credit data), but don't tear them up after you decide you don't want to accept the offer, identity thieves could retrieve the offers for their own use without your knowledge.

To opt out of receiving pre-screened credit card offers, call: 1-888-5-OPTOUT (1-888-567- 8688). The three major credit bureaus use the same toll-free number to let consumers choose to not receive pre-screened credit offers.

Marketing Lists

In addition, you can notify the three major credit bureaus that you do not want personal information about you shared for promotional purposes. To ask the three major credit bureaus not to share your personal information, write to:

Equifax, Inc.
Options
PO Box 740123
Atlanta, GA 30374-0123

Experian
Consumer Opt-Out
701 Experian Parkway
Allen, TX 75013

TransUnion
Marketing List Opt Out
PO Box 97328
Jackson, MS 39288-7328

DEPARTMENT OF MOTOR VEHICLES

The Drivers Privacy Protection Act forbids states from distributing personal information to direct marketers. It does allow for the sharing of personal information with law enforcement officials, courts, government agencies, private investigators, insurance underwriters and similar businesses. Check with your state DMV to learn more, or visit www.ftc.gov/privacy/protect.htm#Motor.

DIRECT MARKETERS
Telemarketing

The federal government has created the National Do Not Call Registry—the free, easy way to reduce the telemarketing calls you get at home. To register, or to get information, visit www.donotcall.gov, or call 1-888-382-1222 from the phone you want to register. You will receive fewer telemarketing calls within three months of registering your number. It will stay in the registry for five years or until it is disconnected or you take it off the registry. After five years, you will be able to renew your registration.

Mail

The Direct Marketing Association's (DMA) Mail Preference Service lets you "opt- out" of receiving direct mail marketing from many national companies for five years. When you register with this service, your name will be put on a "delete" file and made available to direct-mail marketers. However, your registration will not stop mailings from organizations that are not registered with the DMA's Mail Preference Service. To register with DMA, send your letter to:

Direct Marketing Association
Mail Preference Service
PO Box 643
Carmel, NY 10512
Or register online at www.the-dma.org/consumers/offmailinglist.html.

Email

The DMA also has an EMail Preference Service to help you reduce unsolicited commercial emails. To "opt-out" of receiving unsolicited commercial email, use DMA's online form at www.dmaconsumers.org/offemaillist.html. Your online request will be effective for one year.

IF YOU'RE A VICTIM

Sometimes an identity thief can strike even if you've been very careful about keeping your personal information to yourself. If you suspect that your personal information has been hijacked and misappropriated to commit fraud or theft, take action immediately, and keep a record of your conversations and correspondence. You may want to use the form, "Chart Your Course of Action," below. Exactly which steps you should take to protect yourself depends on your circumstances and how your identity has been misused. However, four basic actions are appropriate in almost every case.

YOUR FIRST FOUR STEPS

1. Place a fraud alert on your credit reports and review your credit reports.

Call the toll-free fraud number of any one of the three major credit bureaus to place a fraud alert on your credit report. This can help prevent an identity thief from opening additional accounts in your name. As soon as the credit bureau confirms your fraud alert, the other two credit bureaus will automatically be notified to place fraud alerts on your credit report, and all three reports will be sent to you free of charge.

- **Equifax**—To report fraud, call: 1-800-525-6285, and write: P.O. Box 740241, Atlanta, GA 30374-0241
- **Experian**—To report fraud, call: 1-888-EXPERIAN (397-3742), and write: P.O. Box 9532, Allen, TX 75013
- **TransUnion**—To report fraud, call: 1-800-680-7289, and write: Fraud Victim Assistance Division, P.O. Box 6790, Fullerton, CA 92834-6790

Once you receive your reports, review them carefully. Look for inquiries you didn't initiate, accounts you didn't open, and unexplained debts on your true accounts. Where "inquiries" appear from the company(ies) that opened the fraudulent account(s), request that these "inquiries" be removed from your report. (See "Credit Reports" for more information.) You also should check that information such as your SSN, address(es), name or initial, and employers are correct. Inaccuracies in this information also may be due to typographical errors. Nevertheless, whether the inaccuracies are due to fraud or error, you should notify the credit bureau as soon as possible by telephone and in writing. You should continue to check your reports periodically, especially in the first year after you've discovered the theft, to make sure no new fraudulent activity has occurred. The automated "one-call" fraud alert process only works for the initial placement of your fraud alert. Orders for additional credit reports or renewals of your fraud alerts must be made separately at each of the three major credit bureaus.

2. Close any accounts that have been tampered with or opened fraudulently.

Credit Accounts

Credit accounts include all accounts with banks, credit card companies and other lenders, and phone companies, utilities, ISPs, and other service providers.

If you're closing existing accounts and opening new ones, use new Personal Identification Numbers (PINs) and passwords.

If there are fraudulent charges or debits, ask the company about the following forms for disputing those transactions:

- For new unauthorized accounts, ask if the company accepts the ID Theft Affidavit (available at www.ftc.gov/bcp/conline/pubs/credit/affidavit.pdf or in the Appendix below). If they don't, ask the representative to send you the company's fraud dispute forms.
- For your existing accounts, ask the representative to send you the company's fraud dispute forms.
- If your ATM card has been lost, stolen or otherwise compromised, cancel the card as soon as you can. Get a new card with a new PIN.

Checks

If your checks have been stolen or misused, close the account and ask your bank to notify the appropriate check verification service. While no federal law limits your losses if someone steals your checks and forges your signature, state laws may protect you. Most states hold the bank responsible for losses from a forged check, but they also require you to take reasonable care of your account. For example, you may be held responsible for the forgery if you fail to notify the bank in a timely way that a check was lost or stolen. Contact your state banking or consumer protection agency for more information.

You also should contact these major check verification companies. Ask that retailers who use their databases not accept your checks.

TeleCheck—1-800-710-9898 or 927-0188
Certegy, Inc.—1-800-437-5120
International Check Services—1-800-631-9656
Call SCAN (1-800-262-7771) to find out if the identity thief has been passing bad checks in your name.

3. File a report with your local police or the police in the community where the identity theft took place.

Keep a copy of the report. You may need it to validate your claims to creditors. If you can't get a copy, at least get the report number.

4. File a complaint with the FTC.

By sharing your identity theft complaint with the FTC, you will provide important information that can help law enforcement officials track down identity thieves and stop them. The FTC also can refer victim complaints to other appropriate government agencies and companies for further action. The FTC enters the information you provide into our secure database.

To file a complaint or to learn more about the FTC's Privacy Policy, visit www.consumer.gov/idtheft. If you don't have access to the Internet, you can call the FTC's Identity Theft Hotline: toll-free 1-877-IDTHEFT (438-4338); TDD: 202-326-2502; or write: Identity Theft Clearinghouse, Federal Trade Commission, 600 Pennsylvania Avenue, NW, Washington, DC 20580.

U.S. Department of Justice
Federal Bureau of Investigations
Publications

A PARENT'S GUIDE TO INTERNET SAFETY

Dear Parent:

Our children are our Nation's most valuable asset. They represent the bright future of our country and hold our hopes for a better Nation. Our children are also the most vulnerable members of society. Protecting our children against the fear of crime and from becoming victims of crime must be a national priority.

Unfortunately the same advances in computer and telecommunication technology that allow our children to reach out to new sources of knowledge and cultural experiences are also leaving them vulnerable to exploitation and harm by computer-sex offenders.

I hope that this pamphlet helps you to begin to understand the complexities of on-line child exploitation. For further information, please contact your local FBI office or the National Center for Missing and Exploited Children at 1-800-843-5678.

Louis J. Freeh, Former Director
Federal Bureau of Investigation

INTRODUCTION

While on-line computer exploration opens a world of possibilities for children, expanding their horizons and exposing them to different cultures and ways of life, they can be exposed to dangers as they hit the road exploring the information highway. There are individuals who attempt to sexually exploit children through the use of on-line services and the Internet. Some of these individuals gradually seduce their targets through the use of attention, affection, kindness, and even gifts. These individuals are often willing to devote considerable amounts of time, money, and energy in this process. They listen to and empathize with the problems of children. They will be aware of the latest music, hobbies, and interests of children. These individuals attempt to gradually lower children's inhibitions by slowly introducing sexual context and content into their conversations.

There are other individuals, however, who immediately engage in sexually explicit conversation with children. Some offenders primarily collect and trade child-pornographic images, while others seek face-to-face meetings with children via on-line contacts. It is important for parents to understand that children can be indirectly victimized through conversation, i.e.

"chat," as well as the transfer of sexually explicit information and material. Computer-sex offenders may also be evaluating children they come in contact with on-line for future face-to-face contact and direct victimization. Parents and children should remember that a computer-sex offender can be any age or sex—the person does not have to fit the caricature of a dirty, unkempt, older man wearing a raincoat to be someone who could harm a child.

Children, especially adolescents, are sometimes interested in and curious about sexuality and sexually explicit material. They may be moving away from the total control of parents and seeking to establish new relationships outside their family. Because they may be curious, children/adolescents sometimes use their on-line access to actively seek out such materials and individuals. Sex offenders targeting children will use and exploit these characteristics and needs. Some adolescent children may also be attracted to and lured by on-line offenders closer to their age who, although not technically child molesters, may be dangerous. Nevertheless, they have been seduced and manipulated by a clever offender and do not fully understand or recognize the potential danger of these contacts.

This guide was prepared from actual investigations involving child victims, as well as investigations where law enforcement officers posed as children. Further information on protecting your child on-line may be found in the *National Center for Missing and Exploited Children's* Child Safety on the Information Highway and Teen Safety on the Information Highway pamphlets.

WHAT ARE SIGNS THAT YOUR CHILD MIGHT BE AT RISK ON-LINE?

Your child spends large amounts of time on-line, especially at night.

Most children that fall victim to computer-sex offenders spend large amounts of time on-line, particularly in chat rooms. They may go on-line after dinner and on the weekends. They may be latchkey kids whose parents have told them to stay at home after school. They go on-line to chat with friends, make new friends, pass time, and sometimes look for sexually explicit information. While much of the knowledge and experience gained may be valuable, parents should consider monitoring the amount of time spent on-line.

Children on-line are at the greatest risk during the evening hours. While offenders are on-line around the clock, most work during the day and spend their evenings on-line trying to locate and lure children or seeking pornography.

You find pornography on your child's computer.

Pornography is often used in the sex victimization of children. Sex offenders often supply their potential victims with pornography as a means of opening sexual discussions and for seduction. Child pornography may be used to show the child victim that sex between children and adults is "normal." Parents should be conscious of the fact that a child may hide the pornographic files on diskettes from them. This may be especially true if the computer is used by other family members.

Your child receives phone calls from men you don't know or is making calls, sometimes long distance, to numbers you don't recognize.

While talking to a child victim on-line is a thrill for a computer-sex offender, it can be very cumbersome. Most want to talk to the children on the telephone. They often engage in "phone sex" with the children and often seek to set up an actual meeting for real sex.

While a child may be hesitant to give out his/her home phone number, the computer-sex offenders will give out theirs. With Caller ID, they can readily find out the child's phone number. Some computer-sex offenders have even obtained toll-free 800 numbers, so that their potential victims can call them without their parents finding out. Others will tell the child to call collect. Both of these methods result in the computer-sex offender being able to find out the child's phone number.

Your child receives mail, gifts, or packages from someone you don't know.

As part of the seduction process, it is common for offenders to send letters, photographs, and all manner of gifts to their potential victims. Computer-sex offenders have even sent plane tickets in order for the child to travel across the country to meet them.

Your child turns the computer monitor off or quickly changes the screen on the monitor when you come into the room.

A child looking at pornographic images or having sexually explicit conversations does not want you to see it on the screen.

Your child becomes withdrawn from the family.

Computer-sex offenders will work very hard at driving a wedge between a child and their family or at exploiting their relationship. They will accentuate any minor problems at home that the child might have. Children may also become withdrawn after sexual victimization.

Your child is using an on-line account belonging to someone else.

Even if you don't subscribe to an on-line service or Internet service, your child may meet an offender while on-line at a friend's house or the library. Most computers come preloaded with on-line and/or Internet software. Computer-sex offenders will sometimes provide potential victims with a computer account for communications with them.

WHAT SHOULD YOU DO IF YOU SUSPECT YOUR CHILD IS COMMUNICATING WITH A SEXUAL PREDATOR ON-LINE?

- Consider talking openly with your child about your suspicions. Tell them about the dangers of computer-sex offenders.

- Review what is on your child's computer. If you don't know how, ask a friend, coworker, relative, or other knowledgeable person. Pornography or any kind of sexual communication can be a warning sign.

- Use the Caller ID service to determine who is calling your child. Most telephone companies that offer Caller ID also offer a service that allows you to block your number from appearing on someone else's Caller ID. Telephone companies also offer an additional service feature that rejects incoming calls that you block. This rejection feature prevents computer-sex offenders or anyone else from calling your home anonymously.

- Devices can be purchased that show telephone numbers that have been dialed from your home phone. Additionally, the last number called from your home phone can be retrieved provided that the telephone is equipped with a redial feature. You will also need a telephone pager to complete this retrieval.

- This is done using a numeric-display pager and another phone that is on the same line as the first phone with the redial feature. Using the two phones and the pager, a call is placed from the second phone to the pager. When the paging terminal beeps for you to enter a telephone number, you press the redial button on the first (or suspect) phone. The last number called from that phone will then be displayed on the pager.

- Monitor your child's access to all types of live electronic communications (i.e., chat rooms, instant messages, Internet Relay Chat, etc.), and monitor your child's e-mail. Computer-sex offenders almost always meet potential victims via chat rooms. After meeting a child on-line, they will continue to communicate electronically often via e-mail.

Should any of the following situations arise in your household, via the Internet or on-line service, you should immediately contact your local or state law enforcement agency, the *FBI*, and the *National Center for Missing and Exploited Children:*

1. Your child or anyone in the household has received child pornography;
2. Your child has been sexually solicited by someone who knows that your child is under 18 years of age;
3. Your child has received sexually explicit images from someone that knows your child is under the age of 18.

If one of these scenarios occurs, keep the computer turned off in order to preserve any evidence for future law enforcement use. Unless directed to do so by the law enforcement agency, you should not attempt to copy any of the images and/or text found on the computer.

WHAT CAN YOU DO TO MINIMIZE THE CHANCES OF AN ON-LINE EXPLOITER VICTIMIZING YOUR CHILD?

- Communicate, and talk to your child about sexual victimization and potential on-line danger.

- Spend time with your children on-line. Have them teach you about their favorite on-line destinations.

- Keep the computer in a common room in the house, not in your child's bedroom. It is much more difficult for a computer-sex offender to communicate with a child when the computer screen is visible to a parent or another member of the household.

- Utilize parental controls provided by your service provider and/or blocking software. While electronic chat can be a great place for children to make new friends and discuss various topics of interest, it is also prowled by computer-sex offenders. Use of chat rooms, in particular, should be heavily monitored. While parents should utilize these mechanisms, they should not totally rely on them.

- Always maintain access to your child's on-line account and randomly check his/her e-mail. Be aware that your child could be contacted through the U.S. Mail. Be up front with your child about your access and reasons why.

- Teach your child the responsible use of the resources on-line. There is much more to the on-line experience than chat rooms.

- Find out what computer safeguards are utilized by your child's school, the public library, and at the homes of your child's friends. These are all places, outside your normal supervision, where your child could encounter an on-line predator.

- Understand, even if your child was a willing participant in any form of sexual exploitation, that he/she is not at fault and is the victim. The offender always bears the complete responsibility for his or her actions.

- Instruct your children:

  - to never arrange a face-to-face meeting with someone they met on-line;

  - to never upload (post) pictures of themselves onto the Internet or on-line service to people they do not personally know;

  - to never give out identifying information such as their name, home address, school name, or telephone number;

  - to never download pictures from an unknown source, as there is a good chance there could be sexually explicit images;

  - to never respond to messages or bulletin board postings that are suggestive, obscene, belligerent, or harassing;

  - that whatever they are told on-line may or may not be true.

Frequently Asked Questions:
My child has received an e-mail advertising for a pornographic web site, what should I do?

Generally, advertising for an adult, pornographic web site that is sent to an e-mail address does not violate federal law or the current laws of most states. In some states it may be a violation of law if the sender knows the recipient is under the age of 18. Such advertising can be reported to your service provider and, if known, the service provider of the originator. It can also be reported to your state and federal legislators, so they can be made aware of the extent of the problem.

Is any service safer than the others?

Sex offenders have contacted children via most of the major on-line services and the Internet. The most important factors in keeping your child safe on-line are the utilization of appropriate blocking software and/or parental controls, along with open, honest discussions with your child, monitoring his/her on-line activity, and following the tips in this pamphlet.

Internet Predators

Should I just forbid my child from going on-line?

There are dangers in every part of our society. By educating your children to these dangers and taking appropriate steps to protect them, they can benefit from the wealth of information now available on-line.

Helpful Definitions:

Internet – An immense, global network that connects computers via telephone lines and/or fiber networks to storehouses of electronic information. With only a computer, a modem, a telephone line and a service provider, people from all over the world can communicate and share information with little more than a few keystrokes.

Bulletin Board Systems (BBSs) – Electronic networks of computers that are connected by a central computer setup and operated by a system administrator or operator and are distinguishable from the Internet by their "dial-up" accessibility. BBS users link their individual computers to the central BBS computer by a modem which allows them to post messages, read messages left by others, trade information, or hold direct conversations. Access to a BBS can, and often is, privileged and limited to those users who have access privileges granted by the systems operator.

Commercial On-line Service (COS) – Examples of COSs are America Online, Prodigy, CompuServe and Microsoft Network, which provide access to their service for a fee. COSs generally offer limited access to the Internet as part of their total service package.

Internet Service Provider (ISP) – Examples of ISPs are Erols, Concentric and Netcom. These services offer direct, full access to the Internet at a flat, monthly rate and often provide electronic-mail service for their customers. ISPs often provide space on their servers for their customers to maintain World Wide Web (WWW) sites. Not all ISPs are commercial enterprises. Educational, governmental and nonprofit organizations also provide Internet access to their members.

Public Chat Rooms – Created, maintained, listed and monitored by the COS and other public domain systems such as Internet Relay Chat. A number of customers can be in the public chat rooms at any given time, which are monitored for illegal activity and even appropriate language by systems operators (SYSOP). Some public chat rooms are monitored more frequently than others, depending on the COS and the type of chat room. Violators can be reported to the administrators of the system (at America

On-line they are referred to as terms of service [TOS]) which can revoke user privileges. The public chat rooms usually cover a broad range of topics such as entertainment, sports, game rooms, children only, etc.

Electronic Mail (E-Mail) – A function of BBSs, COSs and ISPs which provides for the transmission of messages and files between computers over a communications network similar to mailing a letter via the postal service. E-mail is stored on a server, where it will remain until the addressee retrieves it. Anonymity can be maintained by the sender by predetermining what the receiver will see as the "from" address. Another way to conceal one's identity is to use an "anonymous remailer," which is a service that allows the user to send an e-mail message repackaged under the remailer's own header, stripping off the originator's name completely.

Chat – Real-time text conversation between users in a chat room with no expectation of privacy. All chat conversation is accessible by all individuals in the chat room while the conversation is taking place.

Instant Messages – Private, real-time text conversation between two users in a chat room.

Internet Relay Chat (IRC) – Real-time text conversation similar to public and/or private chat rooms on COS.

Usenet (Newsgroups) – Like a giant, cork bulletin board where users post messages and information. Each posting is like an open letter and is capable of having attachments, such as graphic image files (GIFs). Anyone accessing the newsgroup can read the postings, take copies of posted items, or post responses. Each newsgroup can hold thousands of postings. Currently, there are over 29,000 public newsgroups and that number is growing daily. Newsgroups are both public and/or private. There is no listing of private newsgroups. A user of private newsgroups has to be invited into the newsgroup and be provided with the newsgroup's address.

Federal Bureau of Investigation
Crimes Against Children Program
935 Pennsylvania Avenue, NW Room 11163
Washington, D.C. 20535
Telephone (202) 324-3666

APPENDIX C

SELECTED U.S.
CODE PROVISIONS

In addition to the separately titled federal laws described in Chapter 2, the U.S. Code has a section relating to computer crimes. Appropriate provisions can often be combined with more specific laws in charging offenses. (For notes and amendments see the Legal Information Institute page at http://www4.law.cornell.edu/uscode/18/1030.notes.html.)

Sec. 1030.—Fraud and related activity in connection with computers
(a)
Whoever —
(1)
having knowingly accessed a computer without authorization or exceeding authorized access, and by means of such conduct having obtained information that has been determined by the United States Government pursuant to an Executive order or statute to require protection against unauthorized disclosure for reasons of national defense or foreign relations, or any restricted data, as defined in paragraph y. of section 11 of the Atomic Energy Act of 1954, with reason to believe that such information so obtained could be used to the injury of the United States, or to the advantage of any foreign nation willfully communicates, delivers, transmits, or causes to be communicated, delivered, or transmitted, or attempts to communicate, deliver, transmit or cause to be communicated, delivered, or transmitted the same to any person not entitled to receive it, or willfully retains the same and fails to deliver it to the officer or employee of the United States entitled to receive it;
(2)
intentionally accesses a computer without authorization or exceeds authorized access, and thereby obtains —

Appendix C

(A)
information contained in a financial record of a financial institution, or of a card issuer as defined in section 1602(n) of title 15, or contained in a file of a consumer reporting agency on a consumer, as such terms are defined in the Fair Credit Reporting Act (15 U.S.C. 1681 et seq.);

(B)
information from any department or agency of the United States; or

(C)
information from any protected computer if the conduct involved an interstate or foreign communication;

(3)
intentionally, without authorization to access any nonpublic computer of a department or agency of the United States, accesses such a computer of that department or agency that is exclusively for the use of the Government of the United States or, in the case of a computer not exclusively for such use, is used by or for the Government of the United States and such conduct affects that use by or for the Government of the United States;

(4)
knowingly and with intent to defraud, accesses a protected computer without authorization, or exceeds authorized access, and by means of such conduct furthers the intended fraud and obtains anything of value, unless the object of the fraud and the thing obtained consists only of the use of the computer and the value of such use is not more than $5,000 in any 1-year period;

(5)

(A)

(i)
knowingly causes the transmission of a program, information, code, or command, and as a result of such conduct, intentionally causes damage without authorization, to a protected computer;

(ii)
intentionally accesses a protected computer without authorization, and as a result of such conduct, recklessly causes damage; or

(iii)
intentionally accesses a protected computer without authorization, and as a result of such conduct, causes damage; and

(B)
by conduct described in clause (i), (ii), or (iii) of subparagraph (A), caused (or, in the case of an attempted offense, would, if completed, have caused)
—

(i)
loss to 1 or more persons during any 1-year period (and, for purposes of an investigation, prosecution, or other proceeding brought by the United

States only, loss resulting from a related course of conduct affecting 1 or more other protected computers) aggregating at least $5,000 in value;

(ii)

the modification or impairment, or potential modification or impairment, of the medical examination, diagnosis, treatment, or care of 1 or more individuals;

(iii)

physical injury to any person;

(iv)

a threat to public health or safety; or

(v)

damage affecting a computer system used by or for a government entity in furtherance of the administration of justice, national defense, or national security;

(6)

knowingly and with intent to defraud traffics (as defined in section 1029) in any password or similar information through which a computer may be accessed without authorization, if —

(A)

such trafficking affects interstate or foreign commerce; or

(B)

such computer is used by or for the Government of the United States; "or".

(7)

with intent to extort from any person any money or other thing of value, transmits in interstate or foreign commerce any communication containing any threat to cause damage to a protected computer;

shall be punished as provided in subsection (c) of this section.

(b)

Whoever attempts to commit an offense under subsection (a) of this section shall be punished as provided in subsection (c) of this section.

(c)

The punishment for an offense under subsection (a) or (b) of this section is —

(1)

(A)

a fine under this title or imprisonment for not more than ten years, or both, in the case of an offense under subsection (a)(1) of this section which does not occur after a conviction for another offense under this section, or an attempt to commit an offense punishable under this subparagraph; and

(B)

a fine under this title or imprisonment for not more than twenty years, or both, in the case of an offense under subsection (a)(1) of this section which occurs after a conviction for another offense under this section, or an attempt to commit an offense punishable under this subparagraph;

(2)

(A)

except as provided in subparagraph (B), a fine under this title or imprisonment for not more than one year, or both, in the case of an offense under subsection (a)(2), (a)(3), (a)(5)(A)(iii), or (a)(6) of this section which does not occur after a conviction for another offense under this section, or an attempt to commit an offense punishable under this subparagraph;

(B)

a fine under this title or imprisonment for not more than 5 years, or both, in the case of an offense under subsection (a)(2), or an attempt to commit an offense punishable under this subparagraph, if —

(i)

the offense was committed for purposes of commercial advantage or private financial gain;

(ii)

the offense was committed in furtherance of any criminal or tortious act in violation of the Constitution or laws of the United States or of any State; or

(iii)

the value of the information obtained exceeds $5,000; and

(C)

a fine under this title or imprisonment for not more than ten years, or both, in the case of an offense under subsection (a)(2), (a)(3) or (a)(6) of this section which occurs after a conviction for another offense under this section, or an attempt to commit an offense punishable under this subparagraph;

(3)

(A)

a fine under this title or imprisonment for not more than five years, or both, in the case of an offense under subsection (a)(4) or (a)(7) of this section which does not occur after a conviction for another offense under this section, or an attempt to commit an offense punishable under this subparagraph; and

(B)

a fine under this title or imprisonment for not more than ten years, or both, in the case of an offense under subsection (a)(4), (a)(5)(A)(iii), or (a)(7) of this section which occurs after a conviction for another offense under this section, or an attempt to commit an offense punishable under this subparagraph;

(4)

(A)

except as provided in paragraph (5), a fine under this title, imprisonment for not more than 10 years, or both, in the case of an offense under subsection (a)(5)(A)(i), or an attempt to commit an offense punishable under that subsection;

(B)

a fine under this title, imprisonment for not more than 5 years, or both, in the case of an offense under subsection (a)(5)(A)(ii), or an attempt to commit an offense punishable under that subsection;

(C)

except as provided in paragraph (5), a fine under this title, imprisonment for not more than 20 years, or both, in the case of an offense under subsection (a)(5)(A)(i) or (a)(5)(A)(ii), or an attempt to commit an offense punishable under either subsection, that occurs after a conviction for another offense under this section; and

(5)

(A)

if the offender knowingly or recklessly causes or attempts to cause serious bodily injury from conduct in violation of subsection (a)(5)(A)(i), a fine under this title or imprisonment for not more than 20 years, or both; and

(B)

if the offender knowingly or recklessly causes or attempts to cause death from conduct in violation of subsection (a)(5)(A)(i), a fine under this title or imprisonment for any term of years or for life, or both.

(d)

(1)

The United States Secret Service shall, in addition to any other agency having such authority, have the authority to investigate offenses under this section.

(2)

The Federal Bureau of Investigation shall have primary authority to investigate offenses under subsection (a)(1) for any cases involving espionage, foreign counterintelligence, information protected against unauthorized disclosure for reasons of national defense or foreign relations, or Restricted Data (as that term is defined in section 11y of the Atomic Energy Act of 1954 (42 U.S.C. 2014(y)), except for offenses affecting the duties of the United States Secret Service pursuant to section 3056(a) of this title.

(3)

Such authority shall be exercised in accordance with an agreement which shall be entered into by the Secretary of the Treasury and the Attorney General.

(e)

As used in this section —

(1)

the term "computer" means an electronic, magnetic, optical, electrochemical, or other high speed data processing device performing logical, arithmetic, or storage functions, and includes any data storage facility or communications facility directly related to or operating in conjunction with such device, but such term does not include an automated typewriter or typesetter, a portable hand held calculator, or other similar device;

(2)

the term "protected computer" means a computer —

(A)

exclusively for the use of a financial institution or the United States Government, or, in the case of a computer not exclusively for such use, used by or for a financial institution or the United States Government and the conduct constituting the offense affects that use by or for the financial institution or the Government; or

(B)

which is used in interstate or foreign commerce or communication, including a computer located outside the United States that is used in a manner that affects interstate or foreign commerce or communication of the United States;

(3)

the term "State" includes the District of Columbia, the Commonwealth of Puerto Rico, and any other commonwealth, possession or territory of the United States;

(4)

the term "financial institution" means —

(A)

an institution, with deposits insured by the Federal Deposit Insurance Corporation;

(B)

the Federal Reserve or a member of the Federal Reserve including any Federal Reserve Bank;

(C)

a credit union with accounts insured by the National Credit Union Administration;

(D)

a member of the Federal home loan bank system and any home loan bank;

(E)

any institution of the Farm Credit System under the Farm Credit Act of 1971;

(F)

a broker-dealer registered with the Securities and Exchange Commission pursuant to section 15 of the Securities Exchange Act of 1934;

(G)

the Securities Investor Protection Corporation;

(H)

a branch or agency of a foreign bank (as such terms are defined in paragraphs (1) and (3) of section 1(b) of the International Banking Act of 1978); and

(I)

an organization operating under section 25 or section 25(a) of the Federal Reserve Act;

(5)

the term "financial record" means information derived from any record held by a financial institution pertaining to a customer's relationship with the financial institution;

(6)

the term "exceeds authorized access" means to access a computer with authorization and to use such access to obtain or alter information in the computer that the accesser is not entitled so to obtain or alter;

(7)

the term "department of the United States" means the legislative or judicial branch of the Government or one of the executive departments enumerated in section 101 of title 5;

(8)

the term "damage" means any impairment to the integrity or availability of data, a program, a system, or information;

(9)

the term "government entity" includes the Government of the United States, any State or political subdivision of the United States, any foreign country, and any state, province, municipality, or other political subdivision of a foreign country;

(10)

the term "conviction" shall include a conviction under the law of any State for a crime punishable by imprisonment for more than 1 year, an element of which is unauthorized access, or exceeding authorized access, to a computer;

(11)

the term "loss" means any reasonable cost to any victim, including the cost of responding to an offense, conducting a damage assessment, and restoring the data, program, system, or information to its condition prior to the offense, and any revenue lost, cost incurred, or other consequential damages incurred because of interruption of service; and

(12)

the term "person" means any individual, firm, corporation, educational institution, financial institution, governmental entity, or legal or other entity.

(f)

This section does not prohibit any lawfully authorized investigative, protective, or intelligence activity of a law enforcement agency of the United

States, a State, or a political subdivision of a State, or of an intelligence agency of the United States.

(g)

Any person who suffers damage or loss by reason of a violation of this section may maintain a civil action against the violator to obtain compensatory damages and injunctive relief or other equitable relief. A civil action for a violation of this section may be brought only if the conduct involves 1 of the factors set forth in clause (i), (ii), (iii), (iv), or (v) of subsection (a)(5)(B). Damages for a violation involving only conduct described in subsection (a)(5)(B)(i) are limited to economic damages. No action may be brought under this subsection unless such action is begun within 2 years of the date of the act complained of or the date of the discovery of the damage. No action may be brought under this subsection for the negligent design or manufacture of computer hardware, computer software, or firmware.

(h)

The Attorney General and the Secretary of the Treasury shall report to the Congress annually, during the first 3 years following the date of the enactment of this subsection, concerning investigations and prosecutions under subsection (a)(5)

APPENDIX D

HELEN REMSBURG V. DOCUSEARCH (2003)

THE SUPREME COURT OF NEW HAMPSHIRE

U.S. District Court
No. 2002-255

HELEN REMSBURG, ADMINISTRATRIX OF THE ESTATE OF
AMY LYNN BOYER

v.

DOCUSEARCH, INC., d/b/a DOCUSEARCH.COM *& a.*
Argued: November 14, 2002
Opinion Issued: February 18, 2003

DALIANIS, J. Pursuant to Supreme Court Rule 34, the United States District Court for the District of New Hampshire (*Barbadoro*, C.J.) certified to us the following questions of law:

1. Under the common law of New Hampshire and in light of the undisputed facts presented by this case, does a private investigator or information broker who sells information to a client pertaining to a third party have a cognizable legal duty to that third party with respect to the sale of the information?

2. If a private investigator or information broker obtains a person's social security number from a credit reporting agency as a part of a credit header without the person's knowledge or permission and sells the social security number to a client, does the individual whose social security number was sold have a cause of action for intrusion upon her seclusion against the private investigator or information broker for damages caused by the sale of the information?

3. When a private investigator or information broker obtains a person's work address by means of a pretextual telephone call and sells the

work address to a client, does the individual whose work address was deceitfully obtained have a cause of action for intrusion upon her seclusion against the private investigator or information broker for damages caused by the sale of the information?

4. If a private investigator or information broker obtains a social security number from a credit reporting agency as a part of a credit header, or a work address by means of a pretextual telephone call, and then sells the information, does the individual whose social security number or work address was sold have a cause of action for commercial appropriation against the private investigator or information broker for damages caused by the sale of the information?

5. If a private investigator or information broker obtains a person's work address by means of a pretextual telephone call, and then sells the information, is the private investigator or information broker liable under N.H. Rev. Stat. Ann. § 358-A to the person it deceived for damages caused by the sale of the information?

For the reasons expressed below, we respond to the first, second and fifth questions in the affirmative, and the third and fourth questions in the negative.

I. Facts

We adopt the district court's recitation of the facts. Docusearch, Inc. and Wing and a Prayer, Inc. (WAAP) jointly own and operate an Internet-based investigation and information service known as Docusearch.com. Daniel Cohn and Kenneth Zeiss each own 50% of each company's stock. Cohn serves as president of both companies and Zeiss serves as a director of WAAP. Cohn is licensed as a private investigator by both the State of Florida and Palm Beach County, Florida.

On July 29, 1999, New Hampshire resident Liam Youens contacted Docusearch through its Internet web site and requested the date of birth for Amy Lynn Boyer, another New Hampshire resident. Youens provided Docusearch his name, New Hampshire address, and a contact telephone number. He paid the $20 fee by credit card. Zeiss placed a telephone call to Youens in New Hampshire on the same day. Zeiss cannot recall the reason for the phone call, but speculates that it was to verify the order. The next day, July 30, 1999, Docusearch provided Youens with the birth dates for several Amy Boyers, but none was for the Amy Boyer sought by Youens. In response, Youens e-mailed Docusearch inquiring whether it would be possible to get better results using Boyer's home address, which he provided. Youens gave Docusearch a different contact phone number.

Later that same day, Youens again contacted Docusearch and placed an order for Boyer's social security number (SSN), paying the $45 fee by credit card. On August 2, 1999, Docusearch obtained Boyer's social security number from a credit reporting agency as a part of a "credit header" and provided it to Youens. A "credit header" is typically provided at the top of a credit report and includes a person's name, address and social security number. The next day, Youens placed an order with Docusearch for Boyer's employment information, paying the $109 fee by credit card, and giving Docusearch the same phone number he had provided originally. Docusearch phone records indicate that Zeiss placed a phone call to Youens on August 6, 1999. The phone number used was the one Youens had provided with his follow-up inquiry regarding Boyer's birth date. The phone call lasted for less than one minute, and no record exists concerning its topic or whether Zeiss was able to speak with Youens. On August 20, 1999, having received no response to his latest request, Youens placed a second request for Boyer's employment information, again paying the $109 fee by credit card. On September 1, 1999, Docusearch refunded Youens' first payment of $109 because its efforts to fulfill his first request for Boyer's employment information had failed.

With his second request for Boyer's employment information pending, Youens placed yet another order for information with Docusearch on September 6, 1999. This time, he requested a "locate by social security number" search for Boyer. Youens paid the $30 fee by credit card, and received the results of the search—Boyer's home address—on September 7, 1999.

On September 8, 1999, Docusearch informed Youens of Boyer's employment address. Docusearch acquired this address through a subcontractor, Michele Gambino, who had obtained the information by placing a "pretext" telephone call to Boyer in New Hampshire. Gambino lied about who she was and the purpose of her call in order to convince Boyer to reveal her employment information. Gambino had no contact with Youens, nor did she know why Youens was requesting the information.

On October 15, 1999, Youens drove to Boyer's workplace and fatally shot her as she left work. Youens then shot and killed himself. A subsequent police investigation revealed that Youens kept firearms and ammunition in his bedroom, and maintained a web site containing references to stalking and killing Boyer as well as other information and statements related to violence and killing.

II. Question 1

All persons have a duty to exercise reasonable care not to subject others to an unreasonable risk of harm. *See Walls v. Oxford Management Co.*, 137 N.H.

653, 656 (1993). Whether a defendant's conduct creates a risk of harm to others sufficiently foreseeable to charge the defendant with a duty to avoid such conduct is a question of law, *Iannelli v. Burger King Corp.*, 145 N.H. 190, 193 (2000), because "the existence of a duty does not arise solely from the relationship between the parties, but also from the need for protection against reasonably foreseeable harm." *Hungerford v. Jones*, 143 N.H. 208, 211 (1998) (quotation omitted). Thus, in some cases, a party's actions give rise to a duty. *Walls*, 137 N.H. at 656. Parties owe a duty to those third parties foreseeably endangered by their conduct with respect to those risks whose likelihood and magnitude make the conduct unreasonably dangerous. *Hungerford*, 143 N.H. at 211.

In situations in which the harm is caused by criminal misconduct, however, determining whether a duty exists is complicated by the competing rule "that a private citizen has no general duty to protect others from the criminal attacks of third parties." *Dupont v. Aavid Thermal Technologies*, 147 N.H. 706, 709 (2002). This rule is grounded in the fundamental unfairness of holding private citizens responsible for the unanticipated criminal acts of third parties, because "[u]nder all ordinary and normal circumstances, in the absence of any reason to expect the contrary, the actor may reasonably proceed upon the assumption that others will obey the law." *Walls*, 137 N.H. at 657-58 (quotation omitted).

In certain limited circumstances, however, we have recognized that there are exceptions to the general rule where a duty to exercise reasonable care will arise. *See Dupont*, 147 N.H. at 709. We have held that such a duty may arise because: (1) a special relationship exists; (2) special circumstances exist; or (3) the duty has been voluntarily assumed. *Id.* The special circumstances exception includes situations where there is "an especial temptation and opportunity for criminal misconduct brought about by the defendant." *Walls*, 137 N.H. at 658 (quotation omitted). This exception follows from the rule that a party who realizes or should realize that his conduct has created a condition which involves an unreasonable risk of harm to another has a duty to exercise reasonable care to prevent the risk from occurring. *Id.* The exact occurrence or precise injuries need not have been foreseeable. *Iannelli*, 145 N.H. at 194. Rather, where the defendant's conduct has created an unreasonable risk of criminal misconduct, a duty is owed to those foreseeably endangered. *See id.*

Thus, if a private investigator or information broker's (hereinafter "investigator" collectively) disclosure of information to a client creates a foreseeable risk of criminal misconduct against the third person whose information was disclosed, the investigator owes a duty to exercise reasonable care not to subject the third person to an unreasonable risk of harm. In determining whether the risk of criminal misconduct is foreseeable to an investigator, we examine two risks of information disclosure implicated by this case: stalking and identity theft.

It is undisputed that stalkers, in seeking to locate and track a victim, sometimes use an investigator to obtain personal information about the victims. *See* Note, *Stalking Humans: Is There A Need For Federalization Of Anti-Stalking Laws In Order To Prevent Recidivism In Stalking?*, 50 Syracuse L. Rev. 1067, 1075 (2000) (discussing two high profile California cases where the stalkers used investigators to obtain their victims' home addresses).

Public concern about stalking has compelled all fifty States to pass some form of legislation criminalizing stalking. Approximately one million women and 371,000 men are stalked annually in the United States. P. Tjaden & N. Thoennes, Nat'l Inst. of Justice Ctr. for Disease Control and Prevention, *Stalking in America: Findings from the National Violence Against Women Survey*, Apr. 1998, at 2. Stalking is a crime that causes serious psychological harm to the victims, and often results in the victim experiencing post-traumatic stress disorder, anxiety, sleeplessness, and sometimes, suicidal ideations. *See* Mullen & Pathe, *Stalking*, 29 Crime & Just. 273, 296-97 (2002). Not only is stalking itself a crime, but it can lead to more violent crimes, including assault, rape or homicide. *See, e.g., Brunner v. State*, 683 So. 2d 1129, 1130 (Fla. Dist. Ct. App. 1996); *People v. Sowewimo*, 657 N.E.2d 1047, 1049 (Ill. App. Ct. 1995); *Com. v. Cruz*, 675 N.E.2d 764, 765 (Mass. 1997).

Identity theft, *i.e.*, the use of one person's identity by another, is an increasingly common risk associated with the disclosure of personal information, such as a SSN. Komuves, *We've Got Your Number: An Overview of Legislation and Decisions to Control the Use of Social Security Numbers as Personal Identifiers*, 16 J. Marshall J. Computer & Info. L. 529, 534 (1998). A person's SSN has attained the status of a quasi-universal personal identification number. *Id.* at 531-32. At the same time, however, a person's privacy interest in his or her SSN is recognized by state and federal statutes, including RSA 260:14, IV-a (Supp. 2002) which prohibits the release of SSNs contained within drivers' license records. *See also* Financial Services Modernization Act of 1999, 15 U.S.C. §§ 6801–6809 (2000); Privacy Act of 1974, 5 U.S.C. § 552a (2000). "[A]rmed with one's SSN, an unscrupulous individual could obtain a person's welfare benefits or Social Security benefits, order new checks at a new address on that person's checking account, obtain credit cards, or even obtain the person's paycheck." *Greidinger v. Davis*, 988 F.2d 1344, 1353 (4th Cir. 1993).

Like the consequences of stalking, the consequences of identity theft can be severe. The best estimates place the number of victims in excess of 100,000 per year and the dollar loss in excess of $2 billion per year. LoPucki, *Human Identification Theory and the Identity Theft Problem*, 80 Tex. L. Rev. 89, 89 (2001). Victims of identity theft risk the destruction of their good credit histories. This often destroys a victim's ability to obtain credit from any source and may, in some cases, render the victim unemployable or even cause the victim to be incarcerated. *Id.* at 91.

The threats posed by stalking and identity theft lead us to conclude that the risk of criminal misconduct is sufficiently foreseeable so that an investigator has a duty to exercise reasonable care in disclosing a third person's personal information to a client. And we so hold. This is especially true when, as in this case, the investigator does not know the client or the client's purpose in seeking the information.

III. Questions 2 and 3

A tort action based upon an intrusion upon seclusion must relate to something secret, secluded or private pertaining to the plaintiff. *Fischer v. Hooper*, 143 N.H. 585, 590 (1999). Moreover, liability exists only if the defendant's conduct was such that the defendant should have realized that it would be offensive to persons of ordinary sensibilities. *Id.* "It is only where the intrusion has gone beyond the limits of decency that liability accrues." *Hamberger v. Eastman*, 106 N.H. 107, 111 (1964) (quotation omitted); *see Restatement (Second) of Torts* § 652B comment *d* at 380 (1977).

In addressing whether a person's SSN is something secret, secluded or private, we must determine whether a person has a reasonable expectation of privacy in the number. *See Fischer*, 143 N.H. at 589–90. SSNs are available in a wide variety of contexts. *Bodah v. Lakeville Motor Express Inc.*, 649 N.W.2d 859, 863 (Minn. Ct. App. 2002). SSNs are used to identify people to track social security benefits, as well as when taxes and credit applications are filed. *See Greidinger*, 988 F.2d at 1352–53. In fact, "the widespread use of SSNs as universal identifiers in the public and private sectors is one of the most serious manifestations of privacy concerns in the Nation." *Id.* at 1353 (quotation omitted). As noted above, a person's interest in maintaining the privacy of his or her SSN has been recognized by numerous federal and state statutes. As a result, the entities to which this information is disclosed and their employees are bound by legal, and, perhaps, contractual constraints to hold SSNs in confidence to ensure that they remain private. *See Bodah*, 649 N.W.2d at 863.

Thus, while a SSN must be disclosed in certain circumstances, a person may reasonably expect that the number will remain private.

Whether the intrusion would be offensive to persons of ordinary sensibilities is ordinarily a question for the fact-finder and only becomes a question of law if reasonable persons can draw only one conclusion from the evidence. *See Swarthout v. Mutual Service Life Ins. Co.*, 632 N.W.2d 741, 745 (Minn. Ct. App. 2001). The evidence underlying the certified question is insufficient to draw any such conclusion here, and we therefore must leave this question to the fact-finder. In making this determination, the fact-finder should consider "the degree of intrusion, the context, conduct and circumstances surrounding the intrusion as well as the intruder's motives and objectives, the setting into which he intrudes, and the expectations of those whose privacy is invaded." *Bauer v. Ford Motor Credit Co.*, 149 F. Supp. 2d 1106, 1109 (D. Minn. 2001). Accordingly, a person whose SSN is obtained by an investigator from a credit reporting agency without the person's knowledge or permission may have a cause of action for intrusion upon seclusion for damages caused by the sale of the SSN, but must prove that the intrusion was such that it would have been offensive to a person of ordinary sensibilities.

We next address whether a person has a cause of action for intrusion upon seclusion where an investigator obtains the person's work address by using a pretextual phone call. We must first establish whether a work address is something secret, secluded or private about the plaintiff. *See Fischer*, 143 N.H. at 590.

In most cases, a person works in a public place. "On the public street, or in any other public place, [a person] has no legal right to be alone." W. Page Keeton *et al.*, *Prosser and Keeton on the Law of Torts* § 117, at 855 (5th ed. 1984).

A person's employment, where he lives, and where he works are exposures which we all must suffer. We have no reasonable expectation of privacy as to our identity or as to where we live or work. Our commuting to and from where we live and work is not done clandestinely and each place provides a facet of our total identity.

Webb v. City of Shreveport, 371 So. 2d 316, 319 (La. Ct. App. 1979). Thus, where a person's work address is readily observable by members of the public, the address cannot be private and no intrusion upon seclusion action can be maintained.

Appendix D

"One who appropriates to his own use or benefit the name or likeness of another is subject to liability to the other for invasion of his privacy." *Restatement (Second) of Torts* § 652C at 380. In *Hamberger*, we noted that the law of invasion of privacy consists of four separate causes of action, including appropriation. *Hamberger*, 106 N.H. at 110–11. However, we have not had occasion to recognize appropriation as a cause of action within the State. We now hold that New Hampshire recognizes the tort of invasion of privacy by appropriation of an individual's name or likeness, and adopt the *Restatement* view. "The interest protected by the rule . . . is the interest of the individual in the exclusive use of his own identity, in so far as it is represented by his name or likeness, and in so far as the use may be of benefit to him or to others." *Restatement (Second) of Torts* § 652C comment *a* at 381.

Tortious liability for appropriation of a name or likeness is intended to protect the value of an individual's notoriety or skill. Thus, the *Restatement* notes, in order that there may be liability under the rule stated in this Section, the defendant must have appropriated to his own use or benefit the reputation, prestige, social or commercial standing, public interest or other values of the plaintiff's name or likeness. The misappropriation tort does not protect one's name *per se;* rather it protects the value associated with that name.

Matthews v. Wozencraft, 15 F.3d 432, 437 (5th Cir. 1994) (citation, brackets and quotation omitted). Appropriation is not actionable if the person's name or likeness is published for "purposes other than taking advantage of [the person's] reputation, prestige or other value" associated with the person. *Restatement (Second) of Torts* § 652C comment *d* at 382-83. Thus, appropriation occurs most often when the person's name or likeness is used to advertise the defendant's product or when the defendant impersonates the person for gain. *Matthews*, 15 F.3d at 437; *see Restatement (Second) of Torts* § 652C comment *b* at 381.

An investigator who sells personal information sells the information for the value of the information itself, not to take advantage of the person's reputation or prestige. The investigator does not capitalize upon the goodwill value associated with the information but rather upon the client's willingness to pay for the information. In other words, the benefit derived from the sale in no way relates to the social or commercial standing of the person whose information is sold. Thus, a person whose personal information is sold does not have a cause of action for appropriation against the investigator who sold the information.

V. Question 5

The last issue relates to the construction of the Consumer Protection Act, RSA chapter 358-A. "On questions of statutory interpretation, this court is the final arbiter of the intent of the legislature as expressed in the words of a statute considered as a whole." *Franklin Lodge of Elks v. Marcoux*, 147 N.H. 95, 96 (2001) (quotation omitted). We begin by considering the plain meaning of the words of the statute. *Snow v. American Morgan Horse Assoc.*, 141 N.H. 467, 471 (1996). In conducting our analysis "we will focus on the statute as a whole, not on isolated words or phrases." *Id.* "[W]e will not consider what the legislature might have said or add words that the legislature did not include." *Minuteman, LLC v. Microsoft Corp.*, 147 N.H. 634, 636 (2002) (quotation omitted). RSA 358-A:2 (1995) states, in pertinent part:

It shall be unlawful for any person to use . . . any unfair or deceptive act or practice in the conduct of any trade or commerce within this state. Such . . . unfair or deceptive act or practice shall include, but is not limited to, the following:

. . .

III. Causing likelihood of confusion or of misunderstanding as to affiliation, connection or association with . . . another.

Pretext phone calling has been described as the use of deception and trickery to obtain a person's private information for resale to others. *See Com. v. Source One Associates, Inc.*, 763 N.E.2d 42, 47–48 n.8 (Mass. 2002). The target of the phone call is deceived into believing that the caller is affiliated with a reliable entity who has a legitimate purpose in requesting the information. RSA 358-A:2, III explicitly prohibits this conduct. The pretext clearly creates a misunderstanding as to the investigator's affiliation.

The defendant argues that our holding in *Snow* bars recovery in cases such as this because an investigator who makes a pretextual phone call to obtain information for sale does not conduct any "trade" or "commerce" with the person deceived by the phone call. The Consumer Protection Act defines "trade" and "commerce" as including "the advertising, offering for sale, sale, or distribution of any services and any property . . ." RSA 358-A:1, II. There is no language in the Act that would restrict the definition of "trade" and "commerce" to that affecting the party deceived by the prohibited conduct. In fact, the Act explicitly includes "trade or commerce directly or *indirectly* affecting the people of this state." *Id.* (emphasis added). In *Snow*, we held that the registering of foals, alone, was not a transaction involving trade or commerce. *Snow*, 141 N.H. at 471. Such is not the case here. Here, the investigator used the pretext phone call to complete the sale of information to a client. Thus, the investigator's pretextual phone call occurred in the conduct of trade or commerce within the State.

The defendant argues that a person deceived by a pretextual phone call lacks standing to maintain a private cause of action under RSA chapter 358-A because only a buyer or seller in privity with the defendant may recover under the statute. We disagree. According to the statute, "*[a]ny* person injured by another's use of any method, act or practice declared unlawful under this chapter may bring an action for damages. . ." RSA 358-A:10 (emphasis added). The statute defines who may bring a private action broadly, *Milford Lumber Co. v. RCB Realty*, 147 N.H. 15, 17 (2001), and by its plain meaning does not limit the class of persons who have standing to those in privity with the defendant.

We find support for this conclusion in the Massachusetts Consumer Protection Act, which is similar in many respects to the New Hampshire statute. *See Milford Lumber Co.*, 147 N.H. at 18; *see also* Mass. Gen. Laws ch. 93A (1997). When the Massachusetts Consumer Protection Act was amended in 1979, section 9 was changed to permit "any person" (other than commercial entities covered under a separate section) to recover for damages, which "substantially broadened the class of persons who could maintain actions under [the statute]." *Van Dyke v. St. Paul Fire and Marine Ins. Co.*, 448 N.E.2d 357, 360 (Mass. 1983). Consequently, Massachusetts courts have permitted third parties who were not in privity with the defendant to recover for damages caused by the defendant's violation of the statute. *Maillet v. ATF-Davidson Co., Inc.*, 552 N.E.2d 95, 99 (Mass. 1990); *see also Ellis v. Safety Ins. Co.*, 672 N.E.2d 979, 985–86 n.13 (Mass. App. Ct. 1996) (permitting the housemates of an insurance policyholder to maintain an action claiming racial harassment during an insurance investigation despite lack of privity).

Accordingly, we conclude that an investigator who obtains a person's work address by means of pretextual phone calling, and then sells the information, may be liable for damages under RSA chapter 358-A to the person deceived.

Remanded.

NADEAU and DUGGAN, JJ., concurred.

INDEX

Locators in **boldface** indicate main topics. Locators followed by *c* indicate chronology entries. Locators followed by *b* indicate biographical entries. Locators followed by *g* indicate glossary entries.

Index

Index

291

Index

293

Index

Index

297